Second Edition

Developing IEPs:

The Complete Guide to Educationally Meaningful Individualized Education Programs for Students with Disabilities

Keith J. Hyatt ▪ **John W. Filler**

Kendall Hunt
publishing company

Cover image © Shutterstock.com
All Chapter Opener Images © Shutterstock.com

Kendall Hunt
publishing company

www.kendallhunt.com
Send all inquiries to:
4050 Westmark Drive
Dubuque, IA 52004-1840

Copyright © 2013, 2016 by Kendall Hunt Publishing Company

ISBN 978-1-4652-9775-4

Printed in the United States of America
10 9 8 7 6 5 4 3 2 1

Table of Contents

About the Authors

Keith J. Hyatt, Ed.D. is a Professor of Special Education at Western Washington University. He earned his doctorate in Special Education at the University of Nevada, Las Vegas. Dr. Hyatt's professional interests include special education law, inclusion, and evidence-based practices. Before working in higher education, Dr. Hyatt was a GED instructor in a program for migrant/seasonal farmworkers, a special education teacher, school psychologist, behavior interventionist, and elementary school principal.

John Filler Ph.D. received his doctorate in Developmental Psychology from Peabody College of Vanderbilt University. Currently, he is a Professor of Special Education and Early Childhood Education at the University of Nevada, Las Vegas. Previously, he served as a Senior Research Scientist at the Illinois Institute on Developmental Disabilities; Assistant Professor and Coordinator of Early Childhood Special Education at Virginia Commonwealth University in Richmond, VA; Assistant to Associate Professor of Special Education at California State University, Hayward and while there also as Assistant Chair of the Department of Educational Psychology and as Assistant Vice President for Research; and finally, as a Professor and Chair of the Department of Counseling and Special Education at the University of Idaho. He has published extensively in the fields of psychology and special education.

Chapter 1

Introduction

Purposes of this Book

In many teacher education programs, preservice general education teachers are required to take just one survey course on special education. The course is frequently completed at the beginning of the teacher education program or wherever it will conveniently fit in the schedule with little consideration of its relationship to other pedagogical coursework. Like other introductory or survey courses, such as an introduction to geology or astronomy, it typically provides a limited amount of information across a wide range of topics—just barely scratching the surface. An introductory course in special education generally covers very basic issues of special education legislation and the need for special education, the referral process, assessment, basic instructional strategies, information on the different eligibility categories, and a cursory overview of the Individualized Education Program (IEP). As a result, many general education teachers complete their teacher training program and begin their teaching careers with relatively limited information regarding special education and frequently lack the skills and confidence needed to be significant contributors to the IEP for the students with whom they work. Given that the education of students with disabilities is not solely an educational issue, but also a civil rights issue, it is imperative that general education teachers be well versed in their responsibilities to children with disabilities, especially as a greater number of students with disabilities are served in the general education setting. One goal of this book is to provide general education teachers with the background information and skills needed to be meaningful participants on IEP teams.

Given the number of legal challenges to poorly written IEPs, it is evident that many special educators enter the workforce with limited training in the development of educationally relevant and legally compliant IEPs. Thus, a second goal of this book is to provide special education teachers with the knowledge and technical skills needed to work collaboratively with general education teachers and families to develop educationally meaningful and legally compliant IEPs. Our overarching purpose is for the book to serve as an ongoing reference for both general and special education teachers who require explicit information in order to understand and meaningfully participate in the IEP process. We also believe the book would be valuable reference for administrators, related service providers, and other professionals who work with children in educational settings.

We begin addressing our goals by providing a brief overview of the recent historical background of special education in this chapter as well as a general review of the referral and eligibility process in Chapter 2. While not technically parts of the IEP process, an understanding of important historical issues will serve as valuable reference points for the development of the IEP and the provision of effective special education services. Additionally, an understanding of the entire process helps clarify the importance of your contribution. Subsequent chapters will provide an in-depth review of different components of the IEP and describe how teachers can work together to address those aspects of the IEP. Upon completion of the book, you will have acquired the necessary skills and understandings to participate in the development of educationally relevant and legally correct IEPs. (This should not be read to imply that we are providing professional legal advice, since neither of the authors is an attorney.)

At the end of the book, you will find appendices with information that will support your continued refinement of skills and understandings needed to be a confident and effective member of an IEP team, and throughout the text, you will find hyperlinks to valuable resources. Since this book is available electronically, active hyperlinks are imbedded in the test, and a listing of hyperlinks used in all chapters in included in Appendix F.

Technical Jargon

The field of special education, like other professions, is replete with technical jargon and acronyms. In many instances they are quite useful and refer to a common set of understandings thereby facilitating communication among team members. For example, members of the IEP team would understand that the acronym "ESY" stands for Extended School Year and would have at least a common understanding or reference from which to work when considering ESY eligibility. (The actual meaning of ESY and its purpose will be discussed in detail in Chapter 3).

In other cases, acronyms and jargonistic expressions appear to provide more accurate information than is possible. For example, the term "specific learning disability" is an eligibility category in special education as well as a descriptor of a particular disability. (In practice, the term "learning disability" is used interchangeably with "specific learning disability.") Educators frequently talk about students with learning disabilities as if those students all exhibited the same learning challenges and required use of the same educational interventions. However, if you think about it for a minute, you will recognize how ridiculous it is to assume that all children with the label of "learning disability" have the same instructional needs. (This assumption is no more true of all students identified as having learning disabilities than it is of all children identified as third grade students.) Some students identified as having a learning disability may require assistance in mathematics only while others may require assistance in reading or other academic, behavioral, or communicative skill areas.

A relatively recent and unfortunate result of this faulty use of labels has been the proliferation of "autism" programs, particularly at the early childhood and elementary levels. Development of "autism" programs implies that autism is a specific disability and all children with autism require the same intervention. While children with autism may share some common characteristics, autism is more accurately viewed as a condition that ranges across a spectrum, impacting some students with significant cognitive delays and others who have average to above average cognitive skills. The point is that a label simply doesn't provide sufficient information to develop a successful and effective educational program and often carries with it unintended or simply incorrect connotations. We really won't know what the child needs to learn until we know the child and have meaningful assessment information (Filler et al., 1975).

In addition to the risk of overgeneralizing characteristics based on label, acronyms and technical jargon can be a source of alienation for individuals. This is of particular concern when parents and general education teachers may not know the meaning of the term and don't want to ask for clarification out of fear of appearing ignorant at a meeting. In fact, acronyms and jargon can also be a source of confusion to trained special educators who may lack training in school psychology, speech therapy, physical therapy, or other specialties that have their own discipline specific jargon but aren't yet familiar with the jargon used in those disciplines. It is crucial that all members of an IEP team or other educational team be "informed consumers" and understand that the terminology being bantered about in meetings has significant implications for students. So, while acronyms and jargon can be useful, care should be taken to ensure that their meanings are understood by all, including parents, and not be used to overgeneralize behavioral characteristics or presume educational needs for any individual child. It is also important to remember that many terms and labels are little more than shorthand notations for a broad range of characteristics that may or may not be accurate when used in reference to any given individual. In this text, we will invariably use acronyms and jargon, but will make every effort to explain the terms. A listing of commonly used abbreviations and terminology is contained in Table 1-1 for your reference.

TABLE 1-1. Abbreviations Commonly Used in Special Education

Abbreviation	Term
ADHD	Attention Deficit Hyperactivity Disorder
BD	Behavior Disorder
BIP	Behavior Intervention Plan
CBM	Curriculum-Based Measurement
DD	Developmental Delay
EAHCA	Education for All Handicapped Children Act
ECSE	Early Childhood Special Education
ED	Emotional Disturbance
EBD	Emotional/Behavioral Disorder
EI	Early Intervention
ESY	Extended School Year
FAPE	Free Appropriate Public Education
FBA	Functional Behavior Assessment
ID	Intellectual Delay
IDEA	Individuals with Disabilities Education Act
IEP	Individualized Education Program
IFSP	Individualized Family Service Plan
IQ	Intelligence Quotient
LD	Learning Disability
LRE	Least Restrictive Environment
MDT	Multi-disciplinary Team
MR	Mental Retardation*
OHI	Other Health Impaired
OT	Occupational Therapy
PBS	Positive Behavioral Supports
PLEP	Present Levels of Educational Performance
PLOP	Present Levels of Performance
PT	Physical Therapy
RtI	Response to Intervention

*NOTE: The term "mental retardation" was recently changed to "intellectual disability" in federal law as required by Rosa's Law (20 USC 1400) which was enacted on October 5, 2010.

People First Language

Before beginning a discussion of the recent historical background of special education, the practice of using "people first language" deserves mention as we will be using it extensively, and we want to encourage our readers to make the use of "people first language" part of their vernacular if it isn't already (**http://www.disabilityisnatural.com/**). This verbiage is consistent with the prevailing view in the field that the individual should be recognized before the disability (Snow, 2012; Turnbull & Turnbull, 1998). It is based upon the belief that using labels before referring to the person evokes preconceptions, and especially negative stereotypes when used with individuals with disabilities, since disability has traditionally been viewed as a deviation from the norm, and not a deviation exemplifying superior talent such as a musician or artist, but a deviation that refers to something undesired and less worthy. For example, for many people, referring to someone as a "retarded person" tends to conjure negative mental images and stereotypes of individuals with cognitive delays who are struggling to succeed in life. Just take a minute to think of the societal images the term "retarded" or "retard" evokes in your mind. Chances are those representations are of anything but an individual living a meaningful life and making important contributions to the community. Generally, those images elicit feelings of pity and sympathy and a belief that the individual must be cared for and may be a perpetual child. These feelings reinforce misconceptions and may result in further marginalization of individuals with disabilities.

While people may still have negative preconceptions regarding disability, the use of people first language tends to provide a focus on the individual, with the disability being a secondary characteristic. Thus disability is not the sole defining characteristic of the person or even the most important of the many characteristics which make each of us unique. Simply stated, people-first language operates from the belief that a disability is something that a person "has" not what a person "is." Throughout this text, we will use people first language. We will refer to a "student with a learning disability" rather than a "learning disabled student." If you are not accustomed to using people first language, it can be a challenge at first, because it requires a change of verbal habits and frequently requires a more wordy response. At the end of this chapter, we will include some practice exercises to help you develop the habit of using people first language.

We also want you to know that the term "handicapped" is no longer acceptable when referring to an individual with disabilities. An individual is not handicapped; the etiology of the term comes from an English game of chance but has been frequently and erroneously equated to a person with a disability standing on a street corner with a cap in her hand, begging for money. While the terms impairment, disability, and handicap are frequently used synonymously, this practice is inaccurate. Heward (2013) differentiated the terms as follows.

> *Impairment*: any loss or reduced function of a body part or organ;
>
> *Disability*: any restriction on ability to perform an activity or task due to an impairment; and
>
> *Handicap*: a disadvantage or problem dealing with the environment that is encountered by a person with an impairment or disability interacting with the environment.

See Table 1-2 for a scenario that provides a clear description of the terms using a preschool child as the subject. Note how the child's circumstances may change as he gets older.

Similarly, when referring to public school students with disabilities who receive special education services, we will not call them special education students. Doing so may imply that they are not really members of the regular education world but belong to a separate system. This view is clearly in conflict with declarations from the President's Commission on

TABLE 1-2. Differences between Impairment, Disability, and Handicap

<u>Student characteristics:</u> David is a 4-yr.-old who has a form of cerebral palsy (CP) called spastic diplegia. David's CP causes his legs to be stiff, tight, and difficult to move. He cannot stand or walk.

Impairment: The inability to move the legs easily at the joints and inability to bear weight on the feet is an impairment. Without orthotics and surgery to release abnormally contracted muscles, David's level of impairment may increase as imbalanced muscle contraction over a period of time can cause hip dislocation and deformed bone growth. No treatment may be currently available to lessen David's impairment.

Disability: David's inability to walk is a disability. His level of disability can be improved with physical therapy and special equipment. For example, if he learns to use a walker, with braces, his level of disability will improve considerably.

Handicap: David's cerebral palsy is handicapping to the extent that it prevents him from fulfilling a normal role at home, in preschool, and in the community. His level of handicap has been only very mild in the early years as he has been well-supported to be able to play with other children, interact normally with family members and participate fully in family and community activities. As he gets older, his handicap will increase where certain sports and physical activities are considered "normal" activities for children of the same age. He has little handicap in his preschool classroom, though he needs some assistance to move about the classroom and from one activity to another outside the classroom. Appropriate services and equipment can reduce the extent to which cerebral palsy prevents David from fulfilling a normal role in the home, school and community as he grows.

From Carter, S. (2001). "Common Developmental Problems." http://www.pediatrics.emory.edu/divisions/neonatology/dpc/defn.html#cp. Reprinted with permission.

Excellence in Special Education (U.S. Department of Education Office of Special Education and Rehabilitative Services, 2002) which noted that students with disabilities are general education students and that special education is a service that follows students and not a place to send students. In addition, we will not use terms such as challenged when referring to an individual with a disability. In our opinion, labels such as "emotionally challenged" fail when it comes to people first language and tend to trivialize the disability. While we all have challenges in our lives, these are typically things that we overcome and then move on to the next challenge whether it be losing an additional five pounds or spending an extra five minutes on the treadmill. However, having a disability is more than a simple challenge. People with disabilities frequently encounter multiple challenges throughout their lives just trying to access the societal rights and privileges that those without disabilities enjoy on a daily basis.

Labels also group or categorize people, so we must use care when affixing labels to students. Spend a short time in a school and you are likely to hear groups of children referred to as "learning disabled students." This label is problematic, because it does not use people first language and implies students with learning disabilities are a homogeneous group with the label providing all the information teachers need. In the past, many educators believed that if they put students with the same diagnostic label in the same classroom, then the teacher could provide more effective instruction. However, students with learning disabilities vary greatly in the types and levels of support they require and this approach of trying to group them together based on label has not proved effective. Thus, as alluded to earlier, the term really isn't helpful in a programmatic sense.

Howell (1976) noted two definitions of special education. One is the education of students with disabilities. The other is the application of exceptional instruction. We strongly adhere to the second definition and believe that the strategies and techniques used by special educators trained in current, research-based assessment and instructional strategies are valuable when used with any student, identified as eligible for special education or not.

We have provided numerous guidelines for referring to individuals with disabilities. These guides do not just reflect the current trend, they promote accurate use of terminology in the manner that is considered most respectful of individuals with disabilities. Absent a personal request, such as a person who is deaf asking to be called a deaf person, the most respectful way to refer to a person with a disability is through the use of people first language.

Historical Background

Others have provided discussion of the history of the provision of services to individuals with disabilities (e.g., Turnbull, Stowe, & Huerta, 2007; Yell, 2006) and there are entire volumes devoted to the history of special education (Osgood, 2008; Winzer, 2009). Our goal here is simply to highlight major legislative issues related to the provision of public education to students with disabilities. We believe it is important for all teachers to have at least a rudimentary understanding of the challenges individuals with disabilities face when trying to exercise the civil rights that most Americans take for granted. In the not too distant past, there was blatant discrimination against individuals with disabilities, and an understanding of that fact may help one understand that while people with disabilities and their families may appear impatient at times, there really is no reason for them to be patient when being denied basic civil rights. We recognize that much has changed for individuals with disabilities, yet there remains much work to be done. Education is a strong value in our society, and public schools are prime venues for promoting educational practices that provide people with the skills needed to meaningfully contribute and participate in our society. As you will see throughout this book, the IEP provides a vehicle for making changes and providing supports, thereby enabling children with disabilities to benefit from education and guaranteeing their civil rights in the public school arena.

Much of the impetus for changes in the treatment of individuals with disabilities within the last sixty years can be traced to a considerable growth in advocacy actions, including the founding of the ARC, formerly the National Association for Retarded Citizens, (**http://www .thearc.org/**) in the 1950s and their subsequent work on behalf of individuals with intellectual disabilities. The 1954 U. S. Supreme Court decision in *Brown v. Board of Education* provided a recognition of the importance of the equal protection clause in the 14th amendment (**http:// www.loc.gov/rr/program/bib/ourdocs/14thamendment.html**) as it pertained to Black children attending public schools and found that segregation based on race was unconstitutional. (We use the term Black rather than African-American because not all who would identify themselves as Black would consider themselves African-American—some students may have come from the Caribbean or France. Yet, the same discriminatory practices and prejudices applied to them.) In their strongly worded decision, the U.S. Supreme Court rejected the separate but equal doctrine that had been the law of the land:

> We come then to the question presented: does segregation of children in public schools solely on the basis of race, even though the physical facilities and other "tangible" factors may be equal, deprive the children of the minority group of equal educational opportunities? We believe it does.
>
> To separate them from others of similar age and qualifications solely because of their race generates a feeling of inferiority as to their status in the community that may affect their hearts and minds in a way unlikely ever to be undone.
>
> Segregation of white and colored children in public schools has a detrimental effect upon the colored children. The impact is greater when it has the sanction of the law; for the policy of separating the races is usually interpreted as denoting the inferiority of the Negro group. A sense of inferiority affects the motivation of a child to learn. Segregation with the sanction of law, therefore, has a tendency to retard the educational and mental development of Negro Children and to deprive them of some of the benefits they receive in a racially integrated school system.

The Brown decision has been viewed by many as a major decision supporting the provision of educational services to children with disabilities. In fact, as noted by Turnbull and Turnbull (1998), if you substitute the words "disabled" for "negro" and "nondisabled" for "white", the decision reads as if it were written for children with disabilities. While this decision was ultimately important for the disability community, it took several more years before children with disabilities were guaranteed a public education. In fact, until the late 1960s, many states had legislation specifically prohibiting some students with disabilities from attending public schools and excluding them from compulsory attendance laws (Yell, 2006).

During that time, many people with disabilities were institutionalized with little or no hope of participating in society. In essence, they were sentenced to living in substandard conditions ... sentenced without having committed any crime and for a characteristic they had no role in creating. A groundbreaking photo exposé of life inside an institution for individuals with disabilities was published by Blatt and Kaplan in 1966. They documented the significant deficiencies in the system and the abusive treatment encountered by individuals with disabilities who had been forced to reside in state institutions, and in 1972, Rivera took a film crew into the Willowbrook State School in New York State. Both of these works graphically depicted the dismal and hopeless conditions in which people with disabilities had been placed and forced to live, because there were few other options in this country or any other for that matter. These appalling living conditions that were captured in photographs taken from a hidden camera, along with graphic descriptions, are included in Blatt and Kaplan's book, *Christmas in Purgatory*. This work depicts the conditions that existed for many individuals with disabilities and would show the interested reader why advocacy groups and families were battling the system with such urgency to make changes that would ensure appropriate treatment of their loved ones with disabilities.

Interest in promoting services for individuals with disabilities continued to gain support in the 1960s as evidenced by President Kennedy's creation of the President's Committee on Mental Retardation and the passage of legislation that provided grant money to improve the education of children with disabilities. As previously noted, the Brown decision was instrumental in providing support for the education of students with disabilities. In reaching a decision in Brown, the Supreme Court was influenced by the 14th Amendment to the Constitution which stated, "... nor shall any State deprive any person of life, liberty, or property, without due process of law; nor deny to any person within its jurisdiction the equal protection of the laws ..." When a state develops laws regarding mandatory school attendance, a property interest is created by the state. The 14th amendment prohibits a state from depriving an individual from life, liberty without due process, or denying individuals equal protection under the laws. Advocates for individuals with disabilities were successful in demonstrating that state practices of excluding students with disabilities from public education violated their constitutional rights.

The momentum gained by the disability rights movement continued into the 1970s and resulted in significant legal action, in the form of both court cases and passage of new federal laws. While there were several court cases at that time, we present just a couple of the more significant cases here. The first was a 1972 consent decree which represented agreement between two parties that avoided the necessity of continuing the issue in court. In that case, *Pennsylvania Ass'n of Retarded Citizens (PARC) v. Pennsylvania*, the state agreed to provide a meaningful program of education and training to individuals with intellectual disabilities and noted that placement in the general class was preferable to placement in a special class and placement in the regular school was preferable to placement in a separate school. These were significant findings at a time when many with cognitive disabilities were not receiving a meaningful education and were routinely segregated in institutions and special schools. In a similar court case, *Mills v. D.C. Board of Education* (1972), the court extended the findings in PARC to all children with disabilities, not just those with intellectual delays. Mills also identified many of the procedural safeguards that would provide a foundation for future special education law, established that placement based on a disability label was inappropriate, and recognized that cost would not be a sufficient reason for denying a public education to children with disabilities. Both PARC and Mills made effective use of the 14th Amendment and influenced the forthcoming special education law.

However, Congress was dissatisfied with lack of progress made by states in the provision of educational services to children with disabilities. In response to the sparse educational opportunities provided to children with disabilities, Congress developed legislation designed to rectify this problem. In 1975, President Gerald Ford signed Public Law 94-142, the Education for All Handicapped Children Act (EHA or EAHCA), the first federal law guaranteeing a Free Appropriate Public Education (FAPE) to children with disabilities. When recognizing the necessity of this landmark legislation in the preamble to the law, Congress noted that there were approximately eight million children with disabilities in the country, with one million receiving absolutely no educational programming, and an additional three million receiving less than adequate programming. By not being afforded the educational opportunities provided to children without disabilities, children with disabilities were functionally discriminated against solely on the basis of their disability.

The EAHCA, now called the Individuals with Disabilities Education Act (IDEA), is a permanent law but is reviewed periodically to allow for amendments and to affirm financial support for the law. When initially passed, the law contained six major principles designed to ensure that a child with a disability was provided with FAPE. These principles which are still in effect and will be discussed in depth in subsequent chapters in this book are:

(1) *Zero reject*—the recognition that if a child meets the eligibility criteria and needs special education, that student will receive special education and related services. This provision prevents states or districts from trying to claim that a child has such a severe a disability that s/he cannot benefit from special education.

(2) *Nondiscriminatory Assessment*—assessments must be conducted in a manner that does not discriminate against a student due to ethnicity, cultural background, primary language, mode of communication, or physical capability, among other things. Essentially, the assessment must be fair and measure what it purports to measure.

(3) *Individualized Education Program (IEP)*—a written document identifying the learning goals and what special education and related services will be provided by the public agency. It is more complex than this, but then that is exactly what this book is about—unraveling the complexities and providing you with the skills and understandings needed to develop a meaningful IEP.

(4) *Least Restrictive Environment (LRE)*—the presumption that children will be educated in the regular education setting. This is a rebuttable presumption which means that the IEP team can remove a child from the regular education setting in those *very limited circumstances* when the child's needs cannot be met in the regular education setting even with the use of supplementary aids and services. This has been a contentious issue and we have devoted an entire chapter to this important protection.

(5) *Due Process Safeguards*—a set of procedures that provides parents with specific information regarding a school's proposed actions with their child and allow parents to challenge the proposed actions of the district. Children with disabilities are afforded special protections to help prevent past discriminatory practices, and we describe the safeguards in a later chapter.

(6) *Parent and student participation and shared decision-making*—a recognition of the importance of parents and students in developing the IEP and making educational decisions.

Since its passage in 1975, the EAHCA has been amended five times. Major aspects of the legislation and amendments are contained in Table 1-3. The information in the table is presented to highlight the fact that special education law is dynamic and amendments may include significant changes that teachers must understand and follow. Typically, school districts provide training on new aspects of the law, but if that training is not provided, it is still incumbent upon teachers to remain aware of changes. An easy place to find information about the federal law is at the U. S. Department of Education webpage for IDEA (**http://idea.ed.gov/**).

TABLE 1-3. Major Attributes of PL 94-142 and Subsequent Amendments

Law	Year	Title	Attributes
PL 94-142	1975	Education for All Handicapped Children Act	<ul><li>11 disability categories</li><li>Special education for eligible children age 6 through 21 years</li><li>Zero reject</li><li>Nondiscriminatory Assessment</li><li>Procedural Due Process</li><li>Parent Participation</li><li>Individualized Education Program</li><li>Least Restrictive Environment (Rebuttable Presumption)</li><li>Free Appropriate Public Education</li></ul>
PL 99-457	1986	Education for All Handicapped Children Act – Amendments of 1986	<ul><li>Special education (IEP) for eligible children age 3–5 (preschool services)</li><li>Early Intervention Services for young children (age birth – 3) with disabilities and their families</li><li>Individualized Family Service Plan (IFSP)</li></ul>
PL 101-476	1990	Individuals with Disabilities Education Act (IDEA '90)	<ul><li>Renamed law and replaced "handicap" with "disability"</li><li>Incorporated people first language</li><li>Transition Services at age 16</li><li>Added Autism and Traumatic Brain Injury as eligibility categories</li></ul>

continued

Law	Year	Title	Attributes
PL 105-17	1997	Individuals with Disabilities Education Act Amendments of 1997 (IDEA '97)	• Discipline procedures added • Increased Parental role in eligibility decision making • Role of general education teacher in IEP development • Increased focus on general education curriculum and setting
PL 108-446	2004	Individuals with Disabilities Education Improvement Act of 2004 (IDEA '04)	• Allowed Response to Intervention framework for LD eligibility • Early Intervening Services • Allowed for changes in IEP team required membership • Short-term IEP objectives not required for all students • Transition planning at age 16 • Disciplinary procedures modified • State option of using IFSP until Kindergarten

Section 504 of the Rehabilitation Act of 1973

Another federal law that has had significant impact on the education of individuals with disabilities is Section 504 of the Rehabilitation Act of 1973, commonly referred to as Section 504 (**http://www2.ed.gov/about/offices/list/ocr/504faq.html**). This legislation differs significantly from IDEA, and a major discussion of the law is beyond the scope of this book. However, it is important to mention for at least two reasons. First, special educators are frequently considered experts in the law and must have at least a general familiarity of its requirements. Second, the law provides protections for all children with disabilities, including those who are technically not eligible for special education and related services. It is actually more focused on the responsibilities of general educators than special educators. Thus both general and special education teachers should have a familiarity with the legislation and know the difference between the important aspects of both Section 504 and IDEA. Rich (2010) developed an excellent manual explaining Section 504 that includes sample documents. The manual is published in English and Spanish and is available free of charge at **http://www.psesd.org/index.php?option=com_content&task=view&id=586&Itemid=342**

Basically, and foremost, Section 504 is civil rights legislation that prohibits agencies receiving federal funds from discriminating against otherwise qualified individuals solely on the basis of disability. Since public schools receive federal funds, they must not engage in any activity considered to be discriminatory toward students with disabilities, or adults with disabilities for that matter. Enforcement of Section 504 in the public schools is the responsibility of the Office of Civil Rights (OCR) in the Department of Education and, should a school district's actions be determined to be discriminatory, OCR can require remediation of the issue. Failure to comply with OCR directions may result in immediate suspension of all federal funds awarded to the district. This represents a considerable amount of money for most school districts. Unlike IDEA, which provides federal funds to assist districts in providing special education supports, Section 504 does not provide federal funding. As a civil rights law, it is expected that districts will comply with the responsibility to behave in a nondiscriminatory manner without any financial incentive to do so.

Eligibility categories for IDEA will be discussed in the next chapter and you will notice that they differ significantly from the eligibility required for 504. While IDEA requires that a child meet state eligibility criteria in specified categories **and** need special education and related services, Section 504 uses the following much broader definition of disability. We won't go into specific detail here, but the definition under Section 504 is that a student must be determined to: (1) have a physical or mental impairment that substantially limits one or more major life activities; or (2) have a record of such an impairment; or (3) be regarded as having such an impairment. This broad definition means that all children eligible for special education services under IDEA would be protected by Section 504, so districts could not discriminate against them solely on the basis of disability. However, not all children covered by Section 504 are eligible for special education services under IDEA, because not all children covered by Section 504 need special education and therefore do not meet the two-part eligibility criteria specified in IDEA. The two-part criterion for IDEA is: 1) does the child meet the eligibility criteria for one of the identified disability categories; and 2) does the child need special education? Consider the following example of a student who would likely meet the first criterion for IDEA but not the second because she does not need special education. She would not be eligible for an IEP; however, she would meet the eligibility under Section 504 and would be eligible for a 504 plan as appropriate.

Sarah attends a large public high school that is four stories tall. She had bone cancer and, as a result, she had one leg amputated just above the knee. With the exception of stairs she can easily maneuver with the use of a prosthetic device and/or crutches. She does not require any special education services, but does have a Section 504 accommodation plan to address her very specific need for assistance regarding stair climbing. The 504 plan is very simple and states that she will have access to the elevator, typically used only by faculty, in order to get to her upper floor classes. That is the only disability related support she requires. Had the school failed to provide her with an elevator key or make other suitable accommodations, thereby denying her access to her courses, one could have made the case that she was being discriminated against solely on the basis of her disability and she could have sought a remedy under Section 504.

Students who are eligible for special education receive an IEP while those eligible for 504 only, receive a 504 plan. The IEP is much more complex than the 504 plan and contains all of the components that would be contained in a 504 plan plus additional required content from IDEA. Thus, students who receive special education do not have both an IEP and a 504 plan, because the IEP would address all requirements under both laws. As you will see, an IEP is several pages long to ensure that it covers all required items. However, 504 plans are typically much shorter and may only be one page. Consider the student in the previous scenario. Her 504 plan would only require a couple of sentences to document that the reasonable accommodation for her was access to the elevator and a provision for permission to use or have a key to do so. A brief listing of differences between Section 504 and IDEA is contained in Table 1-4.

TABLE 1-4. IDEA and Section 504: A Brief Comparison

Component	IDEA	Section 504
WHAT IS IT?	A federal funding law and regulation.	A federal civil rights law and regulation.
WHAT IS ITS PURPOSE?	To provide federal funds to state education agencies and districts to educate disabled students.	To eliminate disability discrimination in all programs and activities that receive federal funds.
WHO IS A "DISABLED STUDENT"?	Both regulations provide protections to "disabled students" but each regulation defines "disabled student" differently. Section 504 defines "disabled student" more broadly than does IDEA.	
	Defines disabled student as a child aged 3-21 who has one or more of 14 specific disabilities (i.e., autism, deaf-blindness, developmental delay, deafness, emotional behavioral disability, hearing impairment, mental retardation, multiple disabilities, orthopedic impairment, other health impairment, specific learning disability, speech or language impairment, traumatic brain injury, and visual impairment, including blindness) and, due to disability, needs special education.	Defines disabled student as a school-aged child who has a physical or mental impairment that substantially limits one or more major life activities. The terms "physical or mental impairment," "substantially limits," and "major life activities" are to be interpreted broadly.
WHAT IS A "FREE APPROPRIATE PUBLIC EDUCATION" (FAPE)?	Both regulations require a district to provide FAPE to each disabled student in its jurisdiction but each regulation defines FAPE differently. Section 504 defines FAPE more broadly than does IDEA.	
	Defines FAPE as special education and related services. Students can receive related services under IDEA only if they need related services to benefit from special education.	Defines FAPE as regular or special education and related aids and services that are designed to meet a student's individual educational needs and are based upon procedures that satisfy required evaluation, placement, and due process procedures. Students can receive related aids and services under Section 504 even if they are not provided any special education.

From "A Parent and Educator Guide to Free Appropriate Public Education Under Section 504 of the Rehabilitation Act of 1973" by Jim Rich, Director of Program Development and Review, Puget Sound ESD. Reprinted by permission of Puget Sound ESD.

Chapter Summary

The history of education for persons with disabilities maps in many ways the history of how any minority group has fared in the schools. With the first European settlers came the notion that children with ostensible disabilities were little more than defective products of an evil that could only be banished by a host of harsh treatments. Education, to the extent that it existed as an institution at all, was the product of the dominant institutions of the time, i.e, the church. Children with disabilities were, at best ostracized, stigmatized, and definitely separated from their peers both by neglect and by design. What followed over the next 200 years was a much more focused view of difference which evolved to the understanding that to be different was accepted as characteristic of the human condition. The work of Itard (translation 1932) and Seguin (1856) gave rise to the optimism that was reflected in the work of Maria Montessori (1917). Montessori's efforts to include children with mental retardation in her early education programs in Italy influenced Alexander and Mabel Bell to try Montessori's methods in the United States (Bell, 1914).

But children with disabilities, although known to benefit from education, were not part of the responsibility of general education. Those with the most severe disabilities were either totally rejected or served in separate residential facilities, but many children whose disabilities were not readily apparent made their way into the public schools. The public schools of America began to recognize these children as a population whose needs were "special". Public school programs for children with disabilities were established as part of the public education system in Chicago as early as 1900 but they were underfunded, staffed by minimally trained teachers, and often located in the oldest and most distant facilities. This trend for separate services kept children in different buildings, different rooms, or even at home. Contact with peers who were participants in the general education program was minimal to nonexistent.

But this began to change as a result of a series of landmark court cases and with legislation that began by establishing the premise that a child with a disability should, if at all possible, be educated with his or her typically developing peers (the LRE requirement). And that is what this book is all about. Just how do we, as educators of all children, those with and those without disabilities, plan for the best possible outcome for each and every child regardless of the nature of the personal or circumstantial conditions that he or she presents. In this chapter we have given you some background, cautioned you to rethink how we talk about people with disabilities and in the process, just maybe, caused you to consider your place in history - what a special role you play in making our society work for all its members, especially those least able or likely to advocate for themselves.

Chapter Activities

1. Rewrite the following statements using people first language:

   Michael is a special education student.

   There is Maria's retarded sister.

   Ms. Lee has an emotionally disturbed student in her class.

   My Down syndrome grandson is in first grade with typically developing peers.

   Martin is schizophrenic.

   Joaquin is developmentally delayed.

   Serafina is crippled.

2. You are in the teacher's lounge and one of your fellow teachers says "that's so retarded." What could you say that would denote the insensitivity of the statement yet maintain your professional relationship with the teacher?

   What might you do if it was the principal?

   If it was a student in your classroom? Or an unknown student in the hallway?

   If it was a parent dropping off her child at school at the beginning of the day?

3. John is a new student in your class. His previous teacher has written a note alerting you to the fact that he is "retarded."

   (a) Write down your immediate perceptions and description of John. Now compare your notations with that of peers. How did your perceptions differ? Did the word "retarded" have different connotations for different individuals?

   (b) Would you find the label "retarded" sufficient in helping you determine what to teach John?

   (c) What kind of information, if any, could the prior teacher provide that would help you be successful with John?

   (d) Why do you think the term was changed from "mental retardation" to "intellectual disability?"

4. A colleague informs you that he dislikes going to IEP meetings because the other teachers and professionals at the meeting use terms that he really doesn't understand and feels foolish asking questions. He doubts the parent understands,

either. Since you know that important decisions regarding children are made at these meetings, all participants, including him and the parent, must understand the topics. How might he resolve this dilemma?

5. Check out the book "Christmas in Purgatory. "What are your initial perceptions? Remember this when you read Chapter 5 and consider the issue of Least Restrictive Environment.

6. Review the site **http://www.disabilityisnatural.com** and develop a presentation that you might use at a teacher workshop.

Chapter 2

Eligibility and Referral Procedures

Chapter Overview

In the previous chapter, we discussed foundational issues including those related to terminology and the practice of using people first language as both an indication of respect and as a way to encourage focus on the individual rather than the disability. We also provided a brief review of the major pillars or components of special education law and provided a brief contrast with Section 504 of the Rehabilitation Act of 1973. Now that we have developed some common understandings, we turn briefly to selected issues related to a referral to special education and eligibility decisions, the precursors to the development of an IEP and subsequent provision of special education services.

These topics are important for a number of reasons: First, a clear understanding of both the referral and eligibility processes will enable you to be a more effective team member, whether you are a special or a general educator. Second, a basic understanding of Early Intervention services provided to eligible children and their families from birth through two years of age (B–3), will help preschool teachers better understand the transition process for children moving from Early Intervention (Part C) to Special Education (Part B) services for students age three through 21 years of age (3–22). Equally important is the need to help parents understand that the nature of services changes from a focus upon development (Part C) to one anchored in preparation for the general education curriculum (Part B). Finally, a basic understanding of the referral process and eligibility determination procedures will help teachers ensure that students with disabilities are afforded equitable educational opportunities.

To accomplish our goals for this chapter, we will provide a brief overview of Early Intervention Services and also contrast eligibility criteria for Early Intervention Services (B–3) with Special Education (3–22) eligibility criteria. This is not a book about eligibility determination, but since preschool teachers are commonly involved in determining whether a child has a developmental delay and elementary level teachers frequently assist with determinations of learning disability, we will discuss eligibility criteria for those two categories at some depth. We do so to provide a description of how the system may function, with the hope that greater understanding will allow you to focus on child-centered issues during the meeting rather than expend your energy figuring out the system. In addition, we will provide a brief description of the referral process and the requirements for special education eligibility evaluations, including an overview of evaluation procedures. But first, we describe the practice followed throughout this book when referring to the law, regulations, and parents.

All states have agreed to the conditions required by IDEA and receive federal funding to support the education of children with disabilities. In addition to Congress creating the law, the U. S. Department of Education developed regulations that provide legal interpretations and recommendations to help ensure that the law is implemented in a manner that is consistent with Congressional intent. The regulations generally provide more in-depth implementation guidance than the law, are easier to use, and include clarifying commentary regarding selected issues of concern. For those reasons, we will typically refer to the regulations rather than the law itself, but you can readily access both the law and regulations governing Part B and Part C at **http://idea.ed.gov/** The regulations covering Part C, Early Intervention Services, are found in Part 303 of the 34th volume of the Code of Federal Regulations (34 CFR Part 303). So, if we refer to specific regulatory language and it is identified as §*303.26 Natural Environments*, you would know that we were writing about Early Intervention Services (B–3) because the section began with the Part number 303. Alternatively, the regulations for Special Education, Part B, are in the 34th volume of the Code of Federal Regulations, Part 300 (34 CFR Part 300). So a reference to §*300.114 Least Restrictive Environment* would indicate that we were writing about Special Education (3–22) because the referenced section began with the Part number 300. We will also refer to commentary that accompanies the Federal Regulations and provide the regulation and page where you can find the comments. For example, Fed. Reg. 71, 46670, 2006 would indicate that the comment is on page 46670 of the Fed. Reg. 71 published in 2006 (Assistance to States for the Education of Children with Disabilities and Preschool Grants for Children with Disabilities; Final Rule, 71 Fed. Reg., Monday, August 14, 2006).

The law and regulations both refer to the State Education Agency (SEA) and Local Education Agency (LEA) when discussing legal responsibilities. We will most commonly refer to school district since this is a common way to refer to the LEA. The federal law and regulations are the same throughout the nation, but states are allowed to develop their own regulations as long as they are consistent with federal law. Since federal law mandates that states develop specific eligibility criteria for different disability categories, prudent special educators should be familiar with the regulations from their own state. These are typically available at state department of education websites.

Throughout this text, we refer to the child's parent. Consistent with both the legal requirements and the intent of IDEA, we will emphasize the importance of parental involvement.

Given the difficulty in determining who should act as parent for some children, IDEA §300.30 has defined parent as follows:

(1) A biological or adoptive parent of a child;

(2) A foster parent, unless prohibited by state law, regulations, or contractual obligations,

(3) A guardian authorized to act as the child's parent or make educational decisions (but not the State if the child is a ward of the state). *Please note that this restriction specifically prohibits child welfare workers from acting as the parent. The authors have been in IEP meetings where state workers tried to act as the parent – in direct violation of the law – and had to be reminded (not so gently at times) that they did not have the authority to act as the child's parent.* Children who do not have an individual to act as parent are assigned a surrogate according to the guidelines in §300.519.

(4) An individual acting in the place of a biological or adoptive parent (including a grandparent, stepparent, or other relative) with whom the child lives, or an individual who is legally responsible for the child's welfare.

In a case where more than one person is qualified to meet the criteria for parent, the regulations (§300.30(b)(1)) provide that the biological or adoptive parent must be afforded parental rights and responsibilities unless the individual does not have legal authority to make educational decisions. The regulations clarify the responsibilities and provide valuable assistance to schools trying to identify the parent or assign a surrogate and begin the evaluation process or work through the IEP process. In a later chapter, we will discuss the transfer of parental rights to a child who has reached age of majority.

We begin our discussion of the major aspects of this chapter with a brief description of Part C services followed by an in-depth discussion of Part B. As a reminder, we are discussing Part C services, because an understanding of the services and supports parents of young children (B–3) were accustomed to receiving can be helpful to a preschool teacher helping a family and child transition from Part C to Part B services.

Part C, Early Intervention (Birth to 3 Years Old)

Services for eligible infants and toddlers between the ages of birth and three years old are far more comprehensive than are those for eligible students between the ages of 3 and 22 years. There are 14 specific services referred to as Early Intervention (EI) services, which both the eligible child and the child's family may receive if needed. This is one of the big differences between Part B and Part C. In Part C, what most would consider to be "special education" is only one of those 14 EI services, service #12 Special Instruction, and it is not a required service for all children. However, all children who are served under Part B must receive specially designed instruction. All of the services provided in Part C are to be "family focused" and as such are delivered according to a formal plan referred to as the Individualized Family Service Plan or IFSP. So whereas older students in public school programs who are eligible for special education and related services have an IEP that is child-focused young children who are eligible for EI services have an IFSP which is family-focused. We will go into more detail regarding the differences between the IEP and the IFSP in a later chapter.

The determination of both eligibility and areas of need proceeds in a fashion similar to that for older students but the categories of eligibility are quite different. Whereas special education and related services are provided to the 3- to 22-year old students who have one of the 13 different identified disabilities (see table 2-2), and need special education and related services because of the disability, any infant or toddler and that child's family can receive the benefit of services listed in the IFSP if the child fits into one of the following three categories. According to §303.21, a child from birth to 3 years old who, according to the results of a formal assessment, is experiencing a developmental delay in one of five named areas (cognitive development, physical development, communication development, social or emotional development, and adaptive development) and that child's family may receive early intervention services. We often refer to these children as being *children with a developmental delay*. A second category of eligibility includes children with a diagnosed physical or mental condition that has a high probability of resulting in developmental delay even though that delay may not yet be reflected in an assessment of developmental status. Children born with chromosomal abnormalities such as Down syndrome would fit into this category regardless of current functioning level as indicated from a formal assessment. We refer to these children as being infants or toddlers with *a high risk* for subsequent delay. The third category of eligibility for infants and toddlers includes children who are *at-risk for developmental delays*. These young children are those who are at-risk for a substantial delay if they do not receive EI services. States have the discretion to either provide services for this at-risk population of children or not and are responsible for determining what factors go into the determination of *at-risk*.

By the time a child who is receiving EI services reaches the age of 2 years, 9 months his or her IFSP must include a transition plan to facilitate the movement of child and family from Part C early intervention services to Part B special education, or, in the event that the child does not qualify for Part B special education, to another program option such as a public or private preschool program. The transition plan must include a specification of steps and services to be taken and provided to support the smooth transition of the child from EI services to the next placement and may go so far as to involve training of parents regarding the difference between Part C and Part B services, future placement options and steps that are required to help the child adjust to a new environment.

Part B, Special Education (3 to 22 Years Old)

For Part B services, children are usually identified and enter the special education system through one of three routes. First, as noted in the previous section, children who receive Early Intervention Services under Part C are evaluated to determine whether they will meet the different eligibility criteria under Special Education as part of the transition process. Those children who are deemed to be eligible because they meet both required requisites: 1) have one of 13 named disabilities or qualify as having a developmental delay in locales where that categorical classification is permitted, and 2) need special education are transitioned into Part B services where they are provided with an IEP which in all but a very few cases replaces the IFSP. This process is intended to fulfill the Congressional desire for a seamless system of service for young children with disabilities. The law is permissive and allows the state the option to authorize use of an IFSP in lieu of an IEP for children age 3 through 5 (§300.323(b)). Exercising this option would require a considerable amount of work and coordination at the state level, because this could result in a mix of young children some with IEPs and others with IFSPs in a classroom. Management of different services provided under each program would present a challenge, and in this text, we will assume that all eligible preschool children receive special services provided in accordance with an IEP.

Second, the law requires states to identify all eligible children with disabilities and operate a Child Find system designed to facilitate that identification process (§300.111). The specific activities carried out through Child Find are not delineated in the law, rather they vary according to local needs and may include informational activities such as 1) placing posters in grocery stores and doctors' offices encouraging parents to contact the school district for an eligibility assessment if there are concerns regarding a child's development, 2) providing necessary information regarding referrals to private preschool and K–12 providers, and 3) conducting screening activities where parents can bring young children for routine screenings. These screening activities, in particular, are frequently collaborative ventures where young children receive developmental, communication, vision, and hearing screenings as well as immunizations. The results from these screenings are designed to indicate whether a child's development is progressing as expected or identify concerns that merit further educational assessment in physical, cognitive, communication, social-emotional, and adaptive domains. In those cases, children are sent to the school district for a more complete and comprehensive evaluation to determine special education eligibility and/or to a medical service provider if there are health concerns.

> A simple illustrative example of a screening procedure is the vision screening typically conducted with all children in elementary schools. A child who fails the screening is referred for additional vision assessment by a specialist, and if needed the appropriate intervention is implemented i. e., the child is prescribed glasses. Similarly, a child who fails a developmental screening for communication may be referred to the local school district for a comprehensive evaluation to determine whether the child is eligible to receive special education and needs those services.

The third major gateway to special education services is through a pre-referral process operated at the school. Most children with severe or evident disabilities were identified before attending school and transitioned into Part B services, whereas, children who were not identified as having a disability until they experienced significant learning and/or behavioral difficulty at elementary school are commonly involved in a referral process. Due to the numerous possibilities regarding pre-referral team composition and operation, we present a relatively generic approach with the understanding that there are unique situations depending upon the needs of the child and district operations.

A pre-referral team can be composed of teachers only (Overton, 2011; Salvia, Ysseldyke, & Bolt, 2013) or include other professionals and parents (Gargiulo & Metcalf, 2013) and serves as the first line of assistance for both the student and the teacher. The purpose of the team is to review/clarify concerns, develop and identify strategies, and assist with the implementation of interventions that will facilitate the child's development before the skill deficits are of such severity that they result in his or her identification as a child with a disability. A pre-referral procedure is recommended or required in numerous states and serves to both prevent disability and to reduce the number of unnecessary referrals for expensive special education assessment (Buck, Polloway, Smith-Thomas, & Cook, 2003). However, the pre-referral team process must not have the effect of delaying the identification and eligibility determination of a child who qualifies for services, and its use would not be appropriate in all cases. For example, if a student lost his or her vision, it would be ludicrous to require that the child proceed through the pre-referral process to determine if the lack of vision really constituted a disability and if an educational intervention could renew his or her sight. That child could proceed to the special education evaluation without going through a pre-referral process and should be seen without delay. A common framework for school-based referrals is depicted in the flow chart contained in Figure 2-1.

As indicated in Figure 2-1, the pre-referral process proceeds in the following manner. First, the concern is brought to the attention of the pre-referral team by the child's teacher or parent. The team typically reviews all relevant information, determines whether additional information or a classroom observation is warranted, identifies research-based interventions, assigns responsibilities for implementation of interventions, and agrees upon a follow-up meeting. At follow-up, the team reviews the data to determine efficacy of the implemented intervention(s) and may recommend a continuation of the intervention, revise or discontinue the intervention, or refer the child for a special education eligibility evaluation or a 504 evaluation. A list of items that a regular education teacher might bring to a pre-referral meeting or provide to team members before the meeting is contained in Table 2-1.

The efficacy of pre-referral intervention in decreasing the need for special education was specifically noted in the preamble of P.L. 105–17, the 1997 Amendments to IDEA. This is particularly true when the strategies recommended by the pre-referral team are research-based to the extent possible, as required by both IDEA and the No Child Left Behind Act (NCLB). (An excellent source for free material and interventions strategies is available at **http://www.interventioncentral.org/**). Additionally, the current special education law (P. L. 108-446 or IDEA 04) allows districts to use 15% of special education funds on Early Intervening Services (EIS) for struggling students in kindergarten through twelfth grade who are not currently identified as eligible for special education or receiving special education services. If funds are used for EIS, the regulations specify that kindergarten through third grade students experiencing academic or behavioral difficulty and requiring supports in addition to those typically provided should be the priority for receiving the support (§300.226). The goal is clear—to promote the use of scientifically-based interventions to prevent a student's behavioral or academic difficulty from becoming so severe that it is ultimately judged to be a disability.

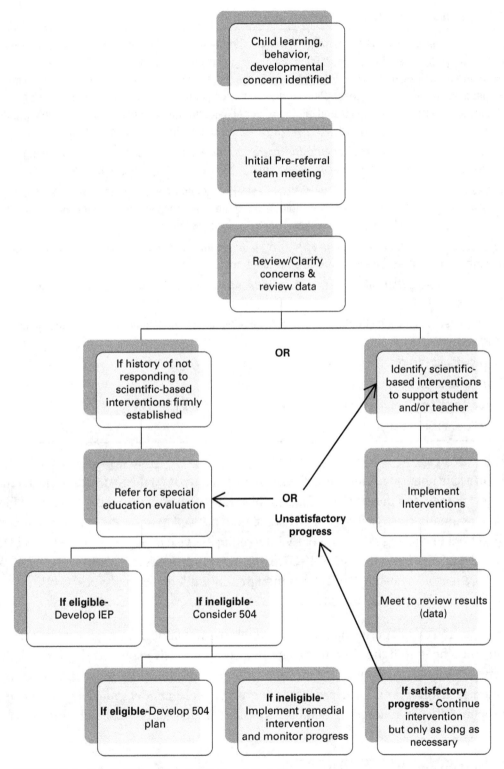

FIGURE 2-1. Special Education Pre-Referral Activities

TABLE 2-1. Items to Bring to a Pre-referral Meeting

- *Specific concerns described in behavioral terms* – Clearly and specifically describe the concerns, do not use generalized descriptions. For example, a general description such as Sara has trouble with math is useless, because it does not provide the team with sufficient detail from which to make suggestions. An acceptable description would be: Sara has one-to-one correspondence to 10, recognizes the numerals 1 and 5, and when presented with groups of items does not identify greater than, less than or equal to. This description provides the team with useful information.

- *Clear descriptions of student strengths and interests.* These might be helpful when developing interventions. Be sure to include sources of support, such as a sibling, parent, best friend, etc.

- *Representative samples of student work if available.* If the concern is about an academic skill, then you should be able to provide a work sample(s), but if the concern is about behavior, you should be able to describe how frequently the behavior occurs and how long it lasts.

- *Representative sample of work done by typical student.* Samples of work done by a student performing at average in the class. This will provide a basis for comparison.

- *Results of on-going (formative) academic assessments.* (ex. math fluency tests, oral reading fluency measures, etc.)

- Specific descriptions of instructional strategies implemented, including materials and grouping strategies.

- Past academic records, if appropriate

- *Behavior records*, if appropriate

- *Any pertinent health records*, such as vision or hearing screenings

- Other relevant information

On a side note, one of the authors was asked if EIS funds could be used to fund a remedial test preparation program for high school students who had not passed the state high school graduation test. Clearly, one would be hard pressed to make the case that teaching high school test-taking skills is an Early Intervening Service of any sort. Unfortunately for some of those students, the use of effective intervention appears to have come too late—all the more reason to ensure that IEPs are thoughtfully written to cover critical skills.

Tracking the child's performance on pre-referral interventions is important, as that information could be used if the child moves on to a comprehensive special education eligibility evaluation. Schools can implement pre-referral interventions without parental permission, but parental involvement in the process is certainly recommended, makes good sense, and is consistent with the required parental involvement components of special education law.

Special Issues in Eligibility

An understanding of the eligibility criteria and associated issues helps clarify the process thereby minimizing confusion that many teachers experience at both pre-referral and special education eligibility meetings. We will provide descriptions of all disability eligibility categories included in Part B, but for a more detailed discussion, interested readers are encouraged to consult assessment texts that deal with eligibility assessment in detail (e.g., Overton, 2011; Salvia et al., 2013). Unlike Part C which has two required and one optional eligibility category, Part B contains 13 mandatory eligibility categories and allows states to use the term Developmental Delay rather than one of the 13 eligibility categories until the child is 9 years old. It is crucial to note that in addition to meeting eligibility criteria for one of the Part B categories or Developmental Delay, a child must also demonstrate a need for special education. So, the special education eligibility determination for a particular child requires an affirmation of the following two points: 1) Does the child meet eligibility criteria; and 2) Does the child need special education? (§300.8) (If a child does meet the criteria for one of the disability categories, but only needs a related service, then the team would be wise to consider eligibility under Section 504).

A brief description of each of the Part B eligibility categories as contained in the regulations is contained in Table 2-2. As you will note from reading the descriptions, the federal regulations provide only the briefest description of the conditions, not the specific criteria that must be met for a child to be considered to have one of the special education eligible disabilities. Those decisions regarding criteria are left to the states, and due in part to that freedom granted to states, it should come as no surprise that eligibility criteria varies by geographic location. This means that there are students who are eligible in one state, move to another state that has more stringent eligibility criteria, and find that they are no longer considered as students with a disability. This frequently causes frustration, making it difficult for parents and teachers to understand why a child is no longer eligible yet still requires assistance. In addition to specific eligibility criteria that may vary by location, the states also have liberty to adjust eligibility criteria. So, it is possible for states to tighten up the eligibility criteria, making it more difficult to be found eligible thereby decreasing the number of eligible students and the associated costs. Alternatively, states could relax the criteria and thereby identify more students as having a disability (Howell & Davidson, 1997). As noted by Kavale and Forness (1997), our ability to identify students with disabilities is less than perfect, particularly those whose disabilities inferred from a child's performance on a test, such as the common practice with Learning Disability.

Before describing eligibility issues related to Developmental Delay or Learning Disability, we will briefly contrast a medical model with an educational model for identifying disabilities. The medical model certainly has a use in medicine, but as we hope to demonstrate, its applicability to education is limited. We will then describe a common approach for determining eligibility for Developmental Delay followed by a review of procedures used to determine eligibility for Learning Disability. We chose to discuss Developmental Delay because it is a common eligibility label that preschool teachers will encounter and Learning Disability because it continues to be the most common eligibility category (U.S. Department of Education, 2011), and elementary level teachers will likely teach numerous students with learning disabilities.

TABLE 2-2. Special Education Eligibility Categories (§300.8)

1. **Autism** means a developmental disability significantly affecting verbal and nonverbal communication and social interaction, generally evident before age three, that adversely affects a child's educational performance. Other characteristics often associated with autism are engagement in repetitive activities and stereotyped movements, resistance to environmental change or change in daily routines, and unusual responses to sensory experiences.
 	
    (ii) Autism does not apply if a child's educational performance is adversely affected primarily because the child has an emotional disturbance
 	
    (iii) A child who manifests the characteristics of autism after age three could be identified as having autism if the criteria in paragraph (c)(1)(i) of this section are satisfied.

2. **Deaf-blindness** means concomitant hearing and visual impairments, the combination of which causes such severe communication and other developmental and educational needs that they cannot be accommodated in special education programs solely for children with deafness or children with blindness.
3. **Deafness** means a hearing impairment that is so severe that the child is impaired in processing linguistic information through hearing, with or without amplification that adversely affects a child's Educational performance.

4. **Emotional disturbance** means a condition exhibiting one or more of the following characteristics over a long period of time and to a marked degree that adversely affects a child's educational performance:
 	
    (A) An inability to learn that cannot be explained by intellectual, sensory, or health factors.
 	
    (B) An inability to build or maintain satisfactory interpersonal relationships with peers and teachers.
 	
    (C) Inappropriate types of behavior or feelings under normal circumstances.
 	
    (D) A general pervasive mood of unhappiness or depression.
 	
    (E) A tendency to develop physical symptoms or fears associated with personal or school problems.
 	
    (ii) Emotional disturbance includes schizophrenia. The term does not apply to children who are socially maladjusted, unless it is determined that they have an emotional disturbance

5. **Hearing impairment** means an impairment in hearing, whether permanent or fluctuating, that adversely affects a child's educational performance but that is not included under the definition of deafness in this section.
6. **Mental retardation** means significantly subaverage general intellectual functioning, existing concurrently with deficits in adaptive behavior and manifested during the developmental period, that adversely affects a child's educational performance.
7. **Multiple disabilities** means concomitant impairments (such as mental retardation-blindness or mental retardation-orthopedic impairment), the combination of which causes such severe educational needs that they cannot be accommodated in special education programs solely for one of the impairments. Multiple disabilities does not include deaf-blindness.
8. **Orthopedic impairment** means a severe orthopedic impairment that adversely affects a child's educational performance. The term includes impairments caused by a congenital anomaly, impairments caused by disease (e.g., poliomyelitis, bone tuberculosis), and impairments from other causes (e.g., cerebral palsy, amputations, and fractures or burns that cause contractures).

9. **Other health impairment** means having limited strength, vitality, or alertness, including a heightened alertness to environmental stimuli, that results in limited alertness with respect to the educational environment, that—

    (ii) Is due to chronic or acute health problems such as asthma, attention deficit disorder or attention deficit hyperactivity disorder, diabetes, epilepsy, a heart condition, hemophilia, lead poisoning, leukemia, nephritis, rheumatic fever, sickle cell anemia, and Tourette syndrome; and

10. **Specific learning disability** means a disorder in one or more of the basic psychological processes involved in understanding or in using language, spoken or written, that may manifest itself in the imperfect ability to listen, think, speak, read, write, spell, or to do mathematical calculations, including conditions such as perceptual disabilities, brain injury, minimal brain dysfunction, dyslexia, and developmental aphasia.

    Disorders not included. Specific learning disability does not include learning problems that are primarily the result of visual, hearing, or motor disabilities, of mental retardation, of emotional disturbance, or of environmental, cultural, or economic disadvantage.

11. **Speech or language impairment** means a communication disorder, such as stuttering, impaired articulation, a language impairment, or a voice impairment, that adversely affects a child's educational performance.

12. **Traumatic brain injury** means an acquired injury to the brain caused by an external physical force, resulting in total or partial functional disability or psychosocial impairment, or both, that adversely affects a child's educational performance. Traumatic brain injury applies to open or closed head injuries resulting in impairments in one or more areas, such as cognition; language; memory; attention; reasoning; abstract thinking; judgment; problem-solving; sensory, perceptual, and motor abilities; psychosocial behavior; physical functions; information processing; and speech. Traumatic brain injury does not apply to brain injuries that are congenital or degenerative, or to brain injuries induced by birth trauma.

13. **Visual impairment including blindness** means an impairment in vision that, even with correction, adversely affects a child's educational performance. The term includes both partial sight and blindness.

Optional Terminology: Developmental Delay. This option is available only from children age three through nine (or any age subset) and is subject to the following restrictions. First, the state must adopt the classification. Second, if the state does not adopt the definition, a local school district could not independently decide to use the term. Third, the state cannot force local school districts to use this classification for special education eligibility and is defined as a child

(1) Who is experiencing developmental delays, as defined by the State and as measured by appropriate diagnostic instruments and procedures, in one or more of the following areas: Physical development, cognitive development, communication development, social or emotional development, or adaptive development.

Medical Model or Educational Model-Views of Disability

The medical model has and continues to be used in the eligibility process. If you consider medical specialization and procedures, the model certainly makes sense and can provide multidisciplinary teams with valuable information regarding disabilities that have a definite physical cause. According to this model, if you aren't feeling well, you go to a doctor for an evaluation, receive a diagnosis and treatment that remedies your disease or illness. Accordingly, if an individual had a growth, the surgeon could remove that growth and all would then be fine with the patient. This is exactly what one wants from the medical profession and what doctors want to provide their patients—a cure for what ails them. This model works well in medicine and, as is evident from this brief description, the problem resides within the individual. It is the individual who had the growth and the individual just needed to be fixed. The existence of the growth had no relationship to the doctor's skills.

A medical diagnosis of diabetes or cerebral palsy may assist a school team with determining whether a child would be eligible as a student with a health impairment (e.g. diabetes) or an orthopedic impairment (e.g. cerebral palsy), but it is crucial that the school team understand that the ultimate responsibility for determining special education eligibility rests with the team, not outside sources. For example, it is very possible that there could be three children with the same medical diagnosis, diabetes, enrolled at a single school. No one would argue that medical intervention is necessary for each student to stay healthy, but just the medical diagnosis of diabetes is not sufficient for a special education eligibility determination. It is quite possible that one of those students needs no support, one requires adaptations and modifications available under Section 504, and the third needs specially designed instruction due to the disability. We emphasize that when making an eligibility determination, the team must consider information provided from experts outside the school setting which may include medical doctors as well as psychiatrists and others; however, it is the school team, including the parent, who considers the information and makes eligibility determinations on an individual basis.

The medical model has been used to explain different nonmedical issues and this practice continues to cause concern. For example, one theory explained learning disabilities as a mental processing disorder resulting from a perceptual-motor processing deficit. The treatment was to try and fix the processing deficit. Given this approach, we could equate the student with a patient, the reading problem as a symptom, and the processing deficit as the disease requiring treatment. However, neither this conceptualization of learning disability nor the perceptual-motor based interventions have withstood the rigors of scientific inquiry (Arter & Jenkins, 1979; Hyatt, 2007; Hyatt, Stephenson, & Carter, 2009; Kavale & Forness, 1987). Some unfortunate consequences of this approach were that children with reading difficulties were taught to balance balls or tumble on mats rather than be provided with effective reading instruction. This application of the medical model to academic difficulties supported the belief that the difficulty resided within the student and blame tended to fall on the student for his or her learning problems—making it all too easy for educators to say that a particular student couldn't read because he or she had an irremediable processing deficit. The model failed to consider the impact of the instructional environment or the reading instruction the student was receiving, and all too often allowed educators to place blame for poor reading performance on the student rather than being forced to consider whether their instructional practice played a significant part in the student's not learning to read. In contrast, an educational model for disability encourages consideration of environmental and instructional conditions that may have served as barriers to attainment of educational goals rather than placing blame on student characteristics. This model would certainly recognize relevant medical conditions and make appropriate accommodations. In the following sections, we discuss eligibility for Developmental Delay and for Learning Disability. In the section on Learning Disability, we will discuss the IQ-Achievement Discrepancy Method which is closely related to a medical model and Response to Intervention (RtI) which is more closely related to an educational model.

Developmental Delay Eligibility

The category of Developmental Delay represents one group of students that **must** be identified and served under Part C. This is an optional term for Part B, but its use makes sense with young children. First its use may facilitate the transition from Part C to Part B, but probably more importantly, it is more logical when used with 3 and 4-year old children than some of the other Part B categories, such as Learning Disability or Emotional Disturbance. Failure of a state to use Developmental Delay terminology for Part B service, does not relieve a state from identifying all eligible children, so a child who would have been identified as having a Developmental Delay would have to be identified under one of the 13 mandatory eligibility categories.

For a young child to be identified as having a developmental delay under Part B, he or she must exhibit a delay in one or more of the following areas in accordance with state guidelines: 1) Cognitive, 2) Physical, 3) Social/emotional, 4) Adaptive, or 5) Communication (§300.8(b)(1)). These are the same areas assessed under Part C, but for special education, the eligibility criteria are frequently more stringent. States may also adopt the terminology for students age 3 through 9 or any age subset therein. For example, Washington State allows the use of Developmental Delay for children age 3 through 5 and also allows the use until age 9 if the child had previously been identified as a child with a Developmental Delay. Then at age 9, the child must be found eligible under one of the other disability categories to continue to receive special education services.

Learning Disability Eligibility

The criteria for learning disability as identified in IDEA are contained in Table 2-2. Absent a few wording changes, the definition has remained intact since passage of the initial special education law in 1975. Despite the longevity of the definition, it continues to be a source of lively debate and the identification of causes of learning disability has been elusive (Gargiulo & Metcalf, 2013; Reschly & Hosp, 2004). In spite of the continuing definitional and causal controversies, the most common disability among school age students is learning disability (U.S. Department of Education, 2011).

A review of the definition reveals that while the criterion remains subjective it also contains many restrictions on eligibility. For example, the learning difficulty may not be a primary result of: 1) visual, hearing, or motor impairment; 2) mental retardation; 3) emotional disturbance; 4) cultural factors; 5) environmental or economic disadvantage; or 6) limited English proficiency (§300.309 (a)(3)(i–vi). If the learning problem is a direct result of any of the above, then the child cannot be determined to have a learning disability. This does not mean that a child whose primary language is one other than English can't be identified as having a learning disability; rather, the evaluation must be comprehensive and rule out lack of English proficiency as the primary cause of learning difficulty. In addition to the restrictions noted above, the learning challenge cannot be due to lack of appropriate instruction in reading or math (§300.309 (b)). So if a 12-year old child moved to the U.S. from another country, spoke no English, and had not been to school, the district could not find that child eligible for special education due to a learning disability, despite the high level of support this student would need for academic success. Yet, the district would still be responsible for educating the student. The Response to Intervention (RtI) approach that will be described shortly provides a viable framework for serving children who may not be eligible for special education services but require additional educational supports (National Association of State Directors of Special Education, 2005).

Prior to passage of IDEA amendments of 2004, the determination of a learning disability required that there be a statistically significant difference or discrepancy between a student's IQ and achievement scores. This is referred to as the discrepancy model and operated from the finding that IQ score is a good predictor of school achievement. In this model, the school psychologist or other qualified individual administered a standardized, norm-referenced intelligence test, such as the Wechsler Intelligence Scale for Children—Fourth Edition (Wechsler, 2004). The school psychologist, special education teacher, or other qualified person administered a standardized, norm-referenced achievement test, such as the Woodcock-Johnson Tests of Achievement III (Woodcock, McGrew, & Mather, 2001). A statistical test was then conducted to determine if there was a statistically significant difference between achievement score as predicted by performance on the IQ test and the actual score received on the achievement test.

Figure 2-2 provides a graphic description of this model with three possible outcomes. Student 1 received an achievement score higher than predicted from her IQ score. The difference was statistically significant and she might have been referred to as a "high achiever". Student 2 earned an achievement score that fell within the expected range. Even if he was experiencing academic difficulty there may not have been any special education support available, because there was not a statistically significant difference between actual and predicted performance. According to assumptions inherent in this model, the scores indicate he was "performing as well as could be expected." However, this student continued to be at risk for failure and "falling through the cracks." Student 3 scored significantly lower than predicted, might be considered as having a learning disability, and receive special education support. In many cases there was really no real skill difference between the student with the learning disability (Student 3) and the struggling student (Student 2) whose achievement score was not statistically significantly lower than expected. As depicted in Figure 2-2, the scores of Students 2 and 3 fell at almost the same place, one was just above the cutoff line and one was just below the cutoff line.

The difference could be compared to that of two university students. Student A received 90% of the points in a class and earned a grade of A- and student B earned 89% of the points in

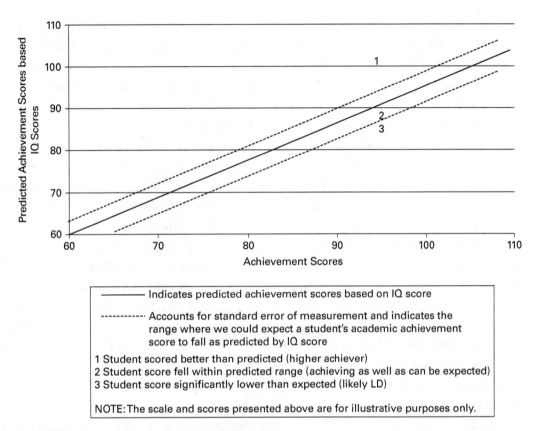

FIGURE 2-2. Illustrative Description of the Discrepancy Model

class and was assigned a grade of B+. Their mastery of course content was almost the same, yet each received a score that was on a different side of the cutoff line and was assigned a different grade. This probably had no discernible effect in the academic or vocational success of the university student who earned the lower grade, but use of this arbitrary cutoff score to determine if a school age child will receive academic support probably has a negative impact on the academic and future vocational success of the student who was struggling academically yet received insufficient or no support.

This discrepancy model has been criticized for numerous reasons (Reschly & Hosp, 2004; Stuebing et al., 2002). As mentioned earlier, the criteria and associated statistical formula varied among states, so it was very common that a student identified as having a disability in one state would be found ineligible in another state due to the differing criteria, not the actual academic skill of the child. If states found that they were identifying too many students as having a learning disability, they could tighten up the criteria by changing the statistical formula and find fewer students eligible.

As significant as these problems seemed, even larger issues were recognized in the field. First, as depicted in Figure 2-2, there was really no meaningful difference between Students 2 and 3, yet Student 3 would likely receive support while Student 2 was left to struggle.

This model was criticized for making a child wait and fail before assistance could be provided. This practice referred to the common scenario where a first grade student was struggling and an evaluation indicated that there was not a statistically significant discrepancy between predicted and actual level of achievement, so the student was found ineligible and generally received little or no support. However, by the time the child reached third grade, the performance gap had ballooned and upon a second special education evaluation, the student was often found eligible. Then the student received special education support, but two years had lapsed and much opportunity for learning had been squandered. The cumulative effect of the lost instruction and learning opportunities that these children experienced made it more difficult for them to benefit from subsequent instructional activities, similar to the Matthew Effect in reading as described by Stanovich (1986). Simply stated, the Matthew Effect equates the saying, "the rich get richer and the poor get poorer," with reading. For a variety of reasons, good readers continue to hone their reading skills and gain access to material covering a wide range of topics. That information is readily available, largely due to their proficient reading skills. In contrast, those with poor reading skills tend to read less (most people don't do things they are not successful with), which limits their access to information. The following hyperlink is to a video by Stanovich titled, "Will reading make you smarter?" which further addresses the issue. **http://www.youtube.com/watch?v=IF6VKmMVWEc**

In response to the problematic use of the discrepancy method for determining a learning disability and active professional advocacy, IDEA 04 incorporated a substantial change in the identification of learning disabilities. The regulations now prohibit states from requiring that school districts use an IQ-Achievement discrepancy model in the process of LD eligibility determination (§300.307(a)(1)) and even allow states to prohibit the use of the discrepancy model entirely. In its place (or in addition to), a state may use a process commonly referred to as Response to Intervention (RtI) that considers a child's response to scientific, research-based intervention (§300.307(a)(2)(3)). There is no single RtI model, but its variations encompass a problem-solving model built upon sound curriculum based assessment, the application of scientific-based intervention, and the provision of targeted instruction as needed (Fuchs, Fuchs, & Vaughn, 2007; Jimerson, Burns, & VanDerHeyden, 2007). Common approaches involve three tiers or levels of support (National Association of State Directors of Special Education, 2008; Salvia et al., 2013). In a 3-tier model, the first tier or level of service represents the general education curriculum that all students receive and serves as the foundation. At the first tier most students (80–90%) achieve satisfactorily. If a student struggles, he or she could receive Level 2 supports which include the general education curriculum as well as targeted supports designed to provide effective instructional support. Level 2 is generally perceived to be a short-term intervention. For some students (1–5%) Level 2 support is not enough and they are provided with Level 3 support which includes more intensive interventions and more frequent assessment to guide instructional decision making. It is important to note that Level 2, and for that matter Level 3, does not imply that the student is removed from the general education setting and Level 3 does not automatically mean a child is eligible for special education. Rather, the levels refer to the amount of support provided to the student. When used to determine eligibility, both the discrepancy model and RtI must document that the student needs special education service and rule out the previously mentioned exclusionary factors as the source of learning problems. Graphic representations of what RtI is and what it is not is contained in Figure 2-3.

An important assumption with RtI is consideration of the child's response to evidence-based interventions that have been implemented with fidelity. Consider the following scenario, but recognize that there is more to RtI than we briefly present here. Let's assume that there are two second grade students who are both performing much lower than their peers in reading. We'll also assume that both have similar skills and both receive evidence-based

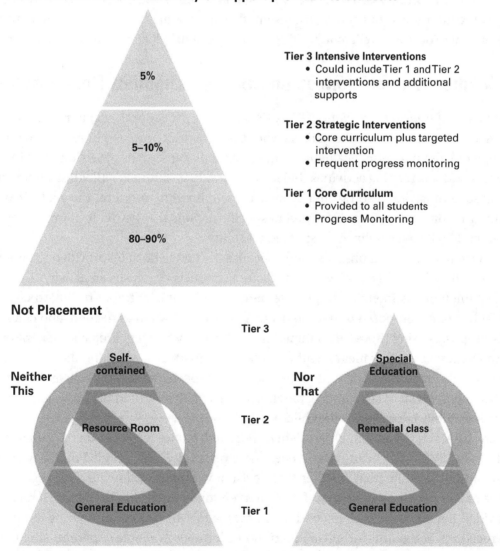

FIGURE 2-3. Response to Intervention Framework

instruction on a consistent basis. The results from frequent formative assessment indicate that student A is not responding to the interventions, but Student B is acquiring reading skill at an acceptable rate. The team may find that Student A should be considered for special education eligibility, but Student B is responding well to the intervention and would likely not be determined eligible for special education services but should continue receiving the supports. (In addition to the references provided above, you can access additional information at Intervention Central **http://www.interventioncentral.org/** and RTI Action Network **http://www.rtinetwork.org/**)

The Procedural Safeguards in the IDEA outline key parental rights and the responsibilities of school districts to keep parents informed and involved in special education issues. We will more fully discuss the procedural safeguards, in a subsequent chapter. However, to provide a contextual basis for our current discussion, we will begin to describe two specific safeguards at this time (prior written notice and informed consent) that are routinely provided before conducting an assessment to determine eligibility and again prior to initial placement in special education.

Prior Written Notice, Informed Consent, and Eligibility Determination

The provision of *Prior Written Notice (PWN)* is one of the procedural safeguards guaranteed by IDEA and must be provided to parents whenever a district proposes or refuses to initiate or change the identification, evaluation, educational placement, or provision of FAPE. It is not necessary for screening activities that schools conduct routinely with all students, such as vision screening, oral reading fluency measures, or hearing tests, etc. The goal of PWN is to ensure that parents are kept informed of specific actions the district is planning regarding their child with a disability or suspected disability.

The term planning is emphasized here, because the notice must be provided to parents a "reasonable time before" (§300.503(a)) the district conducts or refuses an activity. This "reasonable" timeframe is intended to provide parents with sufficient opportunity to consider ramifications of the proposed or refused actions, seek clarification as needed, and challenge district proposals using processes outlined in the procedural safeguards component of the law. We already noted that meaningful parental participation in planning the education of their child with disabilities is a critical component of special education law, and PWN is a significant component of encouraging parental involvement as well as the provision of a Free Appropriate Public Education to the child.

There are several times that PWN might be required, but we will focus on the initial evaluation for now. PWN must be provided once school personnel have decided that they want to conduct an initial evaluation, whether that decision was made following a request directly from the parent or as a result of pre-referral intervention team recommendation. It must also be provided if a school refuses to conduct an evaluation that was requested by the parent. (The Procedural Safeguards include a description of options available to parents should they disagree with the district's proposal outlined in PWN. We will discuss these options in the chapter on Procedural Safeguards.) The regulations specify that PWN must contain the following items in order to keep parents informed:

(1) A description of the action proposed or refused by the agency;

(2) An explanation of why the agency proposes or refuses to take the action;

(3) A description of each evaluation procedure, assessment, record, or report the agency uses as a basis for the proposed or refused action;

(4) A statement that the parents of a child with a disability have protection under the procedural safeguards of this part and, if this notice is not an initial referral for evaluation, the means by which a copy of a description of the procedural safeguards can be obtained;

(5) Sources for parents to contact to obtain assistance in understanding the provisions of this part;

(6) A description of other options that the IEP team considered and the reasons why those options were rejected; and

(7) A description of other factors that are relevant to the agency's proposal or refusal. (§300.503 (b)(1–7))

In addition, the following requirements for PWN to be provided in "understandable language" (§300.503 (c)) reinforce our point that parental involvement is crucial in the provision of FAPE to a child with a disability. These requirements are that PWN be

(i) Written in language understandable to the general public; and

(ii) provided in the native language of the parent or other mode of communication used by the parent, unless it is clearly not feasible to do so.

(2) If the native language or other mode of communication of the parent is not a written language, the public agency must take steps to ensure

(i) that the notice is translated orally or by other means to the parent in his or her native language or other mode of communication;

(ii) that the parent understands the content of the notice; and

(iii) that there is written evidence that the requirements ... have been met.

A sample prior written notice form for an initial evaluation is contained in Table 2-3.

So while PWN serves as notification to parents, it does not grant districts permission to proceed with the initial evaluation. IDEA requires that districts obtain informed parental consent at three specific times. First, it must be obtained before conducting an initial evaluation to determine special education eligibility. Second, informed parental consent must be obtained before the initial provision of special education services (i.e., the first IEP), and third, it must be granted prior to conducting a reevaluation.

TABLE 2-3. Prior Written Notice

This Prior Written Notice is being provided to formally notify you of any actions that the district proposes or refuses to conduct regarding the identification, evaluation, placement, or provision of a Free Appropriate Public Education for your child.

Parent/ Guardian: _____   **Date:** _____

Student: _____   **Student #:** _____

This notice is written to inform you that we are:

☐ Proposing   ☐ Initiate

      or   *To*   or

☐ Refusing   ☐ Change

☐ Identification   ☐ Evaluation   ☐ Placement   ☐ FAPE

1. Description of the action proposed or refused:

   _____

   _____

2. Explanation of Reason for proposed or refused action:

   _____

   _____

3. Description of each evaluation procedure, assessment, record or report used as a basis for the proposed or refused action:

   _____

   _____

4. Other options considered and rejected. Reason(s) for rejection of options:

   _____

   _____

5. Other factors relevant to the proposal or refusal:

   _____

   _____

6. Your child has procedural protections under the Individuals with Disabilities Education Act. If this prior written notice was provided as part of the 1) an initial evaluation or referral, 2) a re-evaluation, or 3) a disciplinary action resulting in a change of placement, a copy of the procedural safeguards is enclosed.

7. We will begin this action on _____

If you did not receive a copy of the procedural safeguards or would like assistance understanding the content, please contact _____

We won't be discussing reevaluations for the purpose of eligibility in this text, other than to note that IDEA requires a reevaluation be conducted to determine continuing eligibility as well as identify academic needs every three years unless the parents and school agree that a reevaluation is unnecessary. However, if a parent or teacher requests a three-year reevaluation, it must be conducted (§300.303). Reevaluations are also required before a school can determine that a child is no longer eligible for special education services unless the child is ineligible because: 1) he or she graduated with a regular diploma, or 2) he or she exceeded age of eligibility for special education services. (§300.305(e)(1)(2)).

Before beginning an evaluation, the district must obtain informed, written consent from the parent. The regulations (§300.9) specify that consent means

(a)   the parent has been fully informed of all information relevant to the activity for which the consent is sought, in his or her native language, or other mode of communication;

(b)   the parent understands and agrees in writing to the carrying out of the activity for which his or her consent is sought and the consent describes any activity and lists the records (if any) that will be released and to whom; and

(c)   (1)   the parent understands that the granting of consent is voluntary on the part of the parent and may be revoked at any time.

(2)   If a parent revokes consent, that revocation is not retroactive.

The provision of consent is an important activity. A few years back, one of the authors accepted a new position as a school psychologist at an elementary school and found the district consent for evaluation forms in the office. The office staff at the school simply gave the form to parents to sign and passed it on to the school psychologist. This practice was clearly not in line with the pre-referral process previously described, failed to ensure that parents were fully informed of the activities that would be conducted with their children (It certainly would be unreasonable to expect that office staff have the background needed to fully describe a special education evaluation), and resulted in a high number of referrals. Clearly, this was not an effective practice. The staff and principal were both surprised and relieved when the school psychologist offered to keep all of those forms in his office and meet with parents to ensure that they were given sufficient information to ensure that any consent provided was fully informed.

IDEA 04 provided a parent the option of revoking consent for evaluations at any time. So if a parent signed a permission to evaluate and the district began the evaluation procedure but the parent subsequently revoked the consent in writing, then the evaluation would have to stop immediately.

Parents must also provide written informed consent prior to their child receiving special education support. The rules guiding revocation of consent are different for initial evaluations than for provision of special education support. If a parent declined to grant consent for an initial evaluation, then a district could utilize the due process procedures (outlined in Procedure Safeguards) and attempt to obtain an order to complete the evaluation. However, districts are not required to do so and could not be found liable for failure to identify a child with a disability under those circumstances (§300.300(c)(i). In fact, our experience suggests that it is unlikely that a district would expend human and fiscal resources trying to get an evaluation ordered. This is probably because a parent may still deny consent for initial provision of special education services and the district would be prohibited from seeking a judicial over-ride of parental refusal for provision of special education (§300.300(3)). In addition, parents can revoke permission for special education services at any time. A sample parental consent form is contained in Table 2-4.

TABLE 2-4. Written Parent Consent

Parent/Guardian: _____ Date: _____

Student: _____ Student #: _____

We are requesting your consent to conduct one of the following actions:

_____ Initial Evaluation

_____ Initial Provision of Special Education and Related Services

_____ Re-evaluation

If this permission is for an **Initial evaluation or Re-evaluation**, we will collect information in areas related to the suspected disability that will assist in eligibility determination and educational planning.

The concerns prompting this evaluation are:

_____

_____

The evaluation will consist of the following types of test and assessments:

_____

_____

If this consent is sought for the **Initial Provision of Special Education and Related Services**, then this permission is granting your consent for implementation of the initial Individualized Education Program.

Description of any records that will be released and to whom: _____

_____

By granting consent, you are acknowledging that you have been fully informed of all information relevant to the activity for which consent is sought. You also understand that your consent tis voluntary and may be revoked at any time; however, if you revoke consent, it is not retroactive. That means it does not negate any actions taken prior to your revocation.

_____ I grant consent

_____ I DO NOT grant consent

_____   _____

Signature   Date

Once a school has provided parents with PWN and received the written, informed parental consent, the actual evaluation can begin. This evaluation is usually conducted by a multidisciplinary team (MDT), consisting of a variety of members from different disciplines who conduct assessments in their relative areas of expertise and share their findings with the MDT. For example, the school psychologist may administer intelligence tests, behavioral rating scales, conduct observations, and obtain information from parents. A graphic depiction of the sequence of events for an evaluation is contained in Figure 2-4.

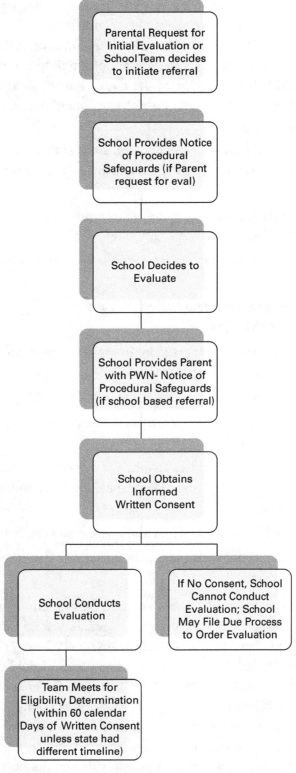

FIGURE 2-4. Sequence of Events for Initial Evaluation

When conducting an initial evaluation, the regulations state that the district must: 1) complete the evaluation within 60 calendar days of receiving informed, written parent consent (§300.301(c)(1)) unless the state has established a different, shorter timeline, and 2) ensure that the evaluation is of sufficient detail to determine eligibility and the educational needs of the child (§300.301(2)(i)(ii)). In addition, the regulations contain specific requirements regarding the assessment procedures that impact assessment practices. In essence, section §300.304 requires the following:

- The team must use a variety of assessment tools and strategies to gather relevant functional, academic, and developmental information about the child, including parental input.

- When making an eligibility decision, the team cannot rely on a single measure or tool which may be used to determine eligibility.

- Instruments used in the evaluation process must be technically sound (reliable and valid).

- Assessment materials are selected and administered so they are not discriminatory on a cultural or racial basis.

- Assessment activities are administered in the child's primary language or mode of communication unless clearly not feasible.

- Assessments are administered by trained and knowledgeable personnel.

- Assessments are administered in accordance with the instructions of the producer of the assessment.

- Assessment activities are selected to ensure that a child's performance is not penalized for impaired sensory, manual, or speaking skills (unless that is the domain being measured).

- The child is assessed in all areas related to the suspected disability.

- The evaluation is sufficiently comprehensive to assist in determining eligibility as well as educational needs.

These guidelines were designed to help ensure that evaluations were comprehensive, included parental input and were conducted in a reliable, valid, and nondiscriminatory manner. For general education teachers, this means that the assessments conducted in the classroom and used to inform the multidisciplinary team should be conducted in a fair manner that will describe the child's actual performance in the area of concern, and not be the simple reflection of subjective observation. It holds the same meaning for special educators, but if those teachers are also administering norm-referenced instruments, such as the Woodcock-Johnson, federal law requires that those instruments be administered and scored in accordance with the standardized procedures provided by the publisher. So, it would be contrary to legal guidelines to use a measure of oral reading fluency to describe the child's reading performance if that child had speech difficulties that interfered with his or her performance. It would also be unfair to use a timed math facts test where a student had to write the answer to as many problems as possible within a set time period if the student had a physical disability that impaired his or her writing skill. In either of the above examples, the impairment would have a negative impact on the student's performance and a low score could actually be the result of the impairment not the student's academic skill. A school psychologist is generally a valuable resource to consult should you have questions regarding assessment.

Once each person of the multidisciplinary team has collected, compiled, and analyzed his or her data, the team typically meets to review results and decide whether the child: 1) meets eligibility criteria and 2) needs special education. It is critical, and a legal requirement, that the parent be part of the team making this decision. If the parent disagrees with the determination, then he or she can appeal through the process available through the procedural safeguards. This is an example of one important reason for ensuring that a copy of the procedural safeguards is provided at the time of initial referral as required (§300.504 (a)(1)). Without provision of that information, parents would likely not be aware of their right to challenge district decisions. Given the emphasis on informed parental consent, it would be advisable to spend a few minutes with the parent briefly reviewing the safeguards and ensuring that the parent knows whom to contact for clarification, if necessary.

As shown in Figure 2-1, once a child has been found eligible, the next step is for the team to initiate the IEP process. We will start the next chapter discussing the IEP team meeting and begin an examination of the various components of the IEP.

Chapter Summary

In this chapter, we offered information that should provide you with a solid understanding of common issues that may precede an IEP meeting. We certainly couldn't cover all possibilities, but wanted to provide you with information that you could use on a frequent basis. We briefly described the difference between Part C and Part B services and will wrap up our investigation of Part C services by contrasting the IFSP with the IEP in the next chapter.

We noted that the majority of students with disabilities are identified after they enter school and encounter academic difficulties, so you will undoubtedly be involved in the referral, eligibility, and IEP process in your professional career. We provided you with a description of just one of many possible school-based assistance team models that may serve as a valuable support for both students and teachers. We also reviewed the procedures that may be used to identify children with Learning Disabilities and encouraged you to further investigate the promising practice of RtI that can provide the structure allowing children with and without disabilities to receive the necessary supports. RtI really does present an exciting opportunity for schools to work effectively with a child before the child is deemed to have a disability. The earlier schools can positively impact the learning of young students, the more likely the children will succeed, learn to value education, and graduate from high school.

We also began our discussion of procedural safeguards—those special protections afforded children with disabilities to help ensure that they are never again locked away in institutions and considered "hopeless cases." Special education is a field that changes, perhaps slowly, but the change tends to be based on the rich research base that informs special education. Practices such as RtI have and continue to be subjected to empirical studies which reveal results that can be trusted much more than a "gut" level feeling. As you progress through this text and read the literature, you will find that the rich research base that continues to inform many but unfortunately not all of special education practices can be aligned with those civil rights and liberties that we value as American citizens.

Chapter Activities

1. Review your state regulations and find any guidance regarding the use of RtI.

2. Does your state still allow the IQ-achievement discrepancy analysis for determination of eligibility?

3. What are the specific eligibility criteria in your state for Developmental Delay, Part C? For Part B? What differences, if any, did you find and why might there be differences between Part C and Part B criteria?

4. In this chapter, we referenced Intervention Central and the RTI Action Network. Review these sites as a beginning step to deepening your understanding of RtI.

Chapter 3

The Individualized Education Program (IEP)

Chapter Overview

The Individualized Education Program (IEP) is a written document that provides a framework for the provision of a Free Appropriate Public Education (FAPE) for an individual child with a disability. Within 30 calendar days after the determination that a child is eligible for special education and related services a meeting must be held to develop an IEP, and as soon as possible after that meeting the provisions of that IEP must be put into effect. Once developed the IEP must be reviewed at least annually and updated during the year if needed. It is important to note that while there are required components to each IEP, the actual content (e.g., special education service, annual goals, related services, accommodations, etc.) is individualized and developed by the IEP team which includes the parents, and the child when appropriate. In other words, there is no such thing as a standard IEP for students with learning disabilities, or students with autism, or students with intellectual disabilities, etc. Each aspect of each IEP must target the "unique needs of the child" that cause the child to require special education services.

The IEP has been described as the heart of IDEA and really is the centerpiece of the law (Bateman & Linden, 2012). It is a contractual agreement between the district and parent in which the district guarantees to provide the services specified in the IEP; however, the actual outcome, or attainment of learning goals by the child, is not guaranteed. Rather, as we shall see, the IEP must be reasonably calculated to produce a meaningful educational benefit, but even with a good faith effort, the child may not achieve all learning targets.

In this chapter, we will discuss the IEP in detail. We will describe the required membership of the IEP team, parent notification, when the IEP must be in effect, specifics of the meeting, and then discuss the required components of the IEP. After reading this chapter, you will have an understanding of IEP team structure, the contents of the IEP, and sufficient understanding to actively participate in the development of an educationally relevant IEP. We believe that some components of the IEP require more in-depth coverage to provide you with the knowledge and skills needed to write truly effective, functional, and legally compliant IEPs. With that in mind, subsequent chapters will build upon the foundational skills presented in this chapter and provide specific guidelines and practice activities focused on developing Present Levels, writing Annual Goals and Short-Term Objectives, applying the LRE requirement of the law, and understanding disciplinary procedures including Functional Behavioral Assessment and Behavior Intervention Plans. Postsecondary transition planning is required to be included in the IEP in effect when the student is 16 years of age. We have devoted a separate chapter to issues regarding transition and the IEP. Finally, since parental involvement is a major pillar of the law, we will devote a chapter to the procedural safeguards (protections) provided to parents to guarantee that they are afforded meaningful opportunities to provide input into the educational programming of their child.

IEP Team Membership

The regulations specify the required participants in an IEP meeting (§300.321). Each of the required members brings with him or her unique understanding of the child and should be prepared to discuss the child's educational needs and be afforded an opportunity to provide meaningful input to the team. The following are typical members of the IEP team, unless postsecondary transition is being addressed (see Chaper 7 for additional information regarding transition): parent, regular education teacher, special education teacher or related service provider, district representative, individual who can interpret assessment results, and others with knowledge or expertise regarding the child. The first four members are required members, but we will discuss the conditions under which required members may be excused and whether a single individual could fulfill more than one role. Before discussing excusal, we will describe IEP team membership.

(1) *Parent*—Parent participation is a particularly important and crucial component required for provision of FAPE. Presenting parents with a completed IEP prior to a meeting and simply informing them of what will happen to their child is not allowed. When this has been attempted by districts and subsequently challenged by parents, courts have found districts in violation of their legal duty to provide FAPE by denying parents an opportunity for meaningful participation in the development of the IEP (*Deal v. Hamilton County Board of Education*, 2004). In Chapter 1, we discussed jargon and the difficulty its use presents in meetings, so to promote meaningful parental participation, school personnel are reminded to take time and explain topics in jargon-free

TABLE 3-1. Parent Participation Form

Date _____

Dear _____,

On _____, we will be meeting to develop an Individualized Education Program (IEP) for _____. In that meeting, we will review your child's progress as well as discuss areas of difficulty and develop learning goals. Your input is very important in this process, and we value your participation in this important activity. Sometimes when at a meeting, it can be easy to forget to ask questions or share information that you wanted to share because the meeting moves too quickly. With that in mind, we would like you to consider the following items and encourage you to ask questions and participate in the meeting. (You don't have to complete this form, and at the IEP meeting, we only ask that you share information you are comfortable sharing.)

1. What questions, if any, do you have about special education and the IEP?

2. What are some of your child's strengths and interests?

3. What concerns do you have regarding your child's learning? Don't feel that you have to limit this to academic skills only. If you have other concerns, such as behavior or communication, please list them.

4. Describe how you would view the ideal school day for your child.

5. Other questions or concerns...

verbiage. Table 3-1 contains a form that could be provided to parents prior to the IEP meeting to help them prepare and facilitate their participation.

(2) *At least one regular education teacher of the child (if the child is, or may be, participating in the regular education environment)*—Prior to IDEA '97, regular education teacher participation was optional, but with the emphasis that IDEA '97 placed on students with disabilities participating in district/state mandated assessments and making progress in the general education curriculum as well as a heightened emphasis on regular education classroom placement, it was only reasonable that regular education teachers be members of the team. The teachers certainly bring a wealth of knowledge regarding the curricular and behavioral expectations of the regular classroom setting and can provide valuable suggestions in the development of the IEP. As a cautionary note, even though the regulations state that a regular education teacher is required only "if the child is, or may be participating in the regular education environment", great care must be exercised when not inviting a regular education teacher since failure to invite the regular education teacher might be considered a predetermined placement—a serious procedural violation that courts have found to result in a denial of FAPE. As you will learn, the presumed placement for all children is the regular education environment, thus it should be a rare instance when a child would

not be expected to participate in the regular education environment to some extent. Only in those rare cases when a child would have zero participation in regular education activities would a regular education teacher not be a required IEP team member. In cases where a child may have more than one regular education teacher, the school is free to select one of those regular education teachers to serve as the required member of the IEP team. Of course when making this selection, the best interests of the child should take precedent over issues such as scheduling or convenience, and the teacher who is in a position to present the most useful information regarding instruction of the child should be selected. It is also permissible for more than one regular education teacher to attend the IEP.

(3) *One special education teacher or special service provider*—The intent behind this requirement is relatively easy to understand. It makes sense that a special education teacher would be required when designing an IEP and determining what special education service will be provided to the child. However, the criteria for special service providers vary by state and the type of service provided. For example, in the case of a speech therapist, if speech therapy was provided as a related service (defined later in this chapter), then annual goals would not need to be written and the speech therapist would not need to attend. (We would recommend that the speech therapist still attend or meet with parents and teachers to discuss how the therapy can be extended into the classroom and home settings, if parents desire.) However, if speech therapy was to be provided as specially designed instruction (special education), then annual goals would need to be developed and the speech therapist should attend the IEP. A potential difficulty with this provision of having either a special education teacher or special service provider attend was addressed in the notes accompanying the regulations (Fed. Reg. 71, 46670, 2006) which referenced Attachment 1 of the 1999 Final Regulations for guidance and noted that the person attending should be the one who is or will be responsible for implementing the IEP.

Fortunately, there is nothing in the law that prohibits attendance of both special educator and other related service provider at the IEP. This would technically be a better arrangement and be consistent with the notion of a transdisciplinary team model where experts share their expertise and cross-train each other. Continuing with our speech and language example, students with speech and language issues typically benefit from support across environments, and it would be beneficial for all educators to address communication issues in a consistent manner, not just try to remediate the communication issue with the all too common practice of a 20 minute per week pull-out session with a speech therapist.

(4) *A representative of the public agency (usually school representative) who: a) is qualified to provide or supervise the provision of special education; b) is knowledgeable about the general education curriculum, c) is knowledgeable about the availability of the resources of the public agency*—This representative is commonly a school administrator but can be a designee, if that person can fulfill all 3 conditions above. In many cases, a special education teacher may serve in this role; however, as Pierangelo and Giuliani (2007) noted, in most states school psychologists, social workers, and guidance counselors could not serve in this role because they are generally not qualified to either provide or supervise the provision of special education. Bateman and Linden (2012) also recognized the importance of the representative as being someone who can commit district resources; a particularly important consideration since, the IEP is a contractual agreement guaranteeing that the district will provide the agreed upon services. For some children, committing resources to meet their needs may not be of great concern, but consider the child who may require a $6000 communication system or 30 hours per week of home-based services. The district could not refuse to supply the support if the team deems it necessary to provide the child FAPE, but we wouldn't recommend that a teacher assume authority to commit those resources on behalf of the district.

(5) *An individual who can interpret the instructional implications of evaluation results*—This person could easily be one of the previously mentioned team members, if that person could explain the evaluation results. IDEA specifically defines "evaluation" as the procedures used to determine if a child is eligible and how the findings help identify the necessary special education and related services (§300.15). So, this is particularly applicable for those times when the IEP is written following an initial evaluation or reevaluation. Based upon the evaluation conducted and expertise of the team, a school psychologist, speech therapist, or other related service provider may be a required member of the team unless a different member could competently explain the results.

(6) *At the discretion of the parent or agency, any other person with knowledge or special expertise regarding the child*—For all practical purposes, the parents can bring anyone to the IEP meeting without informing the district. Following is not an exhaustive list, but the parent could bring a day care provider, another family member, an advocate, or someone else who knows the child.

　　However, the district must notify the parent in writing of anyone who will be attending the IEP at the request of the district. The notification could, but need not contain names of specific people, but it should list titles, such as "physical therapist". Listing titles rather than a person's name is particularly useful in districts that employ numerous related service personnel and may not be able to identify the specific person who will be at the IEP. There can also be unforeseen events, such as an illness, that may prevent a particular individual from attending the meeting.

In the case of a child who will be transitioning from Part C to Part B services, an invitation to attend the initial IEP must be sent to the Part C service coordinator or other representative but only if it is requested by the parent. Absent a district providing this information to parents, it is highly unlikely that parents would be aware of this option to invite their service coordinator. So in the interest of *informed consent* as well as promoting parental involvement and striving to obtain input from individuals familiar with the child, it would behoove a district to inform parents of this option.

(7) *Child, when appropriate*—There may be times when it is appropriate for an elementary age child to attend all or part of an IEP. Student-led IEPs are gaining acceptance as a means to help students develop self-advocacy skills and participate meaningfully in the development of their education (Danneker & Bottge, 2009; Thoma & Wehman, 2010). Of course, attendance may depend on the nature of the discussion and the ability of the child to meaningfully participate. In addition, there would certainly be times when an IEP meeting would be incredibly boring for a child and of little meaning or the content of the conversation may not be appropriate for young children. In those cases, the child would be best excused from the meeting, but participation may become more important as children become older and develop a basic understanding of the schooling process. For example, a student who will be transitioning to middle school may be able to provide some valuable insights to the IEP team regarding supports that will facilitate that change. Student participation is required when postsecondary transition is discussed.

Excusal of Required Member from IEP Meeting

IDEA '04 introduced legislation that allowed required IEP members to be excused from all or a part of an IEP meeting. The professed goal for making this change was to provide flexibility to IEP teams, and it allows individual teams and schools to determine when an excusal is appropriate. Under certain conditions, the following members may be excused: general education teacher, special education teacher or service provider, agency representative, and individual who can interpret evaluation results (numbers 2–5 in our list of required members described in the preceding section). The regulations specify two conditions under which an IEP team member can be excused. Neither option requires permission from the entire IEP team, just the parent and a district representative who has the authority to agree to that excusal. In either case, it is important to note that without a parent's written agreement or consent, the team member must be at the IEP. Furthermore, the parent does not have to provide a reason for not agreeing to the proposal excusal and must not be pressured into agreeing to allow an excusal.

The first option for excusal specifies that an IEP team member may be excused from attending all or part of an IEP meeting if, both the parents and district agree, in writing, to excuse the member because that person's curricular area or related service is not being modified or discussed at the IEP meeting. While the regulations do not prohibit excusal from an initial IEP meeting, we strongly discourage such an excusal, because of the potential negative implications. The initial IEP meetings, in particular, can be a stressful and emotional time for parents who may still be coming to terms with their child having a disability and a supportive meeting with school personnel could be of tremendous benefit.

However, the following scenario for an annual IEP meeting scheduled for the middle of the day when the regular education teacher had a 45-minute preparation period may allow a reasonable option for excusal. The parent and district could discuss the regular education portion of the IEP and excuse the general education teacher when that part of the discussion was over; thereby, allowing the general education teacher to go back to the classroom should the meeting last longer than the 45-minute teacher preparation time. However, if the parent did not agree to the excusal, then the teacher would be required to stay and the district would have the option of either having other faculty cover the class or rescheduling the remainder of the IEP so the teacher could be sent back to cover his or her class and attend at the rescheduled time.

The second option allows excusal from all or part of the IEP, when the team member's curricular area or related service is being discussed or modified. In this case, the district must also obtain written, informed consent from the parent. In addition, the IEP team member must submit, in writing, to the parent and the rest of the IEP team information relative to development of the IEP prior to the IEP meeting. The regulations don't state the detail that must be provided by the excused member or how long before the IEP meeting the information must be provided to parents, but the information should be of such specificity that it will adequately inform the IEP team. As with the prior option, the parents could refuse to provide consent or if they did consent and during the meeting found that additional input from the excused team member was needed, the IEP meeting could be rescheduled when all necessary members could be present.

Parent Notification of the IEP Meeting

Given the importance of parent participation in the IEP process, it makes sense that parents must be provided notice of proposed IEP meetings (§300.332). This notice of an IEP meeting should not be confused with Prior Written Notice (PWN) which is required to inform parents of a district's intent or refusal to initiate an action related to the identification, evaluation, placement, or provision of FAPE. While an IEP is certainly a part of the provision of FAPE, merely meeting to review the current IEP and develop new Annual Goals and Short-Term Objectives for the subsequent IEP does not mean that there is any change in FAPE. The new IEP may result in provision of the same level of service but may simply target more advanced or even different skills.

If as a result of the newly developed IEP, the team does make a change in placement (for example, moves a child from a regular class to a pull-out resource room setting) then the district would be required to provide PWN before implementing the change. So, the IEP could be completed, but the change would not be made immediately and parents would be provided PWN. In such a case, the PWN could be completed at the end of the IEP meeting and given to parents immediately. Giving parents PWN provides them with an opportunity to consider the district proposal, and if they ultimately disagree, to reconvene the meeting and discuss concerns or challenge the district proposal under the procedural safeguards. The PWN must be provided even if parents agreed with the proposed change at the IEP meeting and should be provided prior to initial provision of special education services (the first IEP).

The regulations specify that districts must take specific steps to ensure that parents have an opportunity to participate in the development of their child's IEP. In doing so, districts must invite parents to a meeting at a mutually agreed upon time and place. This invitation should be in writing and inform parents of the purpose, time, and location of the meeting. Since districts are required to tell parents who they will invite to the IEP meeting, (remember, it is best to include title rather than an individual's name) that information should also be included on the invitation as well as the name and number of a person to contact should the meeting need to be rescheduled. For a parent(s) whose primary language is one other than English or require an alternate mode of communication, the district must take whatever action is necessary to ensure that the parent understands the proceedings of the IEP meeting. A sample invitation is contained in Table 3-2.

In rare cases, parents are unable to attend IEP meetings during the regularly scheduled school day. Nothing in the law requires that districts hold evening IEPs. However, the regulations do specify that districts must take steps to ensure participation, by considering alternatives such as conference calls or video conferencing. In fact, nothing in the law prohibits a district representative from meeting with a parent at home or place of employment if needed to ensure parent participation in development of the IEP. A district's failure to include parents in the IEP process may result in denial of FAPE and monetary consequences (*Drobnicki v. Poway*, 2009). Zirkel (2011) recommended that districts place a priority on including parents in decisions related to provision of FAPE with a central focus on the IEP.

One of the authors worked with a teacher who developed a unique solution to obtaining parental participation in the IEP. In this case, the parent's and teacher's travel paths crossed during the morning commute. The parent was unable to meet with school staff during the school day, but the teacher and parent met along the side of the road during their morning commute. This was before the availability of video conferencing technology, such as Skype, and certainly provides an example of a successful effort to keep a parent involved in his child's education instead of assuming that a parent was unconcerned simply because he could not afford to take time off from work to attend the IEP meeting.

TABLE 3-2. IEP Invitation

Parent/ Guardian: _____　Date: _____
Student: _____　Student #: _____
The purpose of this letter is to invite you to an IEP meeting scheduled on _____ at
(Date)
_____. The IEP meeting should be held at a mutually agreed upon time. Should
(Time and Location)
you need to change the meeting time, please contact _____ at _____ to
(Name)　　　　　　　(Phone)
reschedule.
If you are unable to meet at the school, please contact us so we can try to arrange an alternative way for you to participate.
At this meeting, we will be discussing:
_____ Annual IEP Review　　　　　_____ IEP Revision
_____ Manifestation Determination　_____ Placement Issues
_____ Extended School Year　　　　_____ Other: _____
The district is required to notify you of the individuals who will attend the IEP meeting. Following is a listing of those individuals. If your child is transitioning from Early Intervention Services for young children age birth through two years to special education and you would like your Service Coordinator to attend, we will invite that person. Please contact _____ at _____ with the name of your Service Coordinator and contact information.
Individuals who the district will bring to the IEP:
_____　　_____
_____　　_____
_____　　_____
_____　　_____
It is important that you attend the meeting, and we welcome your participation. Once again, please contact us if you need to reschedule.

If the child is currently receiving special education services and a district is unable to obtain parental participation in the development of the IEP, the district will still need to develop an IEP before the current IEP expires and send a copy to the parents. While there is no set rule, you might want to schedule the annual IEP review early enough that should the first scheduled meeting not occur, you would have time to reschedule a second and possibly third meeting time before the current IEP expires. If parents fail to attend the third meeting, even though it was scheduled at a mutually agreed upon time, you might consider having the team write the IEP without the parents. It is important that you carefully track IEP dates, because an IEP must be current if a child is to receive special education services. (Note: this is not an option for students whose parents have not provided informed, written consent for initial placement.)

The regulations provide the following specific guidelines that districts must follow to document efforts to include parental participation:

> 300.322 (d) *Conducting an IEP Team meeting without a parent in attendance.* A meeting may be conducted without a parent in attendance if the public agency is unable to convince the parents that they should attend. In this case, the public agency must keep a record of its attempts to arrange a mutually agreed on time and place, such as—
>
> (1) Detailed records of telephone calls made or attempted and the results of those calls;
>
> (2) Copies of correspondence sent to the parents and any responses received; and
>
> (3) Detailed records of visits made to the parent's home or place of employment and the results of those visits.

As a precautionary measure, districts typically require this documentation be kept for all IEP meeting invitations. Then, should it be necessary to hold an IEP without the parent, the necessary paperwork is in place. Whether an IEP is developed with or without parental participation, the parents must be provided a copy of the IEP at no cost (§300.322 (f)).

Components of the IEP (Without Postsecondary Transition Planning)

Table 3-3 contains a list of the IEP components that are required for all students, including young children (Remember, we discuss postsecondary transition and other issues more commonly addressed on IEPs for secondary age students in Chapter 7.). We have presented the components in tabular format as a reference and will discuss these components and a couple of additional items that must be considered by the IEP team. To help illustrate the concepts presented in this chapter, we will describe the components and then present the appropriate part or parts of a simple initial IEP for a second grade child who receives special education support in the area of math calculation. This uncomplicated example will provide you with an opportunity to see how an IEP is constructed. On a side note, IEPs really should be uncomplicated, because if we expect parents to understand the content it must be jargon free, and if we want teachers to implement IEPs during the busy instructional day, then the documents must also be user friendly.

A copy of the completed IEP for the child we will be discussing is included in Appendix A. As a reminder, we will also discuss the following IEP components in greater depth in subsequent chapters: Present Levels, Annual Goals and Short-Term Objectives/Benchmarks; Least Restrictive Environment, Functional Behavioral Assessment and Behavior Intervention Plans, and postsecondary transition. These tend to be some of the more complex components, but that complexity is often due to a lack of understanding on the part of the IEP team. We will also discuss procedural safeguards in a subsequent chapter. While not technically components of

TABLE 3-3. Contents of the IEP (without postsecondary transition plans for students 16 years and older)

1. A statement of the child's present levels of academic achievement and functional performance
(i) How the child's disability affects the child's involvement and progress in the general education curriculum (i.e., the same curriculum as for nondisabled children) or
(ii) For preschool children, as appropriate, a description of how the disability affects the child's participation in appropriate activities
2.   (i) A statement of measurable annual goals, including academic and functional goals designed to
(A) Meet the child's that result from the child's disability to enable the child to be involved in and make progress in the general education curriculum.
(B) Meet each of the child's other educational needs that result from the child's disability
(ii) For children with disabilities who take alternate assessments aligned to alternate achievement standards, a description of benchmarks or short-term objectives;
3. A description of
(i)   How the child's progress toward meeting the annual goals will be measured and
(ii) When the periodic reports on the progress the child is making toward meeting the annual goals (such as through the use of quarterly or other periodic reports, concurrent with the issuance of report cards) will be provided
4. A statement of the special education and related services and supplementary aids and services, based on peer-reviewed research to the extent practicable, to be provided to the child or on behalf of the child, and a statement of the program modifications or supports for school personnel that will be provided to enable the child
(i) To advance appropriately toward attaining the annual goal;
(ii) To be involved in and make progress in the general education curriculum and to participate in extracurricular and other nonacademic activities
(iii) To be educated and participate with other children with disabilities and nondisabled children in the activities described in this section;
5. An explanation of the extent, if any, to which the child will not participate with nondisabled children in the regular class and activities described in paragraph (a)(4)
6. (i)   A statement of any individual appropriate accommodations that are necessary to measure the academic achievement and functional performance of the child on State and districtwide assessment and
(ii) If the IEP team determines that the child must take an alternate assessment instead of a particular regular State or districtwide assessment of student achievement, as statement of why
(A) The child cannot participate in the regular assessment; and
(B) The particular assessment selected is appropriate for the child; and
7. The projected date for the beginning of the services and modifications described in paragraph (a)(4) of this section, and the anticipated frequency, location, and duration of those services and modifications.

an IEP, the safeguards are important for IEP teams to understand and are a significant source for ensuring informed parental consent. We will now move sequentially through the IEP beginning with demographic information and ending with justification for removal from the regular education environment, if needed (Find more about that later in this chapter and Chapter 5.). We will conclude this chapter with a comparison of the IEP and the IFSP.

Demographic Information

The regulations do not require that demographic information be included on an IEP, but for obvious reasons, we do need to include some basic information, such as student name, address, etc. The form we provided includes only the minimal information that a teacher might consult: student specific information necessary for identification, such as name, student number, birth date. We also included contact information that will be useful when contacting parents and blanks on each page for date and page numbers. (This may seem like an obvious element, but the authors have seen multipage IEPs that did not have page numbers and/or did not have dates on each page. Assuming they were stapled together at one time and then became detached, it can be quite a task to try and piece everything together. We have had to try and do that with several years' worth of IEPs and certainly could have put our time to better use evaluating the IEPs rather than trying to organize a stack of paper.) The demographics section can be completed before the IEP meeting, as long as it is updated if needed at the IEP meeting.

On a majority of IEP forms reviewed by the authors, eligibility category was prominently displayed on the front page as if the categorical designation was related to the type or amount of

Labels seem to get tossed around freely, especially by those who aren't themselves labeled. One of the authors taught elementary students with significant behavioral and emotional needs. On class picture day, one student in each class held a placard identifying the class, such as Ms. Ortiz's First Grade Class. There is no problem with that type of identification as being a first grader does not evoke any negative stigma and it isn't confidential information. However, one student in the author's class was given a placard identifying the class as Mr. X's seriously emotionally disturbed class. Just imagine the possible negative ramifications, not to mention the invasion of privacy, that could have resulted from this picture. We can assure you that the words "seriously emotionally disturbed" were removed from the placard before the class picture was taken. This is not meant to be a negative connotation on the photographer or other school staff, but to emphasize the importance of being extremely careful when attaching labels to a child. In this age of Facebook and pictures/comments on the internet, you must be hyper-vigilant in protecting confidential student information.

service a child would be eligible to receive and in what settings or programs. Districts are required to report the number of students served under each categorical label to the federal government and perhaps that is the origin of this practice. However, when assigning labels that may be stigmatizing, educators must take great care to ensure the confidentiality of that information.

Furthermore, if you recall from our previous discussions, eligibility or the diagnostic indication of a particular disability label should not be taken as determining what specific services a child will need. Decisions regarding service must be made by the IEP team, address all learning needs requiring specially designed instruction, and labels cannot be used to determine what service a child will receive. The label simply has no meaningful programmatic implication and, in our opinion, should not be included on an IEP. Table 3-4 contains a sample demographic statement.

TABLE 3-4. Demographics

Student Name: John Vanberg   Date of Birth: 9-16-2005   Age: 7   Student ID: 154632
Home Address: 1521 1st Ave South Independence   WA   98989   (Street)   (City)   (State)   (Zip)
Phone: 555-9090   Alternate Phone: 555-1475   Primary Language: English
Parent(s)/Guardian(s): Marc and Sylvia Vanberg
Purpose of Meeting: __X__ Initial IEP   ____ Revision   ____ Annual IEP

Present Levels of Academic Achievement and Functional Performance

The second component of the IEP is the Present Levels of Academic Achievement and Functional Performance. These statements are frequently referred to by different names, such as Present Levels of Performance (PLOP) or Present Levels of Educational Performance (PLEP), but for clarity, we will simply refer to them as Present Levels. The regulations (§300.320) provide the following guidance regarding present levels:

> (1) A statement of the child's present levels of academic achievement and functional performance, including—

>> (i) How the child's disability affects the child's involvement and progress in the general education curriculum (i.e., the same curriculum as for nondisabled children); or

>> (ii) For preschool children, as appropriate, a description of how the disability affects the child's participation in appropriate activities.

The Present Levels statement describes how a student is currently performing and will serve as the foundation upon which the rest of the IEP will be structured. Thus, they should include statements that are instructionally relevant and be expressed in measurable terms (Bateman & Linden, 2012; Salvia et al., 2012). This may seem like fairly obvious guidance, but in numerous IEP reviews conducted by the authors, we have seen many statements of Present Levels that fail to abide by this reasonable and responsible recommendation thereby providing meaningless descriptions of student skill. (We will provide examples in Chapter 4.) Since Present Levels represent the starting point for the IEP, an educational plan, it is clear that the statements must be descriptive of the child's current skill level. In addition, the statements must be quantifiable, because they will serve as the baseline measure for determining progress toward the yet to be developed Annual Goals, and we must be able to measure a student's performance in order to judge the efficacy of the instructional program. In essence, the Present Levels statements describe a child's performance and need only be written in those areas in which special education support will be provided.

In the Present Levels statement included in Table 3-5, you will find that we included all of the required components (§300.320) and also incorporated the requirement for parental input

TABLE 3-5. Present Levels

Present Levels of Academic Achievement (Include a description of student strengths, results of initial or most recent evaluation) MATH CALCULATION John adds and subtracts single digit numbers with 100% accuracy at a rate of 35 per minute with 0 errors when given worksheets with only addition or subtraction problems. His speed and accuracy decline when given a worksheet with 30 single digit addition and subtraction problems mixed. Then, he solves 15 per minute with 2 or fewer errors. He adds and subtracts multi-digit numbers without carrying at 100% accuracy but does not add or subtract multi digit numbers with regrouping. On the Woodcock-Johnson III, John received a standard score of 85 (16th percentile) on the math calculation subtest and a standard score of 70 (2nd percentile) on the math fluency subtest.
Present Levels of Functional Performance, for example, communication, behavior, self-help skills, etc. (Include a description of student strengths, results of initial or most recent evaluation) John behaves well in class and is well liked by peers and staff. He communicates clearly.
Description of how the child's disability affects the child's involvement in and progress in the general education curriculum (i.e., the same curriculum as for nondisabled children); or for preschool children, how the disability affects the child's participation in appropriate activities John actively participates in all aspects of the general education math curriculum, but at a level lower than that expected of a student of a student his age and grade. His lack of fluency negatively impacts his acquisition of math skills. He spends a considerable amount of time deciphering basic math facts which interferes with his performance with work and application problems in math. He does understand the questions posed in the application problems when verbally explained to him.
Parental concerns related to enhancing the education of their child Parents are happy with his social performance at school. He has made friends and likes school, except he expresses a dislike for math. Parents would like him to improve his math skills and hope that as he becomes better at math, he will begin to like it more.

regarding their child's education (§300.324(a)(ii)). This is a reasonable place for documenting parental input and fits in nicely with the timing of the IEP meeting. The data in Present Levels will serve as the basis for the development of the Annual Goals, and school personnel are responsible for obtaining parental input throughout the development of the IEP.

The example Present Levels statement makes significant use of data-based descriptions of the child's performance that provide an accurate and understandable explanation of the child's performance on math calculation activities. As we will explain in Chapter 4, results from norm-referenced instruments are of little help when it comes to setting instructional goals and are not required components of every IEP. However, many districts still operate under the faulty assumption that norm-referenced instruments must be used to develop Present Level statements on every IEP. So, in our example, we include results a from child's performance on a norm-referenced instrument, the Woodcock-Johnson Test of Achievement—IV (Schrank, Mather, & McGrew, 2014), after results on curriculum-based measures to demonstrate how to incorporate the norm-referenced data if required by the district. As can be easily seen, the curriculum-based measures provide the specific information needed for development of measurable Annual Goals and associated Short-Term Objectives. There is one other instance in which you might reasonably expect to find scores from norm-referenced tests on an IEP—when the IEP follows an evaluation. IDEA requires that IEP teams consider results of recent evaluations, but references to the child's performance on the norm-referenced tests that may have been used in evaluations could be dealt with in the manner just described, if needed.

Consideration of Special Factors

IDEA requires that IEP teams consider the following "special factors" and plan appropriately: 1) behavior, 2) English proficiency, 3) vision impairment including blindness, 4) special communication needs, and 5) assistive technology needs (§300.324(a)(2)(i–v)). While written documentation verifying consideration of the "special factors" is technically not a required component of the IEP, we have included "special factors" section on the sample IEP form included in the appendix because it provides a convenient place to document that the team addressed the issues as required, and their inclusion on the IEP forms all but ensures that the items will be discussed at the IEP meeting. We placed the item close to the beginning of the IEP, because if any are concerns, they must be addressed appropriately in the IEP. It is more likely that a team will identify appropriate actions if they have necessary knowledge at the beginning of the meeting than if it were presented at the end of a meeting and the participants were required to go back and modify the just completed IEP. The five special factors that must be considered are:

(1) *Does the child's behavior impede the learning of self or others?* An affirmative answer would cue the IEP team to consider developing Annual Goals and Short-Term Objectives to address behavioral needs. (Note: A child does not have to be identified as having a behavioral disorder in order to receive

behavioral support. Student need, not label, drives the identification of services that will be provided). The team may also decide to conduct a Functional Behavioral Assessment (FBA) to determine the actual function of the behavior of concern.

We will discuss the FBA process in an upcoming chapter, but for now, suffice to say that a quality FBA would require the allocation of some resources for observation and should not even be attempted by individuals while sitting around a table developing an IEP. Rather, the team could decide that an FBA was necessary, set a timeline for completing it, and schedule a time to meet again. At that meeting, the results of the FBA could be reviewed and the team could develop a Behavior Intervention Plan (BIP). The IEP could be amended with the attachment of the BIP and any additional Annual Goals and Short-Term Objectives that resulted from the FBA. The clear goal from IDEA is for the IEP team to develop and implement strategies that will benefit the child by supporting the child's behavioral needs without the use of punishment or exclusion as the first options.

(2)   *Does the child have limited English proficiency?* If yes, the IEP team must consider language needs as they relate to student learning and the IEP. Strategies to promote understanding and acquisition of English must be considered and should be implemented on a systematic basis. The following scenario provides a clear example of the importance of working with parents and obtaining parental input in the development of the IEP. Assume that the child had a significant cognitive delay, did not speak English, but did have a vocabulary of 25 words in her primary language. That fact could have serious implications for the instructional program and maybe the teacher would be required to learn some words that are not his or her primary language in order to support the student with his or her transition to English. Absent parental involvement in the IEP process, this important communicative repertoire could have been overlooked and the child's education could have been negatively impacted.

(3)   *Is the child blind or visually impaired?* This question doesn't refer to common refractive problems readily resolved with the use of prescription lenses. Rather, the question refers to students with significant vision problems—including those students who may qualify for special education due to blindness or vision impairment. If the child does have a vision impairment or blindness, the IEP team is required to include instruction in Braille in the IEP unless based on evaluation results it is determined that Braille is not appropriate for the student. So, if an evaluation has not been completed, it should be scheduled without unnecessary delay and a subsequent IEP meeting held to amend the document as necessary.

(4) *Does the child have special communication needs?* This is an important issue and should not be considered in isolation of other learning and behavioral issues. If a child has a unique way (e.g., a signal) of indicating his or her preference but that signal is not understood by school staff and ultimately ignored, it could result in unanticipated behavioral outbursts as the child tries to communicate his or her needs in an alternate manner. For example if a child was nonverbal but used a pictorial communication system, such as the Picture Exchange Communication System (Frost & Bondy, 2002), then it would be important to indicate that in the IEP. Or if a child used a more sophisticated technology device for communication, the teacher may require training to support the child's communication (i.e., the teacher may need to be trained on the operation of the device and that training could be included in the IEP). In both examples presented, staff would need to ensure that the appropriate academic and conversational vocabulary choices were available, and the IEP team could specify what training or support would be provided to the teacher in order to work effectively with the child. For a child who is deaf or hard of hearing, the IEP team must also consider opportunities for direct communication with peers and professionals in the child's language and mode of communication.

(5) *Does the child require assistive technology (AT) devices and services?* Before an IEP team can answer this question, it is critical that the team know what IDEA means by both AT devices and services. Both the definitions of devices and services are quite involved, and the authors are certain that most IEP teams do not consider AT in depth. However a clear and informed understanding of district responsibility regarding provision of AT is critical, because the regulations clearly require its use as needed to ensure FAPE:

> 300.5 *Assistive technology device* means any item, piece of equipment or product system, whether acquired commercially off the shelf, modified, or customized, that is used to increase, maintain, or improve the functional capabilities of a child with a disability. The term does not include a medical device that is surgically implanted or the replacement of such device.
>
> 300.6 *Assistive technology service* means any service that directly assists a child with a disability in the selection, acquisition, or use of an assistive technology device. The term includes—
>
>> (a) The evaluation of the needs of a child with a disability, including a functional evaluation of the child in the child's customary environment;
>>
>> (b) Purchasing, leasing, or otherwise providing for the acquisition of assistive technology devices by children with disabilities,

(c) Selecting, designing, fitting, customizing, adapting, applying, maintaining, repairing, or replacing assistive technology devices;

(d) Coordinating and using other therapies, interventions, or services with assistive technology devices, such as those associated with existing education and rehabilitation plans and programs;

(e) Training or technical assistance for a child with a disability or, if appropriate, that child's family; and

(f) Training or technical assistance for professionals (including individuals providing education or rehabilitation services), employers, or other individuals who provide services to, employ, or are otherwise substantially involved in the major life functions of that child.

Given the broad definition of both AT device and AT service this should be a major consideration for an IEP team. Team members often go to the default position that assistive technology is little more than expensive computer equipment. However a computer based approach to assistive technology is only one of many possibilities. AT can include items as simple as pencil grips that help students with fine motor difficulties hold a pencil and write legibly, talking calculators, magnifying glasses, and a whole host of other items that range in expense. It is helpful to consult with individuals who are familiar with the wide range of AT devices currently available and have kept up with the rapidly changing technologies, particularly for more complex items. For example, some students who were nonverbal used voice synthesizers that cost thousands of dollars and could present quite an expense for districts. However, a cheaper option has become available in recent years using the IPad™ and new communication applications. So, rather than spending several thousands of dollars on a single communication device, a district could spend much less than one thousand dollars on an IPad and software that would provide a very functional and useful communication device. The device would have more uses than a voice synthesizer, and should it become damaged, it would be relatively cheap to replace, but cost is not the overriding consideration. If a child required a more expensive device to meet his or her Annual Goals, then the district would be responsible for securing access to the appropriate device.

In addition to the mere "functional" or "adaptive" examples of AT just provided, there is a growing amount of AT related to academic content. Given the requirement that students with disabilities have access to and make progress in the general education curriculum, academic AT is of increasing importance. Some examples include modified texts, novels controlled for reading skill, voice recognition, and writing software.

The regulations are very clear in permitting the use of district purchased AT in the child's home or other nonschool district environments (e.g., daycare, preschool, community recreation activities, etc.) if their use is needed in those environs for the child to receive FAPE. Since the district maintains ownership of the device should it be damaged or stolen, the district might seek reimbursement from the parents, so parents should be informed of any responsibility they may have regarding safeguarding any AT. Before ending this discussion on AT, it is important to note that a separate section of the regulations outlines school district responsibility for maintaining hearing aids and the external components of surgically implanted devices, such as cochlear implants (§300.113).

Annual Goals, Short-Term Objectives and Report of Progress

Now that the IEP team has developed Present Levels that objectively describe a child's performance and identified any special factors that must be addressed, the team is ready to develop Annual Goals (AG) and Short-Term Objectives (STO). For all children, an IEP must contain measurable Annual Goals tied directly to the child's stated Present Levels of Performance. The Present Levels serve as the starting point, describing the child's level of skill, and the Annual Goals represent how far the IEP team expects the child to advance during the calendar year. Annual goals are written for all areas in which the child will receive special education support but do not need to cover every single thing a child will learn. Rather, the development of Annual Goals is a way for the team to prioritize learning outcomes for the child and provide educators with major foci for instructional planning. So, depending on the needs of the child, not eligibility label, the IEP team might develop Annual Goals for academic skill areas such as reading, math, and written expression as well as behavior and functional skills that cover daily living, including recreation and adaptive physical education. The regulatory language covering Annual Goals, Short-Term Objectives, and progress reporting follows (§300.320):

> (2) (i) A statement of measurable annual goals, including academic and functional goals designed to
>
> (A) Meet the child's needs that result from the child's disability to enable the child to be involved in and make progress in the general education curriculum.
>
> (B) Meet each of the child's other educational needs that result from the child's disability.
>
> (ii) For children with disabilities who take alternate assessments aligned to alternate achievement standards, a description of benchmarks or short-term objectives;
>
> (3) A description of
>
> (i) How the child's progress toward meeting the annual goals will be measured and
>
> (ii) When the periodic reports on the progress the child is making toward meeting the annual goals (such as through the use of quarterly or other periodic reports, concurrent with the issuance of report cards) will be provided.

Prior to IDEA '04, IEP teams had to develop Short-Term Objectives or Benchmarks for each annual goal. Short-Term Objectives or Benchmarks served as intermediary steps to help focus the IEP and provide measurable targets to ensure that the child was making progress toward the Annual Goal. In this chapter, we will focus on Short-Term Objectives and differentiate them from Benchmarks in Chapter 4. Since the amendments of 2004, however, IEP teams are only required to write Short-Term Objectives or Benchmarks for students who take alternate assessments aligned with alternate achievement standards if the state opted to use alternative assessments and alternative standards. Generally, this applies to students with more significant disabilities. It is important, however, to remember that any state may choose to include Short-Term Objectives and/or Benchmarks in any or all IEPs and you should check to see what your state and local policy is in this area. The decision on the type of participation in assessment is made by the IEP team, and is the next component we will discuss. As you can see, due to the interrelated aspects of an IEP, it is difficult to approach in a strictly linear fashion.

Bateman and Linden (2012) described the decision to remove Short-Term Objectives from most IEPs as "... a wildly misguided move to reduce paperwork ... (p. 170)." We concur as it makes no sense to write IEPs for children without Short-Term Objectives, especially when there are no formal assessments as is the case with most children in preschool through second grade or for students who have other learning targets including behavior and self-help skills that are not included on the state and district mandated assessments. IEP teams are not prohibited from writing Short-Term Objectives and Benchmarks for children, whether the students take the regular state/district mandated assessments or not. We agree with Bateman and Linden (2012) that Short-Term Objectives constitute educational "best practice" and should still be written for all children. We address this point further in Chapter 4.

For John, our hypothetical student, we are only addressing math calculation and providing just one Annual Goal that is based upon skills described in the Present Levels and has reasonable projections for annual growth (See Table 3-6). We do this for simplicity, but in all likelihood, an IEP would contain more than a single Annual Goal. For John, the law simply requires that the IEP team develop measureable Annual Goals, because he will be participating in the regular state mandated assessment. However, we have gone a step further and also included Short-Term Objectives in our example. As you will see, the Short-Term Objectives break the Annual Goal into discrete, intermediary steps. At this time, we would also like to call your attention to the fact that the Annual Goal and Short-Term Objectives are written in terms anyone can understand and are measureable. There really is no doubt what skill he will be expected to demonstrate and at what level of proficiency. If a particular skill can't be objectively measured, then the IEP team should not attempt to write a "measureable" Annual Goal or Short-Term Objective.

The regulations require the IEP team to describe how a child's progress toward Annual Goals will be measured, so it is critical that goals be written in objective measurable terms or you couldn't describe progress (See Table 3-6). Essentially this means that they should be written to describe discrete acts or behaviors that are manifestly observable and require little interpretation. Parents must also be advised on a periodic basis of their child's progress toward attainment of the Annual Goals. The regulations don't require any particular timeline for progress reporting, but do offer the very sensible suggestion to provide a report on progress on the IEP at the same interval as progress reports are provided to all students. That decision is left to the IEP team, but we strongly urge that recommendation be followed, because doing so will make your life as a teacher much easier with only one progress report timeline to track.

TABLE 3-6. Sample Annual Goal, Short-Term Objective, Progress Report

Measureable Annual Goals and Short-Term Objectives
Area of Need: _Math Calculation_____
<u>Measurable Annual Goal</u> When presented with 50 single digit, mixed addition and subtraction problems using numerals (0–9), John will write the correct answer to 48 problems within 60 seconds.   <u>Short-Term Objective 1</u> Given a worksheet with 30 single digit **addition** problems (0–9) and a direction to complete it, John will write the correct answer to 29 problems within 60 seconds on three consecutive opportunities.   <u>Short-Term Objective 2</u> Given a worksheet with 30 single digit **subtraction** problems (0–9) and a direction to complete it, John will write the correct answer to 29 problems within 60 seconds on three consecutive opportunities.   <u>Describe how progress will be measured</u>: John's progress will be measured on timed fluency measures.
Progress Report   <u>Identify when periodic progress reports regarding the student's progression on annual goals and/or objectives will be made:</u> Progress reports for IEP goals and objectives will be provided at the regular quarterly report card distribution time.

Participation in State and District Mandated Assessment

IDEA requires that children with disabilities participate in state and district mandated assessments and that student performance will be used in determining Adequate Yearly Progress (AYP) as required by NCLB. This is just one area in which IDEA '04 was aligned with NCLB. While there are many concerns with the method in which AYP is computed and reported as well as with the current practice of wide-scale assessment (worthy discussions, but well beyond the depth of this text), the mandatory inclusion of students with disabilities in state and district mandated assessment, beginning with IDEA' 97, was a fundamentally positive requirement. It was positive because it highlighted the importance of students with disabilities having access to and making progress in the general education curriculum. It also reinforced recognition that students with disabilities must receive a quality education if they are to be afforded opportunities to be happy, productive, successful, and contributing members of American society and their local communities.

In addition, and on a somewhat sarcastic note, it may have been a response to professional concerns that in many pull-out special education classrooms there was no curriculum and nothing special nor educationally relevant happening. In a documentary by Habib (2009), disability rights advocate, Keith Jones, provided an accurate, yet disheartening critique on what happened in many separate educational settings. He attended a special school as a child and complained that he was not being challenged. Instead of learning mathematics or other academic skills, he was involved in making items with craft sticks. So requiring that students have access to and progress in the general curriculum, even if done at a very different level or depth than typically developing peers, recognizes the importance of a meaningful education for all students. Making items with craft sticks may be a fun activity for children, and may be very appropriate for young children, but it should not be a substitute for academic instruction for older students.

Before IDEA '97, IEP teams could excuse a child with a disability from participating in state and district mandated assessments. There may have been good reason for excusing some children, particularly those who could not participate in paper and pencil tests and those who did not have the academic skills necessary to comprehend the grade level test that would be administered. However with IDEA '97, states were required to develop alternative assessment opportunities for students and include all students in assessments. Now, states have five different options for conducting assessments as described by the U. S. Department of Education, Office of Special Education Programs (**http://www.osepideasthatwork.org**/). The first is simply completion of the regular grade level assessment. The second option is the grade level assessment with appropriate accommodations that maintain the validity of the test. For example, a student with a vision impairment may be provided with a test that has enlarged text. As with the first two options, the third still measures a student's performance on grade level standards, but the assessment can be presented in an alternate format. (We will discuss accommodations and modifications shortly.)

The final options reference modified or alternate achievement standards and are available for use only with students with disabilities. The fourth option is for students to complete an assessment that is still based on the standard curriculum, but with a modified achievement standard, which may simply be a lowered level of proficiency or testing at a lower grade level. The fifth option is for the student to complete an alternative assessment using alternative achievement standards. This final option is typically reserved for students with significant cognitive disabilities or preschool age children and may include a portfolio assessment with activities and data collected over several months rather than the usual one or two week testing period commonly associated with the other four assessment options.

The current regulations state the following guidelines and IEP team responsibilities regarding participation in state and district wide assessments (§300.321):

> (6) (i) A statement of any individual appropriate accommodations that are necessary to measure the academic achievement and functional performance of the child on State and district wide assessment and

(ii) If the IEP team determines that the child must take an alternate assessment instead of a particular regular State or district wide assessment of student achievement, as statement of why

(A) The child cannot participate in the regular assessment; and

(B) The particular assessment selected is appropriate for the child.

As you complete the IEP, you will find the terms accommodations and modifications frequently used when referring to supports provided to students with disabilities—whether instructional, environmental, or assessment supports. For assessment, specifically, accommodations generally refer to changes in the input (the way information is provided to the student) or output (the way information is demonstrated by the student). An accommodation does not alter what a student is expected to learn but serves as a means of providing equitable access. For example, a child with a vision impairment may get the accommodation of having the test material presented in large font or braille (input) and may write the letter of the answer to a multiple choice question or indicate choice verbally rather than fill in a bubble sheet (output). In this example the content has not changed from that included in the standard assessment and the accommodation simply allowed the student to participate in the assessment without being discriminated against due to disability.

The term modification refers to a change in performance expectation for a child. The change can be a lower level of academic achievement on the regular curriculum or an individualized performance standard on an alternative curriculum that is tied to the regular education curriculum. For example, a student who participates in a reading assessment but at a much lower grade level has been provided a modification; that is, the instructional expectations have been lowered or modified.

Since states have considerable latitude in conducting assessments, we recommend that you regularly check with your district or state department of education for specific actions that are allowable without jeopardizing the validity of the assessment. But first and foremost it is critical to keep in mind that it is the child's performance relative to the Annual Goals and Short-Term Objectives in the IEP that is most important. Teachers should monitor, above all else, whether or not Annual Goals and Short-Term Objectives are being met in a timely fashion. If they are and if the Annual Goals and Short-Term Objectives were designed to allow progress in the general curriculum, then there should be little concern regarding mandated state and district assessments. The IEP team should also write Annual Goals and Short-Term Objectives for all areas in which the child will receive special education support, not limit themselves to the academic areas covered on the mandated assessments. For areas not covered by mandated assessments, such as behavior, the team should always write Short-Term Objectives for each Annual Goal.

Acceptable accommodations are generally grouped by type: presentation, response, setting, or timing and scheduling. Before moving to the next section of the IEP, we will provide an illustrative (and by no means exhaustive) listing of commonly used accommodations, and Table 3-7 contains an example of an IEP statement regarding participation in state and district mandated assessments. Following is a listing of possible accommodations:

Presentation Accommodations:

- Directions read orally to the student
- Directions reread as often as needed
- Directions provided in primary language or mode of communication
- Large print or braille
- Audio amplification system
- Human readers (except for reading tests)
- Read aloud computer translations
- Assistance tuning page
- Fewer items per page

Response Accommodations:

- Use of pencil grip
- Larger bubbles on answer sheets
- Student dictates answer
- Manipulative to help compute mathematics problems
- Calculators
- Rulers, graph paper, abacus
- Speech activated software
- Word processor

Setting Accommodations:

- Complete test in different location
- Use sound deadening headphones
- Administer test individually or in small group

Timing and Scheduling:

- Provide extra time for writing
- Provide frequent breaks
- Extend test time (3 weeks instead of 2 weeks)
- Break test into smaller increments

TABLE 3-7. Participation in State & District

State and District Mandated Assessments
<u>Student will be taking standard assessment</u>: If the student will be participating in the assessment but needs modifications or adaptations for any of the sections, identify what modifications or adaptions will be allowed and for what assessment.
John will be allowed up to twice the allotted time for completion of math application sections of the assessment that are not timed fluency measures. He will be allowed to complete the assessment in an alternative setting, such as the office or resource room or other quite setting.
<u>Student will **NOT** be taking standard assessment</u>: If the IEP team determined that the standard assessment would not be appropriate, answer the following:
1. Describe why the student cannot participate in the standard assessment.
_____
2. Describe why the particular alternative assessment selected is appropriate for the student.
_____

Statement of Special Education and Related Services

The identification of what special education and related services and supplementary aids and services will be provided to a child is a required component of the IEP, but that determination cannot be made until after the development of Annual Goals and Short-Term Objectives, as appropriate. For obvious reasons, it would be impossible to identify what services will be provided to a child without first identifying the target learning outcomes. The regulations (§300.320) provide the following regarding the content specifically related to special education and related services that must be included in the IEP:

(4) A statement of the special education and related services and supplementary aids and services, based on peer-reviewed research to the extent practicable, to be provided to the child or on behalf of the child, and a statement of the program modifications or supports for school personnel that will be provided to enable the child

(i) To advance appropriately toward attaining the annual goal;

(ii) To be involved in and make progress in the general education curriculum and to participate in extracurricular and other nonacademic activities;

(iii) To be educated and participate with other children with disabilities and nondisabled children in the activities described in this section.

As you may have noticed, there are several components to this requirement, and in order to complete an IEP correctly, you must be familiar with the meaning of each component. We will provide the legal definition of special education and related services, but want to point out a couple of items in the regulatory language that deserve special attention. First, the requirement that special education services be based on practices supported by peer-reviewed research to the extent practicable was a new requirement of IDEA '04 that sought to align this legislation with the No Child Left Behind Act of 2001. At this time, there is not research supporting all practices in schools, but that does not relieve schools of the ethical responsibility of implementing research supported interventions whenever possible. This is a relatively new requirement, but as Bateman and Linden (2012) noted, courts haven't gotten into the point of determining which practice is best, rather they continue to be guided by the standard of benefit set forth by the 1982 US Supreme Court decision in *Hendrick Hudson Dist. Bd. of Ed. v. Rowley* (hereafter Rowley). Commonly known as the Rowley Standard, this ruling made it clear that special education services must be reasonably calculated to provide a child with meaningful educational benefit but need not "maximize" a child's potential. Public schools aren't required to maximize the potential of any student (even if we could measure potential).

We also want to emphasize the importance of items (ii) and (iii). A review of these requirements reveals the clear and overriding Congressional intent that children with disabilities be educated with their typically developing peers in both academic activities (with a particular focus on the general education curriculum) and nonacademic activities (recess, lunch, assemblies, fieldtrips, etc.) and extracurricular activities, such as school clubs. To comply with the law and congressional intent, the IEP team must assume that the child will be educated in the regular education setting with the use of supplementary aids and services as stated in the Least Restrictive Environment (LRE) section of the regulations (§300.114). This is an incredibly important point, from both an educational perspective and a civil rights perspective, which be discussed further in Chapter 5. But we need to mention it here to emphasize that the team must consider regular education placement before considering any other placement. This legal presumption of placement in the regular education environment can only be rebutted if the child's needs cannot be met in the regular education environment with the use of supplementary aids and services, a determination that can only be made at the end of the IEP meeting.

Now that we have covered regulatory guidance for research-based intervention along with the presumption of regular education placement, we can provide the definitions of special education, related services, and supplementary aids and services. First, special education is defined in the regulations as follows:

> 300.39 Special education.
>
> (a) *General.*
>
> (1) *Special education* means specially designed instruction, at no cost to the parents, to meet the unique needs of a child with a disability, including—
>
> (i) Instruction conducted in the classroom, in the home, in hospitals and institutions, and in other settings; and
>
> (ii) Instruction in physical education.

(2) *Special education* includes each of the following, if the services otherwise meet the requirements of paragraph (a)(1) of this section—

(i) Speech-language pathology, or any other related service, if the service is considered special education rather than a related service under State standards;

(ii) Travel training; and

(iii) Vocational education.

(f) *Individual special education terms defined.* The terms in this definition are defined as follows:

(1) *At no cost* means that all specially-designed instruction is provided without charge, but does not preclude incidental fees that are normally charged to nondisabled students or their parents as part of the regular education program.

(5) *Physical education* means—

(i) The development of—

(A) Physical and motor fitness;

(B) Fundamental motor skills and patterns; and

(C) Skills in aquatics, dance, and individual and group games and sports (including intramural and lifetime sports; and (ii) Includes special physical education, adapted physical education, movement education, and motor development.

(3) *Specially designed instruction* means adapting, as appropriate to the needs of an eligible child under this part, the contents, methodology, or delivery of instruction—

(i) To address the unique needs of the child that result from the child's disability; and

(ii) To ensure access of the child to the general curriculum, so that the child can meet the educational standards within the jurisdiction of the public agency that apply to all children.

(4) *Travel training* means providing instruction, as appropriate, to children with significant cognitive disabilities, and any other children with disabilities who require this instruction, to enable them to—

(i) Develop an awareness of the environment in which they live; and

(i) Learn the skills necessary to move effectively and safely from place to place within that environment (e.g., in school, in the home, at work, and in the community).

(5) *Vocational education* means organized educational programs that are directly related to the preparation of individuals for paid or unpaid employment, or for additional preparation for a career not requiring a baccalaureate or advanced degree.

We have provided the legal definition, but need to offer some clarifying commentary on selected items. As is apparent from the definition, special education includes specially designed instruction designed to meet the unique needs of the child. This means that there is no single special education instructional practice that will be appropriate for a child with a specific disability label (as we discussed in Chapter 1), rather service decisions must be made on an individual basis for each child based upon his or her unique needs. Thus, the assessments that were conducted as precursor to the IEP development must be educationally relevant, and the results must be clearly and operationally specified in statements of Present Levels. Only by having a solid understanding of the unique educational needs of a specific child will the team be able to identify what the child will require and develop a truly Individualized Education Program.

It is also important to note that special education is provided at no cost to the parent, regardless of the parent's income level. All states have mandatory attendance laws and provide education at no cost to students without disabilities. To charge parents of students with disabilities tuition or other fees not levied against parents of children without disabilities would be clearly discriminatory. If that were allowed (and it was allowed before legislation in the 1970s specifically prohibited such practice), then a child with a disability could be kept from school due to parents' inability or unwillingness to pay extra for an educational service that the state provides to other children without disabilities free of charge. However, this does not prevent districts from charging students with disabilities fees to participate in activities, such as field trips or sports, if those same fees are required of students without disabilities.

So, we know that special education is specially designed instruction provided free of charge. However, it is important to recognize that it can be provided in a variety of settings. While the presumed placement of the child is the regular education setting, special education supports can be provided in the home or in community preschool settings where the child will have an opportunity to interact with peers without disabilities. For older students placement at a jobsite in the community with nondisabled coworkers could be done in compliance with the LRE mandate and intent. The "continuum at the alternative placements" describes placement options ranging from regular class to very restrictive institutions and will be discussed in detail in Chapter 5. However, it is important for IEP teams to recognize that placement, or the setting(s) in which the child will receive specially designed instruction, is determined annually and on an individual basis after Annual Goals and Short-Term Objectives are developed and with a presumption of placement in the regular education setting.

The regulations offered some guidance on specially designed instruction which provided IEP teams an opportunity to adapt content, methodology, or delivery of instruction. The content requirements could be modified and reflected in the IEP goals and objectives. For example, some children may receive reading instruction on skills typically acquired in earlier grades (content adaptation) or students may receive instruction in content not typically considered part of the formal school curriculum (e.g., eating, toileting, or mobility). Specific methodological practice is generally left to the purview of the school and court decisions have found that if the child benefitted from the special education provided at the school, then parents could not force a district to change methodology (*Lachman v. Illinois State Board of Education, 1988*). However, it is allowable for an IEP team to decide that a specific methodology will be used with a particular child. For example, an IEP team might determine that a particular child requires some home-based Applied Behavior Analysis (ABA) training in order to benefit from special education. In that case, the school would be required to provide that service and ABA would be considered specially designed instruction. Provision of home-based service is an expensive proposition and underscores the importance of having a representative of the public agency at the IEP meeting.

We chose this example because the use of ABA with children with autism has been an area of contention and legal challenge. Many times, districts have tried to avoid the cost associated with home-based ABA, but lost their case in due process hearings and were ordered to provide the service because the child had not been making satisfactory progress in the program provided by the district which meant that the child was not receiving FAPE. However, had the district provided FAPE as indicated by the child making satisfactory benefit from whatever methodology the district had implemented, then it is highly unlikely that a district would have lost a hearing on an issue of methodology just because a parent preferred a different methodology.

We have discussed some major components of the definition of special education that are included in most IEPs. The regulatory language does not require that each item identified in the definition of special education (§300.39) be included in an IEP. For example, not all children require travel training, mobility training, or specially designed instruction in PE. The thing to remember is the supports to be provided are those that enable the child to benefit from special education, have access to the general education curriculum, and interact with typically developing peers to the maximum extent appropriate.

In one of the most egregious practices involving provision of special education services of which the authors are aware, the district would only provide speech and language services to children who had an IQ score above a certain arbitrary level. This practice was clearly illegal because the district policy stripped the IEP team of its right and responsibility to develop a truly individualized IEP. Additionally, the policy made absolutely no sense. In this scenario, children with severe disabilities who had extremely limited communication skills were barred from receiving speech and language therapy (communication skills) because the district had determined that the low IQ score precluded them from benefitting from that intervention. In other words, children who were in greatest need of communication support were denied that support. The district was requiring those students to demonstrate their ability to benefit from special education service—a requirement forcefully negated by the 1st Circuit Court in the 1989 decision in *Timothy W. v. Rochester School District*. **http://law.justia.com/cases/federal/appellate-courts/ F2/875/954/179023/**

In addition to identifying special education services, the IEP must also specify the related services as well as supplementary aids and services that will be provided for the child to benefit from special education. We will continue our discussion by moving on to the topic of related services that are simply defined as services that a child needs in order to benefit from special education. The regulations include the following overarching definition:

> 300.34 Related services.
> (a) General. Related services means transportation and such developmental, corrective, and other supportive services as are required to assist a child with a disability to benefit from special education, and includes speech language pathology and audiology services, interpreting services, psychological services, physical and occupational therapy, recreation, including therapeutic recreation, early identification and assessment of disabilities in children, counseling services, including rehabilitation counseling, orientation and mobility services, and medical services for diagnostic or evaluation purposes. Related services also include school health services and school nurse services, social work services in schools, and parent counseling and training.

This listing is not exhaustive but does identify the most commonly used related services. They are called "related services" because they are related to the child's special education. In other words, the child could receive the services at no cost only if needed to benefit from special education. Giangreco (2011) argued that related services should only involve as much support as is necessary and must be clearly educationally relevant. He provided an interesting example that one of the authors also encountered while consulting with a school district. The related service in question was horseback riding or "equine therapy" for the development of motor skills. There simply was no justifiable reason for provision of horseback riding as a necessary related service. Any motor skills developed through horseback riding could have been addressed during more typical times and activities, such as physical education or recess.

Now, let's consider a couple of very simple scenarios regarding related services without reading anything extra into the description or making any assumptions. These are intended to be simplistic in order to illustrate the basic points. Our first example is very unlikely (not the bicycle accident and sprained ankle, but trying to relate the sprained ankle it to reading support). Suppose you had a student with a learning disability who received special education support for reading. One day, this student had an accident while riding her bike, sprained an ankle, and the doctor ordered physical therapy. Now, just because physical therapy is listed as a related service and she receives special education does not mean that she would now be eligible for physical therapy as a related service. To get the service, she would need it in order to benefit from special education, and it would be nearly impossible to successfully argue that a sprained ankle impacted her ability to benefit from specially designed instruction in reading.

For our next example, assume you work in a district that provides transportation for students who live two miles or more from the school. You have a kindergarten student with an orthopedic impairment who uses a walker, moves very slowly, and tires easily from the walking. She lives less than one-half mile from school, but the IEP team could easily determine that she would need transportation as a related service in order to get to school in a timely manner and have enough energy to participate in instructional activities and benefit from her special education. One final point about transportation, there is no requirement that it be provided on a "short bus". In our example, the full-size bus that transports students without disabilities could make an extra stop and pick her up—this would actually be consistent with the LRE requirements by supporting her participation in nonacademic activities with typically developing peers to the maximum extent.

We will provide the rather lengthy regulatory definitions for each of the related services previously listed. Before presenting that information, we do want to bring your attention to a few items. First, there are some restrictions on many of the services. For example, the list includes both "health services" and "medical services" as related services. School districts must provide "health services," but only need to provide "medical services" if needed for diagnostic purposes. In *Irving Independent School District. v. Tatro* (1984), a case involving Clean Intermittent Catheterization, the U.S. Supreme Court provided guidelines regarding the identification of medical services that districts need not provide. Essentially, the Court determined that medical services are those that must be provided by a licensed physician and unless required for diagnostic purposes, the district is not responsible for their provision. **http://supreme.justia.com/cases/federal/us/468/883/case.html** Second, the regulations specifically limit district responsibility for surgically implanted devices, specifically mapping cochlear implants that many children with hearing impairments use. Our third point is particularly important for preschool teachers who receive children transitioning from Part C services. With the exception of some parent training and provision of information, related services are provided to children only. Under Part C, some adult family members or even siblings may have been recipients of Early Intervention Services that are now considered related services under Part B, so this could be a significant change for some families. Finally, IEP teams should avoid the temptation of thinking that since a particular related service was required by a child on a prior IEP that the related service will always be required and should be included in subsequent IEPs. What is needed one year may not be needed the next year.

Following is the extensive description of related services as provided in the regulations (§300.34).

> **(c) Individual related services terms defined.** The terms used in this definition are defined as follows:
>
> (1) *Audiology* includes—
>
> (i) Identification of children with hearing loss;
>
> (ii) Determination of the range, nature, and degree of hearing loss, including referral for medical or other professional attention for the habilitation of hearing;

(iii) Provision of habilitative activities, such as language habilitation, auditory training, speech reading (lipreading), hearing evaluation, and speech conservation;

(iv) Creation and administration of programs for prevention of hearing loss;

(v) Counseling and guidance of children, parents, and teachers regarding hearing loss; and

(vi) Determination of children's needs for group and individual amplification, selecting and fitting an appropriate aid, and evaluating the effectiveness of amplification.

(2) *Counseling services* means services provided by qualified social workers, psychologists, guidance counselors, or other qualified personnel.

(3) *Early identification and assessment* of disabilities in children means the implementation of a formal plan for identifying a disability as early as possible in a child's life.

(4) *Interpreting services* includes—

(i) The following, when used with respect to children who are deaf or hard of hearing: Oral transliteration services, cued language transliteration services, sign language transliteration and interpreting services, and transcription services, such as communication access real-time translation (CART), C-Print, and TypeWell; and

(ii) Special interpreting services for children who are deaf-blind.

(5) *Medical services* means services provided by a licensed physician to determine a child's medically related disability that results in the child's need for special education and related services.

(6) *Occupational therapy*—

(i) Means services provided by a qualified occupational therapist; and

(ii) Includes—

(A) Improving, developing, or restoring functions impaired or lost through illness, injury, or deprivation;

(B) Improving ability to perform tasks for independent functioning if functions are impaired or lost; and

(C) Preventing, through early intervention, initial or further

(7) *Orientation and mobility services*—

(i) Means services provided to blind or visually impaired children by qualified personnel to enable those students to attain systematic orientation to and safe movement within their environments in school, home, and community; and

(ii) Includes teaching children the following, as appropriate:

(A) Spatial and environmental concepts and use of information received by the senses (such as sound, temperature, and vibrations) to establish, maintain, or regain orientation and line of travel (e.g., using sound at a traffic light to cross the street);

(B) To use the long cane or a service animal to supplement visual travel skills or as a tool for safely negotiating the environment for children with no available travel vision;

(C) To understand and use remaining vision and distance low vision aids; and

(D) Other concepts, techniques, and tools.

(8) (i) *Parent counseling and training* means assisting parents in understanding the special needs of their child;

(ii) Providing parents with information about child development; and

(iii) Helping parents to acquire the necessary skills that will allow them to support the implementation of their child's IEP or IFSP.

(9) *Physical therapy* means services provided by a qualified physical therapist.

(10) *Psychological services* includes—

(i) Administering psychological and educational tests, and other assessment procedures;

(ii) Interpreting assessment results;

(iii) Obtaining, integrating, and interpreting information about child behavior and conditions relating to learning;

(iv) Consulting with other staff members in planning school programs to meet the special educational needs of children as indicated by psychological tests, interviews, direct observation, and behavioral evaluations;

(v) Planning and managing a program of psychological services, including psychological counseling for children and parents; and

(vi) Assisting in developing positive behavioral intervention strategies.

(11) *Recreation* includes—

(i) Assessment of leisure function;

(ii) Therapeutic recreation services;

(iii) Recreation programs in schools and community agencies; and

(iv) Leisure education.

(12) *Rehabilitation counseling services* means services provided by qualified personnel in individual or group sessions that focus specifically on career development, employment preparation, achieving independence, and integration in the workplace and community of a student with a disability. The term also includes vocational rehabilitation service provided to a student with a disability by vocational rehabilitation programs funded under the Rehabilitation Act of 1973, as amended, 29 U.S.C. 701 et seq.

(13) *School health services and school nurse services* means health services that are designed to enable a child with a disability to receive FAPE as described in the child's IEP. School nurse services are services provided by a qualified school nurse. School health services are services that may be provided by either a qualified school nurse or other qualified person.

(14) *Social work services* in schools includes—

(i) Preparing a social or developmental history on a child with a disability;

(ii) Group and individual counseling with the child and family;

(iii) Working in partnership with parents and others on those problems in a child's living situation (home, school, and community) that affect the child's adjustment in school;

(iv) Mobilizing school and community resources to enable the child to learn as effectively as possible in his or her educational program; and

(v) Assisting in developing positive behavioral intervention strategies.

(15) *Speech-language pathology services* includes—

(i) Identification of children with speech or language impairments;

(ii) Diagnosis and appraisal of specific speech or language impairments;

(iii) Referral for medical or other professional attention necessary for the habilitation of speech or language impairments;

(iv) Provision of speech and language services for the habilitation or prevention of communicative impairments; and

(v) Counseling and guidance of parents, children, and teachers regarding speech and language impairments.

(16) *Transportation* includes—

(i) Travel to and from school and between schools;

(ii) Travel in and around school buildings; and

(iii) Specialized equipment (such as special or adapted buses, lifts, and ramps), if required to provide special transportation for a child with a disability.

IEPs must identify the supplementary aids and services that will be provided to support the child in achieving the IEP goals. They are defined as aids, services, and other supports provided in regular education classes, other education related settings, and in extracurricular and nonacademic settings, to enable children with disabilities to be educated with nondisabled children to the maximum extent appropriate (§300.342). This requirement is clearly aligned with the LRE provision of the law which has been in place since passage in 1975. The presumption that children with disabilities would be educated with typically developing peers is not a new idea or some passing fad. These aids, services, and other supports are varied and can include assistive technology, adult support, peer supports, and modification of architectural barriers to allow access, or even access to resource room supports. An example of when a resource room might be considered as a supplementary aid or service rather than a placement would be when a student receives all instruction in the regular class but only goes to resource room to take a test in a quiet setting. The definition is broad and one could make a reasoned argument that it is broad by design, because those who wrote the law could not have foreseen the various types of individualized supports that children might need.

Given that these supports could be quite varied, we thought it might be helpful to provide some illustrative examples. Please remember that these supports may not need to be provided at all times; this is especially true of the assignment of an adult assistant. Since assignment of an adult assistant is so prevalent and beset with difficulty, we want to discuss it at some depth. It often seems that children with significant disabilities are automatically tethered to an adult at all times. Some children may need an adult with them to monitor serious medical issues, such as a ventilator, but even then the adult should only be as close as absolutely necessary. Having adults in constant proximity can have detrimental outcomes as identified by Giangreco, Edelman, Luiselli, and MacFarland (1997) including the unintended effect of causing students without disabilities to avoid the student with a disability or altering or limiting interpersonal interactions (we all know that 11 year olds act differently with other 11 year olds when an adult is present than when an adult is not present). **http://www.uvm.edu/ ~cdci/archives/mgiangre/helpinghovering.pdf** The proximity of the adult may also result in a phenomenon known as "learned helplessness", because the adult, trying to be helpful, overcompensates and does things for the child without requiring that the child complete the task. In some cases, the adult may even speak for the child and/or interpret what the child is saying, which may negatively impact a child's opportunities to improve communication skills. In many cases, there is also the risk that the child with a severe disability, a child who likely requires the most specialized instruction, is instructed by individuals with the least amount of training, teacher assistants. This is not meant to minimize the high quality work done by many teacher assistants, but to point out that unless specifically trained, they may not have the necessary skills. Merely having experience with children with disabilities doesn't equate with instructional competence.

If additional adult support is necessary to ensure that a child with a disability receives the appropriate support, then the adult could work with children without disabilities and support the child with a disability only when he/she needs the support. That additional adult support would likely be welcome in most classrooms. As an aside, and an important point, the regulations do not require that all the additional supports be provided by an adult. The peers of the student with a disability are great sources of support and may provide more natural support than an adult, but they too may need some training or direction for working with a particular child. Or if an adult is required, it may only be for specific support activities at times such as meals or toileting.

The examples of accommodations and modifications previously mentioned for use on assessments could also be used in the classroom; in fact, when used with students on state and district mandated assessments, it is generally required that they must have been used by the student on a regular basis in the education setting and not just selected for use on the assessment. So, it is important that consideration be given to ensure that students have regular access to needed accommodations or modifications during the school year. Some examples of additional supports that may or may not be appropriate for inclusion in assessment activities, but could be included on an IEP, include items, such as

- pencil grips that make it easier for a child with fine motor difficulties to grip a pencil
- provision of an alternate setting to take tests
- heavy paper for writing rather than the newsprint
- preferential seating (not necessarily seating next to the teacher as this is punishing to some students)
- audio amplification
- picture schedule and verbal reminder approximately 5 minutes before change in activity
- picture communication system
- assignment notebook to be checked by teacher at the end of the day
- use of calculator for math computation problems
- audio taping or reading of math application story problems
- seating support and straps on preschool playground toys
- access to nurse's office for toileting assistance
- supervised access to food

- assigned playground area
- use of restroom when no other children are present
- adult assistance with toileting
- taped responses rather than written responses
- text adapted to reading level
- copy of classroom material for use at home

The regulations also require that the IEP include supports that will be provided to the teacher to allow the child to participate and benefit from the regular education setting. As evidenced throughout this chapter, the regulations consistently reference the goal of enabling the child to access and progress in the general education setting and curriculum. This particular requirement may have the effect of minimizing the excuse that many teachers, in the past, used to keep a child out of the classroom—"I don't have the training." This excuse was never acceptable, because no child should have to pay the price for the teacher's lack of training by being relegated to a segregated setting or denied entry to school.

This excuse also implied that if the child was sent to another setting, the teacher in that segregated setting would be appropriately trained. Let us take a minute to disabuse you of this type of thinking. We personally know of situations where students with disabilities have been sent away from regular schools with fully certificated teachers to special education classrooms with uncertified teachers. Consider the following: child rode a "short bus" to attend a bilingual special education program only to find that it was staffed by a substitute teacher who was not fully certificated and only spoke English. There was absolutely no justifiable reason to send that student from his home school where there was a fully certificated special education teacher. Neither teacher spoke Spanish, but the student was removed from his home school under false premise of receiving competent bilingual and special education support from a fully certificated teacher. Consider the case of another student who was sent to a special school that supposedly had faculty with specialized training in the application of applied behavior analysis only to discover that he was placed in a class with a substitute teacher who did not have a bachelor's degree and had no specialization in behavioral intervention. We must avoid the assumption that removal from the regular education setting and placement in a special education setting automatically results in the student receiving highly specialized educational interventions. We must also avoid the temptation of believing that highly specialized services cannot be provided in the regular education setting when in fact, many can and should be provided there.

In addition to identifying the special education, related services, modifications and adaptations and use of supplementary aids and services that will be provided, the IEP team must identify the projected date for the beginning of the services and modifications and the anticipated frequency, location, and duration of those services and modifications.

Location does not need to identify the specific school site, but only include a general specification as to where the services will be provided—whether regular classroom setting, a pull-out setting, or some other setting—is sufficient (71 Fed. Reg. 46588, 2006; Letter to Wessels, 1992). Since districts may have an appropriate placement at more than one location, the district is afforded flexibility in assigning a student to a particular location. Despite these clarifications, in an unpublished decision, which is not precedent setting, the Fourth Circuit Court determined that IEP teams should identify the specific school (*K.J. v. Fairfax County School Board, 2010*) whereas, in a published decision, the Second Circuit Court ruled that IDEA does not require identification of a specific school, merely the placement where the IEP will be implemented (*T. Y. v. New York City Department of Education, 2009/2010*). The Second Circuit decision was appealed to the U.S. Supreme Court who refused to hear the case, indicating that the Second Circuit interpreted the law correctly. Zirkel (2011) noted that a subsequent decision by the Fourth Circuit indicated that identification of a specific school depends upon the circumstances of the case. We mention this issue, not to cause confusion or concern on your part, but to note that schools in the Fourth Circuit may have different practices, based on the court ruling. This difference of opinion among the courts also serves to illustrate the importance of keeping abreast of legal rulings. Should there be decisions that impact your locale, the school district should keep you informed. One last comment regarding the cases mentioned above. These cases were a result of serious disagreements between parents and school districts. You will likely never find yourself in such a position, but if you do, then rest assured that the district will have legal counsel and administrators working to try and resolve the issue. There are plenty of opportunities for the school district and parents to reach a resolution before the case ends up in court.

The team should specify the number of minutes of special education and any related services that the child will receive. The IEP must identify the specific number of minutes that will be provided to the child and cannot simply be a range of time. So, 15 minutes twice per week would be allowable, but 15–20 minutes once per week would not be an acceptable level of specification. The team would need to identify either 15 or 20 minutes.

An exception to this rule would be a service such as transportation; you don't need to identify the number of minutes of transportation provided per day, just identify that the child will be transported to and from school and on what days. Many districts use an additional form for transportation to document information needed by the bus driver including specific directions such as whether the child can be left at home alone. This is important information, and the district should take steps to ensure that the bus driver, including substitute drivers, have the information. The IEP should also specify the number of minutes of special education support services provided, but could also identify that some services will be available as needed. An example of an as needed support could be providing the student access to the resource room for test taking if the regular classroom setting is too distracting.

Table 3-8 contains a Service Summary Matrix that is a useful way of documenting special education, related services, and supplementary aids or services that will be provided to the child. We remind you that this IEP example for John was purposefully simple, because we could show you the IEP components in a straightforward manner. Once you can complete a

TABLE 3-8. Special Ed and Related Services

Special Education, Related Services, and Accommodations/Adaptations

Describe the special education and related services, based on peer-reviewed research to the extent available, that will be provided to enable the student to 1) make adequate progress toward meeting annual goals and/or objectives, 2) to be involved and make progress in the general education curriculum, including extra-curricular and nonacademic activities, 3) to be educated with other students with and without disabilities. Include any modifications or supports provided to school personnel.

Special Education	Begin Date	Frequency	Location	Duration	Person Responsible
Small group instruction	9-10-2012	Daily	Regular Ed Cassroom	20 minutes	Special and Regular Ed. Teachers

Related Service	Begin Date	Frequency	Location	Duration	Person Responsible

Accommodations/Adaptations: None needed

Supports provided to school personnel: None needed

basic IEP, it becomes easier to add on more components. On this form, we did include a place to identify who is responsible for providing the service. The responsible person cannot be the parent or the student. Children and their parents cannot be required to implement the IEP, because it is the duty of the school to provide FAPE.

LRE Statement

Throughout this chapter, we have noted that the law presumes that children with disabilities are educated in the regular education class and have access to extracurricular and nonacademic activities with their typically developing peers. The regulations (§300.320(5)) require that the IEP contain:

> *An explanation of the extent, if any, to which the child will not participate with nondisabled children in the regular class and activities described in paragraph (a)(4)*

We will reserve a discussion of acceptable reasons for removal from the regular education setting for Chapter 5, and just note the requirement here. In Table 3-9, we provide a sample

TABLE 3-9. LRE, ESY, PBS

Least Restrictive Environment Provide an explanation of the extent, if any, that the child will not be participating with children without disabilities in the regular class and extra-curricular or nonacademic activities. _____ _____ _____ _____ Percentage of time in general education setting ____100%_____
Extended School Year Is the child eligible for Extended School Year Services? _____ Yes _____ No Decision will be made by __May 1, 2013_____
Positive Behavioral Supports Does the child have a Behavior Intervention Plan? _____ Yes__X__ No (If yes, attach to the IEP)

LRE statement for John, our hypothetical student. Since he will spend 100% of the time in the regular class, there is no need to make any justification for removal. We have also included a section denoting whether he will receive Extended School Year services (discussed in the next section) and a blank to indicate whether he has a Behavior Intervention Plan (BIP). We will discuss BIP in Chapter 6, but want to include it on the IEP to ensure that the use of such a plan is documented. We recommend attaching the BIP to the IEP, but more of that in a subsequent chapter.

Extended School Year

Extended School Year (ESY) is technically not a component of the IEP, but the decision to provide ESY rests with the IEP team, and it certainly makes sense that the decision be documented on the IEP form. Inclusion on the form provides some assurance that the issue was discussed and assists with record keeping. Extended School Year is defined as:

> 300.106 (b) Definition. As used in this section, the term extended school year services means special education and related services that—

> (1) Are provided to a child with a disability:

>> (i) Beyond the normal school year of the public agency;

>> (ii) In accordance with the child's IEP; and

>> (iii) At no cost to the parents of the child

The determination of ESY is clearly an individualized determination and the regulations specifically prohibit the district from limiting the provision of ESY to particular disability categories, or unilaterally limiting the type, amount, or duration of the ESY services. In the past, hopefully not in the present, some districts have imposed arbitrary limits on ESY services. For example, a district might have stated that the only ESY service available was during a specified 6 week summer session, 4 hours per day, 4 days per week—for a total of 96 hours per student. We hope that you realize that type of restriction on service is clearly not appropriate because it deprives IEP teams of making individualized decisions for the specific child of concern. In fact, the regulations prohibit districts from limiting ESY according to disability category, or limiting the amount, type, or duration of those services (Yell, 2006).

ESY has commonly and erroneously been equated with summer school. Summer school is an optional program offered by school districts during summer break, and districts typically charge tuition and provide limited curricular choices. Elementary age students may participate in enrichment courses, while high school students frequently participate in summer school if they failed a class required for graduation, want to take courses to hasten their completion of required graduation requirements, or take enrichment courses such as driver's education. ESY, on the other hand, is a continuation of special education services as identified in the IEP and is provided free of charge. A school district is not required to provide summer school services, but ESY support must be available to eligible students who need it. In addition, ESY offering need not be restricted to summer months. ESY could also result in a longer school day for a child. Imagine that you were a preschool teacher implementing a traditional toileting strategy with a child. This strategy required a specific procedure be conducted at the "period of maximum likelihood," i.e., when the child was most likely to eliminate. Now, if this time overlapped with school excusal, the IEP team could make a cogent case that ESY service should be implemented and the child's school day lengthened to allow the toilet training procedure to occur during that "period of maximum likelihood." Failure to do so could deprive the child of an important learning opportunity and the instruction needed to achieve an Annual Goal or Short-Term Objective. ESY services could also be offered on weekends or during breaks other than summer vacation.

States can set criteria for determining whether a child is eligible for ESY (Fed. Reg. 71, 46582, 2006). Many states have developed criteria requiring the consideration of regression and recoupment of skills where regression refers to the loss of skills during a break in instruction and recoupment refers to the time it takes for the child to regain skills lost during a break. These conditions regarding ESY eligibility highlight the importance of IEP team members being well versed with state guidelines and regulations and that the school staff collects appropriate data. Of course, if IEP teams are uncertain of particular eligibility criteria or if it is simply too soon to determine if the child will be eligible for ESY, the IEP could be reconvened at a later time to address that issue. A final comment on ESY is that parents cannot be required to send their child to ESY services even though the majority of the members of the IEP team think that it is needed and appropriate. Compulsory attendance laws simply don't apply to ESY services.

IEP Summary

In the previous pages, we have provided you with a detailed description of the components that are contained in the IEP. You should now possess knowledge that will help you be a productive member of an IEP team in the development of an educationally relevant IEP for a young child who requires additional assistance in order to succeed at school. Our intent has been to provide a simple description of the IEP without postsecondary transition and in Appendix B we provide blank sample IEP Forms, and in Appendix C we provide a checklist for completing the IEP which also serves as a brief overview of the steps in developing an IEP—from setting up the meeting thought completing the IEP. In subsequent chapters, we will provide a more detailed discussion of several key items including Present Levels, Goals and Objectives, postsecondary transition, Least Restrictive Environment, and Procedural Safeguards. We will also provide guidelines for implementing the IEP in an inclusive elementary classroom. This strategy could easily be adapted for the secondary setting. A comprehensive set of questions and answers regarding the IEP was revised by the U. S. Department of Education in 2010. **http://www2.ed.gov/policy/speced/guid/idea/iep-qa-2010.pdf** Since you should now have basic understanding of the IEP, we will provide a brief comparison with the IFSP which will be particularly useful for those of you who will be working with children and families who are transitioning from IFSP services to IEP services.

Comparison of IEP with IFSP

As we discussed in Chapter 2, an Individualized Family Service Plan is a document that contains the outline of Early Intervention services for eligible children between the ages of birth and three years. Unlike the IEP that is for students age 3 years to 22 years of age, it is family focused and differs in many significant ways from the IEP. Some of the more important differences include:

(1) Whereas the IEP begins by including a statement of present levels of academic achievement and functional performance, the IFSP must include a statement of the child's development in the areas of physical development (vision, hearing, health, cognitive development, communication development, social development, and adaptive development). Clearly the emphasis in the IFSP is upon child development and not academic achievement as is the case in the IEP.

(2) The IFSP must, with the family's permission, include a statement of family concerns, priorities, and resources relative to the development of the child as identified through a series of assessment procedures detailed in the regulations that govern the administration of EI services (34 CFR 303). The IEP does not include any such statement or reflect a requirement to focus upon the family. Herein is the essence of a major difference referred to above. The family is the focus of the IFSP and the child is the focus of the IEP.

(3)   The IEP must include a statement of measureable Annual Goals and Short-Term Objectives; the IFSP must include a statement of measureable outcomes or results to be achieved for the child and for the child's family. The difference between an Annual Goal and Short-Term Objective versus an Outcome or Result is not as large as it may at first seem. We will address this point more later, but for now it is important to note that both must be observable and measureable.

(4)   While the IEP requires that services be provided in the LRE to the maximum extent appropriate and an explanation for why a child is removed from the regular educational setting, an IFSP must include a statement that each service is provided in the natural environment to the maximum extent appropriate and when that is not the setting for a service or services a justification must be provided as to why not a natural environment. When first exposed to the term "natural environment" the thought may be that for an infant or toddler that must mean the home. But that is not the case. "Natural environment" means any setting that is natural or typical for infants or toddlers the same age without disabilities that may include the home or any one of a host of other community settings such as daycare, the YMCA, a park, etc.

(5)   The IFSP must include the name of a person who will act as the Service Coordinator. The Service Coordinator is an individual who is from a profession closely related to the needs of the child or who is otherwise qualified to fulfill the responsibilities of the position. The Service Coordinator is responsible for insuring that all services specified in the IFSP are delivered in a timely and effective manner. The Service Coordinator is an especially important resource person for parents preparing to transition from Part C to Part B services and must be invited by the district to attend the initial IEP meeting upon parental request. The IEP does include a provision for a Service Coordinator.

(6)   The IFSP must include a transition plan. The transition plan is a list of steps taken to insure the smooth transition of an eligible child and that child's family to preschool Part B services or other services once the child becomes 3 years of age. A transition plan must be in effect for a child with an IEP by age 16 whereas such a plan must be a part of the IFSP when first developed.

(7)   The IEP is written for a calendar year and must be rewritten each year. Gathering the IEP team during the year to review the child's progress toward the Annual Goals is optional and generally done only if revisions are necessary. The IFSP is written annually, but the IFSP must be reviewed and revised as needed every 6 months.

While these seven differences between the content of the IEP and the IFSP are significant, there are also many similarities. Both the IEP and the IFSP statements regarding achievements must be in objective clearly specifiable terms that anyone can understand; both require a clear unequivocal delineation of services to be provided, including a timeline for when they are to begin and how long they are to be provided; both require specification as to when and how progress is to be measured and communicated and as one may conclude from #3 above, both reflect the undeniable preference for the provision of services in inclusive settings with children the same age without disabilities. Finally it is important to note that both the IEP and the IFSP require that the services that are included are based upon peer reviewed research whenever possible.

Chapter Summary

The IEP represents a collaborative effort by numerous people who are involved in the education of the child and the process places a high level of importance on parent participation. That does not mean that parents get whatever they want, rather it means that they are informed participants and the school considers parental opinion and insights. If parents and the district disagree on the IEP, then, as we will describe in Chapter 7, there are safeguards that allow the parents to challenge the proposal. Failure to involve parents in the process can place a district in a precarious position should the IEP be challenged. Legal issues aside, we do know that children benefit when schools and parents are cooperative and work as a team, and cooperation should be a goal, but not at the expense of providing the child FAPE. One step in ensuring meaningful parental participation is ensuring that teachers are well informed on the many aspects of the IEP. We have covered basic issues regarding IEP development and will investigate other topics at more depth in the following chapters. However, the IEP is an individualized document and all possibilities could not be covered in any book, because there will always be a unique, child-specific issue that must be addressed. By having a basic understanding of the process and district responsibilities, you will be in a position to develop high quality IEPs, and should an issue arise that you cannot answer without additional research, then the IEP meeting could be reconvened to discuss that aspect or the team could agree on part of the IEP and then reconvene to address the topic of concern.

Interpretation of the law is an ongoing process, so it is important that part of your ongoing professional development include keeping appraised of any changes. Some options for keeping current include attending professional conferences, school district or state level trainings, and reading professional journals and other publications.

Chapter Activites

1. Why do you think that IFSP focuses upon the family but the IEP focuses almost exclusively upon the child?

2. Why in the IFSP is there a focus upon "development" but in the IEP the focus is upon "academic achievement"?

3. Why isn't every child receiving ESY?

4. Identify the major components of an IEP.

5. Why is it important the Present Levels and Annual Goals be measurable?

6. Find the appropriate website for your state and find the regulations and procedures related to special education. Read the sections on IEP development. Does your state have requirements in addition to those presented in this chapter?

7. What guidance do your state regulations provide for determination of ESY service?

8. Does your state have model IEP forms, including PWN and invitation to IEP meetings?

9. Find and compare an IEP form with an IFSP form.

10. Locate your state guidelines regarding acceptable modifications and adaptations in state and district assessments. Can you think of instances how you might incorporate those modifications or adaptations into instructional activities should you have a student that may require them?

11. Read your state guidelines on the participation of students with disabilities on state and district mandated assessments. Are there separate guidelines for students who have an IEP, students with a 504 plan, or students whose primary language is one other than English? What are the different options that an IEP team could consider?

12. Compare your state options for participation in the regular assessment with the available alternative assessment option.

Chapter 4

Writing Meaningful Present Levels, Annual Goals, and Short-Term Objectives

Chapter Overview

In the previous chapter, we discussed the major provisions of the Individualized Education Program (IEP) with a focus on preschool and elementary age students. While our review was complete and substantive, we also noted that we would pay special attention to the development of Present Levels of Academic Achievement and Functional Performance as well as Annual Goals and Short-Term Objectives or benchmarks in this chapter. Poorly written Annual Goals and Short-Term Objectives may result in a court finding that there was a denial of Free Appropriate Public Education (FAPE) should the IEP ever be challenged, so it is imperative that you develop proficiency at writing them. Since Present Levels of Academic Achievement and Functional Performance, Annual Goals, and Short-Term Objectives are interdependent and foundational parts of the IEP, we felt it important that a book on IEP development provide you with (1) a thorough understanding of these concepts including their relationship to the other components of the IEP and (2) guidelines for writing them in an educationally meaningful manner that promotes the provision of FAPE. To accomplish our goals, we will provide the pertinent legal and professional guidelines, but we will also include some appropriate and inappropriate examples for comparative purposes. We begin by describing present levels and their relationship to Annual Goals.

Defining Present Levels

The first item on an IEP is generally a listing of demographic information, but the first part of the IEP that is directly related to the provision of special education is the description of the child's Present Levels of Academic Achievement and Functional Performance (§300.320(a)(1)). The intended purpose of these present level statements is to provide the IEP team with a sufficient level of descriptive data needed to develop meaningful Annual Goals and Short-Term Objectives. The IEP team can then discuss, what kind of special education and related services will be necessary for the child to achieve those goals and objectives. The present level statements serve as a baseline description of a child's current performance and only need to be provided in areas in which the child will receive special education support. Since the goals and objectives must be measurable and a child's progress towards meeting Annual Goals and must be documented and reported to parents, it is critical that present level statements are both understandable and contain educationally relevant quantitative data (Salvia, Ysseldyke, & Bolt, 2013). "Subjective opinion" or "gut level feelings" should not be substituted for quantitative data as neither opinion nor feelings are valid and reliable measurement methodologies. Examples of terms commonly used in education that are designated as either measurable or nonmeasurable are contained in Table 4-1.

TABLE 4-1. Descriptors that Indicate Measurability

Measurable	Not Measurable
Points	Understand
Read aloud	Read quietly
Write	Listen
Walk	Demonstrate
Say	Appreciate
Name	Improve
Respond	Feel
Initiate	Discover
Take off	Think
Put on	Concentrate

For clarity, we will discuss the development of Present Levels for Academic Achievement and Present Levels for Functional Performance separately. In practice, you may encounter IEP forms that contain one section for you to describe both academic and functional performance, and either format is allowable as the regulations (§300.320(1)) specifically require the IEP to contain the following regarding present levels:

(1) A statement of the child's present levels of academic achievement and functional performance including:

    (i) How the child's disability affects the child's involvement and progress in the general education curriculum (i.e., the same curriculum as for nondisabled children) or

(ii)   For preschool children, as appropriate, a description of how the disability affects the child's participation in appropriate activities

The regulations do not specifically describe "academic achievement" but the following statement is contained in the accompanying notes (71 Fed. Reg, 46662, 2006), the phrase "generally refers to a child's performance in academic areas (e.g., reading or language arts, math, science, and history)." We want to emphasize that the Present Levels of Academic Achievement need only be provided in areas in which the child will receive special education support. For example, if a child reads and writes at grade level, but requires assistance in math calculation, then present levels would only need to written for math calculation. However, if the child's difficulty with math calculation impacted his or her performance in another subject, such as science, then that effect should be noted in the present levels and appropriate accommodations should be noted in the IEP.

The Annual Goals and all services or supports provided through the IEP must have some alignment with the present levels statement(s). For example, consider the student with a disability related difficulty in computing mathematics equations, using the present levels statement as a starting point (i.e., the quantitative description of his skill level), the IEP team should develop an Annual Goal(s) for math calculation skills. Each Annual Goal may be broken down into Short-Term Objectives that represent intermediate steps between where the student is currently (i.e., present levels) and where he is projected to be after one year (Annual Goals). The relationship among these components is depicted in Figure 4-1. As can be seen, present levels inform the development of Annual Goals which, in turn, guide the development of STOs. Thus, it is important that information contained in the present levels be accurate and meaningful. Next, we will provide brief descriptions, differentiation for the Present Levels of Academic Achievement from Present Levels of Functional Performance followed by a discussion of some assessment "Don'ts" and "Dos."

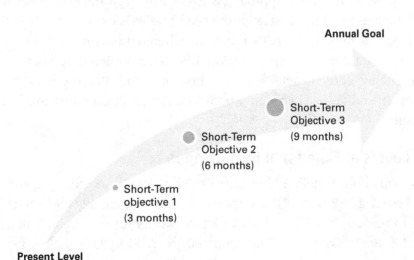

FIGURE 4-1. Progression from Present Level to Annual Goal

Present Levels of Academic Achievement

Present Levels for Academic Achievement describe the child's performance using meaningful and quantifiable data in the areas where the child will receive specially designed instruction. This quantitative data will provide the information needed to write measurable Annual Goals. It is relatively easy to write present level statement for skill areas, such as mathematics that have a clear and sequential skill progression. However, the same cannot be said for other content areas that are more knowledge based, such as science or social studies, than skill based.

For example, a present level statement for math calculation may focus on accurately computing mathematical algorithms, but there is no similar skill sequence to describe with the knowledge based courses. It really makes no sense to include the following objective (poorly written, but from a real IEP): "Mark will recite the names of the last ten presidents." It simply represents a random set of knowledge that is not a major outcome of a social studies curriculum, does not serve as a foundational or prerequisite skill for future learning, and simply isn't a critical skill. That knowledge might be nice to know and the student may even have to learn that content in the class, but it is not important enough to be included in the IEP. (In fact, we would wager that many of you could not name the last 10 presidents, yet you are likely a successful university student despite your lack of mastery of information that is arguably more trivial than critical to everyday life.)

IEPs typically don't contain present levels (or Annual Goals and Short-Term Objectives) for these knowledge based areas. If, however, you do find yourself in a position of needing to write present levels for a knowledge-based content area, you might consider one of the following approaches. First, you could identify a skill that is generalizable across contexts. For example, classification and categorization skills that can be addressed in science class, math class, and other areas of daily living might represent important skills for the child while addressing science standards. Many states have alternate achievement standards for knowledge-based content courses, so you might find valuable suggestions among those alternate standards. A second approach is to describe how the child's performance in one of the content courses, such as science or social studies is being impacted by his or her lack of skill in math, reading, study skills, etc. Then, when writing Annual Goals, you might write a goal for study skills or you might develop different modifications or accommodations for use in the science and/or social studies course to ensure that the child had access to the curriculum. The difference between modifications and accommodations is described later in this chapter.

Present Levels of Functional Performance

The regulations do not define "functional performance". According to the accompanying notes (71 Fed. Reg, 46661(2006)), the term "functional" generally refers to skills that are not perceived to be academic in nature, but are necessary for successful functioning in everyday activities. Some examples of functional skills could include eating, toileting, dressing, mobility, physical education, communication, social skills, and behavior. If the child requires support in functional skills, then those skills must be addressed in the IEP, just as academic skills negatively impacted by the disability are addressed. If there are no concerns, then we recommend that the IEP team document that on the IEP form. Then, at a future date, should there be a question of whether the IEP team discussed the issue, there would be documentation indicating that it had been discussed. If there are not concerns for a particular child, the team need not list every conceivable functional skill, but can just make a statement specifying that the child's functional skills are commensurate with his or her same age peers. In areas where there are disability related concerns, the present levels of performance for each functional skill area of concern should be described in objective, measurable terms, just as required when describing academic skill levels. Most functional skills can be adequately addressed in the regular education setting with the appropriate supports. But it is important to remember that whenever a functional skill is indicated as an area of need there must be at least one Annual Goal for that skill and that goal must be broken down into at least two Short-Term Objectives. Since functional skills are not aligned to state standards, Short-Term Objectives are a requirement not an option.

A Broader Context for "Functional" versus "Academic" and/or "Standards-Based" IEP Content

In the minds of many, particularly, parents and others not familiar with the vernacular and daily challenges faced by educators as they seek to develop curricula, the distinction between what is an *academic skill* and what is a *functional skill* may seem to be rather ridiculous. Why should we ever teach *anything* that is not, in the most basic sense of the word, *functional*, particularly to students who learn more slowly and require additional supports in order to learn. An emphasis upon that which is "practical" or "useful" and goes significantly beyond the boundaries of daily living. Should not the relevance of all content be apparent to both teachers and parents even if it is if not to our students? In a very real sense all of education should be "useful," and so, perhaps what we should embrace is a foundational idea that value in education is measured by a determination of both its proximal and distal significance to the well-being of the individual student and to society more broadly. The goal of the IEP is to provide the framework for an individualized *functional education* that reflects first and foremost the individual needs of the student as determined by the results of assessment including performance in the general education curriculum. Application of standards for the *content* of the IEP (or for the *performance* of an individual student relative to that content) must be viewed from the perspective of value to society and value to the individual. The assumption is that national, state, and local standards should reflect societal values and role of the individual student within that society. Standards, or common core, are in a very real sense the collective view of what states and localities see as important for all students. But this raises a fundamental question; Are those standards (content and performance standards) sufficiently flexible to accommodate the wide range of individual differences that is fundamental to the notion of individualized educational programming?

Arguments have arisen that, almost by definition, *special education* with its emphasis upon individually appropriate content and its reliance upon the long-established principle of individual differences in performance runs counter to the application of a common set of standards or a common core when it comes to the development of IEPs (e.g., Bateman & Linden, 2012; Kaufmann, 2010). Others have stressed the need for a commitment to the overarching standard of, "quality of life," when it comes developing the goals and objectives of the IEP (Hunt, McDonnell, & Crocket, 2012) and others have noted that an ecological curricular framework that reflects a commitment to individual relevance is not necessarily antithetical to standards-based content (Lynch & Adams, 2008). Hunt et al. embrace such a notion by suggesting that the significance of the standard to the student's quality of life be considered when deciding how to address the standard in the IEP. Their discussion is framed for students with moderate to severe disabilities, but we believe that it is relevant for all students with IEPs. In fact, it is this need to question how content (whether, we call it "functional," " standards-based" and/or The often amorphous conglomerate of rules, which face educators as they struggle with notions of what to teach and how to measure progress should not dissuade IEP teams from a commitment to their primary responsibility to address the unique needs of each student respecting both individuality as well as the right of society to set general standards and expectations, which may be expressed in a variety of different forms. A *functional education* is one that reflects the dual commitment to teach that which both enhances quality of life for the individual while at the same time addressing the standards of the society in which that life must be lived; and does so without denying the fundamental right we each have to differ one from another.

An example of how standards can be addressed without ignoring the need to make IEP content immediately relevant to the individual needs of a student is provided by Hunt, McDonnell, and Crockett (2012). They have described, how the IEP of one 10th grade student with significant intellectual disabilities, Jamal, could address the national common core standard for geometry (*use units as way to understand problems and to guide the solution of multi-step problems; choose and interpret the scale and the origin in graphs and data displays, etc.*). Jamal's IEP goal and associated instructional activities for that standard might involve purchasing items at school, selecting and preparing a meal using measuring cups, measuring his weight and height and recording it on a graph for comparison to national height and weight by age comparison. This way of weaving common core standards-based content into the complex fabric of each individual student's immediate life needs is at the heart of what we mean by the term *functional education*.

Writing Educationally Relevant Present Level Statements

Present level statements represent the first step in developing a truly individualized plan, and incomplete or poorly written statements can result in the development of inappropriate Annual Goal and Short-Term Objectives and could lead to a failure to provide FAPE. However, as you will see, writing present level statements should not be a source of anguish. (Unfortunately, judging from many of the poorly written and subjective present level statements reviewed by the authors during consultations, it appears that the development of present levels has not always been taken very seriously and/or their purpose was not well understood.)

The purpose of the present levels statement is to provide a clear description of the child's performance in areas of concern and to serve as an aid for the IEP team in the development of educationally relevant and measurable Annual Goals and/or Short-Term Objectives. If, as required by law, the Annual Goals must be measurable, then it follows that the present levels must provide a data-based description. Without objective data describing the child's current present level, the IEP team would not have information needed to write meaningful Annual Goals or Short-Term Objectives.

Sources of Data: Don'ts

Before describing how to write present level statements, we will make a few points about assessment approaches commonly used to collect data for present levels. We begin by discussing inappropriate practice and provide a detailed explanation of the wrong way to write present levels. We were a bit concerned about devoting so much attention to faulty practice, but believe that providing you with that information first will help you contrast those practices with the recommended practices and appreciate the actual differences inherent in the approaches. We also hope that your knowledge of the practices will help you facilitate the use of recommended practice should you find yourself in a setting where best practice is not implemented, because you will be able to talk intelligently about the various methodologies. We begin with a discussion of two major "don'ts," specifically, copying psychoeducational reports right into the present levels statements and placing an inordinate amount of value in the use of commercially prepared, norm-referenced tests (NRT) to develop present levels.

Psychoeducational Reports

A psychoeducational report is a summary of assessment results in areas, such as cognitive functioning, academic achievement, adaptive skills, socio-emotional behaviors, etc. and is typically conducted when determining whether a child is eligible for special education services. While there may be useful instructional recommendations contained in a psychoeducational report, there may also be several problems with trying to develop present levels from some reports. First, much of the information contained in a psychoeducational report is not necessary for educational planning and therefore not appropriate for inclusion in an IEP. For example, the reports frequently include a child's IQ score in the text. IQ scores are not educationally relevant, because they do not relate directly to the selection of instructional outcomes and are some of the most misunderstood and misused scores, and have been challenged on the basis of racial bias as well as other concerns (See *Mismeasure of Man* by Stephen J. Gould for a comprehensive discussion on the history of intelligence testing). For these reasons, the scores simply don't belong on an IEP. IEPs themselves are confidential and information should only be shared with those who need the information in order to implement the IEP. Really, there is no reason for a teacher to know a student's IQ score in order to implement the IEP. In addition, IQ scores are not useful in developing instructional activities and may, in fact, result in bias against a child with a low IQ score, by lowering expectations.

Additionally, there is no need to keep multiple copies of the same information in different places (Bateman & Linden, 2012). The IEP is an Individualized Education Program, not a depository for the most recent psychoeducational evaluation completed as part of the eligibility process. Including the overly technical report in a document that is supposed to be parent and teacher friendly may, in fact, impede the usefulness of the process and intimidate participants who may already be reluctant to ask for clarifications during meetings out of fear of appearing ignorant. In addition, information contained in these reports is frequently outdated and any information that may have been useful would need to be updated. In the case, where the report is current, any educationally appropriate information that could assist the IEP team in determining the appropriate Annual Goals and special education services should be summarized in parent-friendly language rather than simply dumped into a form.

Commercially Prepared Norm-Referenced Tests

Psychoeducational testing that we just discussed commonly includes the administration of numerous commercially prepared norm-referenced tests (NRTs) such as IQ tests, behavioral scales, and academic achievement tests with those results summarized in a psychoeducational report Unfortunately, the information obtained from NRTs is not always used in the appropriate manner. These tests were developed to compare an individual student's performance on that specific test to the average performance of the students in the standardization sample or norm group. They simply are not of sufficient depth that the results guide instruction in a meaningful way.

Given the common use of NRTs, we will assume that you have a basic familiarity with norm-referenced assessment and the following associated scores—standard scores, percentile scores, and grade- or age-equivalent scores. Readers interested in measurement practices and the specific attributes of NRTs can obtain valuable information from a number of different assessment textbooks (e.g., McClean, Wolery, & Bailey, 2004; Overton, 2011; Salvia, Ysseldyke, & Bolt, 2013). If scores from norm-referenced measures, such as the Woodcock-Johnson Tests of Academic Achievement—IV (Schrack, Mather, & McGrew, 2014), are used on statements of present levels then only standard scores and percentile ranks should be used. Even then, great care is advised as standardized scores obtained from administration of these tests have limited applicability.

Problems associated with the use of NRTs as instructional guides has been recognized and include the following: (1) the emphasis of the scores is on describing the student's relative standing when compared to those in the norm group—an issue more appropriate for eligibility determination than for detailed identification of instructional targets, (2) the instruments measure broad skills and are insensitive to small, yet significant changes that may result from carefully planned instruction, and (3) their content is not directly tied to the actual curriculum taught in the school (Blankenship, 1985; Good & Jefferson, 1998; Hargrove, Church, Yssel, & Koch, 2002). In spite of these longstanding concerns, some publishers of norm-referenced instruments encourage educators to use the instruments to develop educational programs and claim that they are curriculum based; however, we recommend against using them as instructional measures for the reasons listed above. Additionally, these tests do not necessarily match the content being taught in an individual school or to state or local standards. There is no national curriculum and representing the tests as curriculum based may be more of marketing bid to sell more tests and protocols (examiner and examinee booklets) than a source of instructional support (Hyatt & Howell, 2004).

Despite documented concerns, some districts require that scores from NRTs be included on the IEP and require special education teachers to administer NRTs of academic achievement for the purpose of developing an IEP. We will provide you with guidance on how to include those scores should you find yourself in such a predicament. Our admonitions about commercially developed norm-referenced assessments do not mean that we are advocating their total abolition. Rather, if used, they should be used cautiously and only to describe a child's performance on the attribute being measured in relation to the performance of subjects in the standardization sample. In other words, when it comes to determining eligibility they may have value, but when it comes to determining both content and strategies for instruction they may have little or no value.

Experts have issued cautions about the use of two widely used and misused scores commonly used with NRT, age-equivalent and grade-equivalent scores (Bateman & Herr, 2006; Bennett, 1982; Salvia, Ysseldyke, & Bolt, 2013). Despite cautions from scholars and even test authors (Ginsburg & Baroody, 2003; Reid, Hresko, & Hammill, 2001) regarding the inappropriate use of these scores, they continue to be used. Age-equivalent scores are commonly used with preschool students and are presented as hyphenated numerals where 3-4 would indicate that the child's performance was equivalent to that of a child 3 years and 4 months of age. These are typically referred to as indications of the child's developmental level. Grade-equivalent scores are similar and are commonly used with school age children but are presented as decimal numerals, such as 3.2 which would indicate approximately second month of third grade.

Unfortunately, the use of both age-equivalent and grade-equivalent scores is fraught with misinterpretation and misunderstanding. Due to their continued widespread use and the erroneous decisions based upon these poorly developed metrics, we will spend considerable time discussing the scores. Whether we are referring to age- or grade-equivalent scores in our examples in the following text, the same principles apply, and we agree with Bennett (1982) that their use should be abandoned. The following five reasons encompass some of the well-known, yet often ignored, concerns with these scores.

First, grade-equivalent scores merely represent the average number of items a student at a particular grade level answered correctly on a specific test. Assuming that the average kindergarten student in third month answered 10 questions correctly, then any student who answered 10 questions correctly on that test would be assigned a grade-equivalent score of K.3. However, this method of scoring does not account for item difficulty. So, if a first-grade student missed the initial five items (easiest items), but then answered 10 more difficult items correctly that student would be assigned a grade-equivalent score of K.3 which would be the same as a kindergarten student who answered the initial-ten easy items but missed the more difficult items. The level of difficulty represented by each problem would not be illustrated by the score, and these students were not performing the same, even though they were assigned the same grade-equivalent score. In a related example, assume that a second-grade student received a grade-equivalent score of 6.3. This does not mean that the second grader was reading as well as students in the third month of sixth grade. It only means that the child answered the same number of questions correctly. While one could reasonably assume that the second grader was a skilled reader, there can be no assumption that the child understands the material at the same conceptual level as a fourth-grade student.

Second, grade-equivalent scores are generally developed by extrapolation and interpolation. This means that the test developers did not have a sample of students at grade 4.1, 4.2, 4.3, etc. Rather, they used the obtained data from students tested and made "educated" guesses to develop grade-equivalent scores. In a sense, they may not be real scores at all.

Third, grade-equivalent scores operate under the assumption that learning is linear. If learning is linear, then all children learn a particular skill before learning another. However, we know that isn't true; children acquire skills at different rates and sometimes in different order. A view that learning is linear also makes an assumption that the date of acquisition of a particular key skill can be determined. So, if a child is in 4.3, when she goes to bed at night and wakes up as a student in 4.4 then she should have already mastered some new skill or knowledge associated with fourth graders in the fourth month of school.

Fourth, grade-equivalent scores exaggerate small differences in performance. At the lower end of the test, for example, kindergarten, there are typically a number of items, a child must answer correctly in order to receive a higher grade-equivalent score. Hypothetically speaking, a child may have to correctly answer seven questions in order to receive a grade-equivalent score of K.1. So, this means that the child learned seven key concepts during the first month of kindergarten. To move to K.2, the child may have to answer only one additional item for a total of eight items answered correctly. Certainly, one would not assume that kindergarteners learned only one thing during that second month of kindergarten, but that is exactly how it appears using grade-equivalent scores. It gets even more confusing, because to advance to K.3, the child may have to answer two additional questions correctly for a total of 10 items which implies more learning took place during that month. It is also possible that the test does not assign grade-equivalent scores for K.4, K.5, K.6, or K.7 and should the child answer 11 items, then a grade-equivalent of K.8 would be assigned. Here is where the exaggeration of small differences in scores becomes readily apparent, the child certainly learned more than one thing during four months of kindergarten, but the grade-equivalent score indicates that answering one random question equates to 4 months of learning which is significantly different from the seven questions that a child must answer correctly to get a score of K.1. This distorted description of student performance increases as students get older when, for example, answering an additional question could result in a grade-equivalent score that is more than a year greater.

Fifth, use of grade-equivalent scores assumes that we can capture the performance of the typical student. Given the variability of curricula across the nation, there can be no reasonable acceptance of the hypothetical construct of the "typical student" or meaningfulness of grade-equivalent scores. The determination of grade-equivalent scores was based on the students in the standardization sample when the test was developed or revised. Since the different test developers use different sample groups at different times, one cannot assume that the groups of students were equivalent. This is one reason that a student could take two different NRTs covering the same academic content, yet obtain different grade-equivalent scores. Performance across different NRT can be compared using standard scores, but grade equivalents are unacceptable metrics for such comparisons.

In conclusion, grade-equivalent scores may seem to be useful to the uniformed consumer of measurement principles, but experts in measurement have expressed concern with their continued use and the authors of some NRT advise that great caution be used when interpreting those scores. The use of grade-equivalent scores should simply be abandoned, and educators should interpret NRTs using standard scores and percentile ranks, even though percentile ranks should be used cautiously, because like grade-equivalent scores they are not equidistant. There really is no meaningful difference between the 50th and 51st percentile as those scores fall at nearly the same point on a normal bell curve. However, as scores move further away from the mean (50th percentile) the distance between scores greatly increases making comparison somewhat difficult. NRTs should only be used for the purpose for which they were designed—to compare student performance to the standardization sample.

We discussed ineffective data collection practices to encourage you to refrain from using them as well as to serve as a contrast to the recommended measurement practices that will be discussed in the following sections. We are confident that you will realize that the information collected through the following strategies provides sound descriptions of student skill rather than a nebulous grade-equivalent score. The following assessment practices may be appropriate with preschool children, but there are additional issues concerning the assessment of young children that we will address in a separate section before moving to guidelines for writing present levels statements.

Sources of Data: Dos

Curriculum-Based Measurement for Academic Skills

A preferred alternative to using NRTs as the major source of data for describing student performance is the use of information from Curriculum-Based Measurement (CBM). CBM relies upon short, standardized assessments in basic skills for reading, mathematics, spelling, and written expression (Shinn, 1989, 1998). More than 40 years of research on CBM has demonstrated that the approaches are valid and reliable for describing a child's performance. They are quick to administer and allow for progress monitoring within a problem solving model (Hosp, Hosp, Howell, & Allison, 2014; Shinn, 2008). The term curriculum in this context does not mean that the material must come directly from the classroom, but that the material is representative of the curriculum being taught (Shinn, 2008). Results from CBM can yield valid data for instructional decision-making and can also be helpful for helping determine eligibility, especially within the Response to Intervention (RtI) framework.

Hosp, Hosp, and Howell (2007) provide a teacher-friendly guide for the use of CBM to describe a child's performance on a particular skill or set of skills in math, reading, writing, and spelling. The procedures they described are valid and reliable methods for evaluating and monitoring student progress as well as for guiding instructional decision-making (by the way, this is one useful way to collect data for periodic reporting of student progress toward goals and objectives as required by the IDEA 04). We recommend that you consider using these curriculum-based procedures in place of NRTs, when describing specific skills in a student's repertoire, monitoring student progress, making decisions regarding efficacy of the instructional intervention, and assisting with development of the IEP as appropriate. Following is a summary of three key descriptors Hosp, Hosp, and Howell provided when discussing three different types of CBM (General Outcome Measures [GOMs], Skill Based Measures [SBM], and Mastery Measures [MM]) and their possible uses.

First, General Outcome Measures are used to measure performance on the global or capstone skill as an indicator of the child's progress. To improve performance on the GOM, a student must have improved performance on any of the subskills that make up the overall or capstone skill. Oral reading fluency is a commonly used reading GOM and the task requires a student to perform numerous skills involving the use of letters, phonemic awareness, blending, and vocabulary. Rather than describing performance on each specific-skill related to oral reading fluency, the use of GOM provides a way to monitor a child's progress with a single activity. Of course, use of a GOM does not preclude assessment of specific skills as needed to develop viable instructional procedures.

A second type of CBM, Skill Based Measures, is particularly useful for academic tasks in which there is no specific capstone skill. For example, in the mathematics curriculum for the year, a student may be expected to learn numerous skills including adding, subtracting, multiplying, and dividing fractions as well as changing fractions into decimals and decimals into fraction. The SBM for these skills would a random set of mathematical problems that would assess a student's performance on the entire year's curriculum. This type of CBM provides a strong measure of overall skill level, just as a GOM. However, neither SBM nor GOM provide assessments of student performance focused solely on discrete skills such as multiplication facts using nine as the multiplier.

Mastery Measures constitute a third type of CBM and are useful for measuring student performance on specific, discrete skills. For the mathematics example just mentioned, one could develop a separate MM for multiplying fractions, a separate MM for dividing fractions, etc. and use that information to gauge student learning and inform instructional decision-making. There are advantages and disadvantages to each of the procedures, but that discussion is beyond the scope of this book and interested readers are referred to Hosp, Hosp, and Howell (2007) for further information. There are commercially prepared CBM, such as the Dynamic Indicators of Basic Early Literacy Skills (DIBELS), that are useful sources for obtaining measurement instruments, finding appropriate norms and expected growth rates **(https://dibels.uoregon.edu/)** Whatever research supported CBM you use, we hope it is evident that data from any or all could be useful in developing present level statements. We provided the following links in Chapter 2 when we discussed RtI, but provide them again for your convenience, because they provide valuable resources and supports for CBM: Intervention Central, **http://www.interventioncentral.org/** and RTI Action Network, **http://www.rtinetwork.org/**

Assessment Options for Functional Performance

As just noted, we have quality assessments that can assist in developing present level statements for academic skills, especially as related to the general education curriculum. We have fewer options when working with students with more significant disabilities who may be learning skills that are linked, yet significantly modified from the general education curriculum. While the actual definition of functional skills refers to skills that are not academic in nature, we will include some academic skills in our discussion here, because they are frequently described as functional academic skills in the field. In addition, the modified assessment procedures we will discuss here may be used when assessing these functional academic skills. However, if academic in nature, the skills would be more likely included in Present Levels for Academic Achievement rather than Functional Performance.

Many of the procedures described by Hosp, Hosp, and Howell (2007) and Hosp et al. (2014) could be adapted for different content, but would likely require additional time on the part of the teacher to develop a truly reliable and valid assessment for learning tasks that are unique to the individual, such as telling time to the nearest half hour. Spooner and Browder (2006) noted that in the past students with significant cognitive disabilities were rarely provided with instructional opportunities that were focused upon reading or the general education curriculum. Only recently has there been a research focus on those learning opportunities that has yielded positive results. Clearly there is much to be done to identify practices that will allow students with the most significant cognitive disabilities greater access to the general education curriculum; however, new techniques and strategies that can assist an IEP team in identifying what is important for a particular child and how to uniquely tailor his or her educational program are becoming more readily available.

Members of the IEP team may participate in personcentered planning activities, such as McGill Action Planning System aka Making Action Plans (MAPS) (Vandercook, York, & Forrest, 1989), that provide an opportunity for individuals with disabilities and their families to take a lead role in helping the school team identify meaningful and valued learning outcomes that may be incorporated into a subsequent IEP. In addition to the use of MAPS and similar programs, there has been growing interest and support in the implementation of student-led IEPs for all students with disabilities and with a major focus on helping students develop self-advocacy skills (Danneker & Bottge, 2009; Thoma & Wehman, 2010).

As with assessment of academic skills, there are no suitable, commercially prepared NRTs for functional skills. Items on tests, such as the Vineland Adaptive Behavior Scales, Second Edition (Sparrow, Cicchetti, & Balla, 2005), a measure commonly used when determining eligibility for students with cognitive delays, are not presented in a sequential manner and may not address skills that are important for the child, whether that unimportance is related to chronological age, community standards, or agreement with skill prioritization developed in MAPS and/or the IEP process. There really are no official curricula for functional skills and hence, no simple ready-made CBM tools, so collecting objective data describing a child's repertoire of behavioral or functional skills really comes from two major assessment procedures. We have purposely excluded interviews or narrative descriptions from those who know the child as assessment options. That information may be incredibly important and helpful in developing the IEP, but here we want to focus on two methods that are more likely to provide a quantifiable description adequate for use as a baseline measure.

The first is a *direct test* where the situation is arranged and a student is asked to perform a specific skill (Bricker & Waddell, 2002; Brown, Lehr, & Snell, 2011). Examples of some skills that may be assessed using a direct test could be washing hands, asking to join in an activity, or having the child print his or her name. Teachers could easily set up the situation for the child to perform the skill, but there is no way to verify with certainty whether or not the child would perform the skill in the natural environment. So, a direct test would help identify whether a child could perform a particular skill and at what level of proficiency.

A second procedure is an *observation* of the child in the natural environment. These assessment activities allow the observer to determine whether the child completed the skill in the natural environment with naturally occurring stimuli which is strength of the approach. But, as with other assessment procedures, there are drawbacks. First, the assessment takes a considerable amount of time to complete and, second, there may be few or no opportunities for the child to exhibit the skill in the natural environment (Brown, Lehr, & Snell, 2011). Consider the following example. In school, many children are taught safety skills, such as not getting into a car with a stranger. The children may be able to state the reasons for not getting the car and even role-play (direct test); however, it would be impractical to test most children in the natural environment, because the probability of a child finding him or herself in such a situation is incredibly low and purposefully placing a child in a dangerous situation would be out of the question. However, the opportunity to observe skill performance in the natural environment really does depend upon the skill. We could easily conduct a direct test to see if a student wrote his or her name on a paper when requested. If needed, the instructor could provide assistance with spelling or letter formation. Once a child could perform the skill at the acceptable criterion, the instructor could observe the child in the natural environment and see if he or she performed the skill at the usual time under the usual circumstances. If not, then additional instruction or support may be required. To accomplish this, the teacher may be required to conduct ecological inventories, task analyses, discrepancy analyses, and identification of skills to be taught/adapted/modified, and the sequence for such activities (Brown, Lehr, & Snell, 2011).

Our discussion of functional performance has focused primarily on student with significant disabilities, but IEP teams must consider functional performance for all students regardless of severity of disability. There simply aren't many suitable commercially prepared options and observation may be the method of choice. However, commercially prepared option you may want to consider is the Functional Assessment of Academic Behavior (Ysseldyke & Christenson, 2002) which operates from the perspective of evaluating the instructional environment rather than the traditional approach of trying to discover what is "wrong" with the child. As noted, teams should also consider whether the student requires supports in areas such as study skills that will enable them to successfully participate in and benefit from instructional activities.

Unique Issues in Early Childhood Special Education Assessment

The use of well-designed CBM may also provide assistance with the development of Annual Goals and Short-Term Objectives for preschool age children. These measures do not have the long history and as large a research base as do CBM for school age children, but the movement toward using CBM is clearly an area in which there has been a growing interest.

The most recent series of Best Practices in School Psychology published in 2008 is a valuable reference for assessment across all age levels and topics, but the reason for mentioning that publication here is to recognize that several chapters were devoted to the issue of CBM in early childhood. Slentz and Hyatt (2008) described a procedure and rationale for using CBM and used the Assessment Evaluation and Programming System (AEPS) (Bricker et al., 2002) as an exemplar, because the program included assessment activities directly aligned with curricular activities across a wide range of behaviors including communication, fine and gross motor skills, social-emotional development, and academic skills. Slentz and Hyatt stressed the importance of the developmental sequence of the curriculum and the linkage of skills across domains, for example, fine-motor control was directly related to the functional academic skill of writing but still allowed for significant modifications and adaptations to provide opportunities for teaching the skills. It is important to stress that the "developmental curriculum sequence" they described was considerably different from the "developmental approach" described by Bowe (2000) where children were expected to pass through rigid and inflexible stages of development before being "ready" to learn the next higher level skill. Rather, they framed the discussion as using CBM as a support for a curricular approach in which meaningful, sequentially ordered and chronologically age-appropriate practices were routinely implemented with appropriate accommodations and adaptations provided to allow the child to demonstrate the skill or part of the skill.

In addition to the example above referencing a specific program, the AEPS, there are other instruments that can be used to monitor General Outcome Measures for preschool age children. These measures provide information similar to the GOM, we previously described for areas such as oral reading fluency. The Individual Growth and Development Indicators (IGDI) are available at both infant/toddler and preschool levels and provide reliable and valid measures that can be used to monitor child growth and development **(http://www.igdi.ku.edu/)**

As can be deduced from our discussion thus far, there are several sources of data that teachers can access to develop quality statements of present levels that incorporate objective clearly specifiable data that can serve as a basis for the development of measurable Annual Goals and Short-Term Objectives. We do need to stress that there are some areas for which there are no official curricula and teachers will be required to take data on the child's performance during the school day and may use the performance of typically developing peers as a standard for comparison to help determine the level of proficiency that will be expected of the child with a disability. This is particularly true for student requiring support in behavioral areas including social skills and self-help skills. Now that we have covered some "dos" and "don'ts" regarding measurement of skills for development of present levels statements, we turn to a discussion of writing Present Levels of Academic Achievement followed by writing Present Levels of Functional Performance.

Writing Present Levels (Academic Achievement)

We noted that one purpose of present level statements was a description of a child's academic achievement. We provided a lengthy discussion to give you the background information necessary to avoid ineffective use of NRT materials and implement the effective use of CBM and behavioral observations. Our cautions against the use of grade-equivalent scores should not be taken to mean that using grade level performance statements are prohibited in present level statements. It is permissible to state that a student is reading 50 words per minute without error on a one minute oral fluency measure using a passage from a third grade basal. The use of grade reference in this case is simply referring to material commonly used at that grade level, it is not equating that performance with a child's grade equivalence. Plus, this description clearly describes exactly what the child is doing—reading 50 words per minute without error from a specific material. There is no prohibition preventing use of grade-equivalents scores previously discussed, but there is no reason to use scores of such dubious value when there are more meaningful ways to describe skill level.

It may seem that we have taken a long time to get to what will be a relatively simple discussion of writing present level statements. However, the present levels statement serves as a foundation for developing the IEP and the better the present levels are written; the more likely the IEP team will develop meaningful Annual Goals and Short-Term Objectives. As we have previously noted, the statement of present levels should simply describe a child's performance in areas in which the child requires special education support, and the description should be objective, observable, and data based, so that the IEP team can use that information to develop measurable Annual Goals, and the statements should be written in clear language that anyone can understand. We also stressed that present levels should be written for skills rather than content knowledge.

Consider the following three incredibly poor nonexamples of present levels from actual IEPs. As you will find, none of these sample present level statements met minimum acceptable criteria just outlined and many incorporate the measurement "don'ts. They do not provide sufficient detail for developing measurable Annual Goals and Short-Term Objectives, do not sufficiently describe a child's performance, and also use jargon (names of tests) and grade-equivalent scores to try and describe the child's performance. The lack of clarity in the writing along with the grammatical and usage errors also tends to reduce the level of confidence that could be placed in the skill of the teachers who wrote these statements. (If, these were writing samples of the special education teachers, would you trust that one of those individuals has the skills necessary to teach your own child to write? An IEP is a legal document, and it is important that it be written in a professional format.) It is clear that each of the students has experienced some difficulty in school, but that is all we can conclude from the present level statements. We included a few comments and questions following each of the three nonexamples and fully expect that you would have additional comments. After presenting these non-examples, we provide acceptable examples.

Sample 1

Rachel's current math level is 3.0 Brigance. Rachel's current reading level is 1.4. Math—Rachel should be able to master basic skills in math calculation and math applications. Place value, reading, writing, and rounding whole numbers. Word problems should be used with addition and subtraction. Reading—Rachel should work with basic sight vocabulary, vowels, consonants, and blends. She tries with all his difficulties.

Sample 1 merely states what Rachel should be able to do, but fails to provide any description of her current skill level other than grade-equivalent scores, in other words it does not tell us what she is actually doing now. It is unclear if she knows place value or not, and if not, what place value is she working on . . . ones, tens, hundreds, thousands? For reading, what is meant by "basic sight vocabulary?" To which words or list of words does that refer? How does one work with vowels, consonants, and blends? If Rachel has so much trouble reading, will it be realistic for her to complete mathematical story problems (math applications) without penalizing her for her reading difficulties? Perhaps, but the present level is written in such ambiguous language that one couldn't be sure. We are assuming that math application involves reading story problems—an assumption that you may not have made when you read the present level statement. This is an example of why we are stressing that the writing on IEPs be clear and concise. Finally, the last sentence really doesn't make sense and fails to serve any useful purpose.

Sample 2

WRAT 5th grade math, reading comprehension and reading recognition 3rd. In the beginning of the school year, Mark had good attendance. After the first marking quarter, Mark's attendance started to decrease. His performance in his academic classes was satisfactory. Due to his poor attendance his performance has not been evaluated.

Sample 2 has many problems and doesn't provide any description of Mark's skills. There is no indication of what is meant by "good attendance" or the "beginning of the school year." Does "good attendance" mean he attended every day, missed one day every two weeks, or was half an hour late to school every Thursday morning? Then the teacher stated that his attendance started to decrease. Decrease from what and to what? Did it just "start" to decrease or did the attendance get progressively worse? The last sentence in this present level statement makes absolutely no sense. You simply can't write a statement of present levels of performance without having assessed and evaluated a child's performance. The teacher provided some grade-equivalent scores from the Wide Range Achievement Test (WRAT; Wilkinson & Robertson, 2007). Those data are not particularly useful, but if she had time to administer the WRAT, then she could have administered quality CBM in less time than it would have taken to administer the WRAT and come up with more useful descriptions of the student's academic skills.

Sample 3

Quanisha has not had any academic success during this school year. She has very poor attendance and cut classes very often. Once Quanisha does attends class, she is very uncooperative.

Math 3.0 Brigance

Reading 7.6 Slosson

Sample 3 contains no programmatically useful information. We know that in the opinion of the teacher, she is uncooperative and misses much school. However, we don't know the conditions under which she is uncooperative or what this uncooperative behavior looks like. We know nothing about her academic skills, and this statement really does not provide information that would be sufficient for writing an IEP. The first statement is particularly problematic; the teacher's recognition that Quanisha has not had any academic success could be an indicator that the district failed to provide Quanisha with FAPE. (Remember that in Rowley, the US Supreme Court ruled that the district had a responsibility to provide learning opportunities that would likely result in meaningful benefit.)

If you contrast those with the following acceptable samples, you will note significant differences. We start by reviewing Present Levels of Academic Achievement statement for our hypothetical student John that we provided in the last chapter.

Sample 4

John adds and subtracts single digit numbers with 100% accuracy at a rate of 35 per minute with 0 errors when given worksheets with only addition or subtraction problems. His speed and accuracy decline when given a worksheet with 30 single-digit addition and subtraction problems mixed. Then, he solves 15 per minute with 2 or fewer errors. He adds and subtracts multi-digit numbers without carrying at 100% accuracy but does not add or subtract multi-digit numbers with regrouping. On the Woodcock-Johnson Tests of Academic Achievement IV, Jon received a standard score of 85 (16th percentile) on the math calculation subtest and a standard score of 70 (2nd percentile) on the math fluency subtest.

Sample 4 does provide specific descriptions of academic skills with sufficient detail that the data could serve as baseline data for the development of measurable Annual Goals. For the development of the present levels statement, the teacher relied upon the student's performance on CBM. As noted by Hosp, Hosp, and Howell (2007), a strength of CBM is the direct relationship of the measurement to the skills actually being taught to the child. In this example, the IEP team would know exactly how John performs—what he has mastered and how he is performing on subsequent skills. This information would allow them to make reasonable projections of his progress for the Annual Goal statement.

Note that in this example, information from a NRT of academic achievement, the Woodcock-Johnson—IV (Schrack, Mather, & McGrew, 2014), was included in the last sentence. The preference would be not to include information from commercially prepared NRTs in the present levels, but some school districts are still requiring frequent administration of NRTs and the inclusion of those results on the IEP. We wanted to demonstrate how to include those scores without referring to age or grade-equivalents if your district required NRT scores on an IEP. The statement doesn't really provide useful instructional information, so it was purposefully included it at the end of the present level statement. This allows the team to focus on the information that is instructionally relevant and not get side tracked by standard scores and percentile rankings.

Following is one more acceptable example of a present levels statement for academics. In this example, you will probably note that the designation of skills as academic and functional is not always clear. You may have to just select the best option. For example, fine-motor skills could be addressed via academic skills (such as writing) as well as functional skills (such as eating). (Just remember if fine-motor difficulties are addressed through specially designed instruction, goals/objectives will need to be written for fine motor. Otherwise, the appropriate modifications should be noted on the IEP form.) Fortunately, it really doesn't matter if the skill was described in the academic or functional area as long as the child's needs are identified and addressed. It just depends on the IEP form that your district uses and whether it combines academic and functional goals into one present level statement or separates them into academic and functional statements as we did with our sample IEP document.

Sample 5

Academics:

> Reading and writing: Monique names all upper and lowercase letters without error. She points to her own name in print and says the letter sound for the consonants (b, c, d, and f). She holds a primary pencil with a pincer grasp and copies her name in large (approx. 3 inch letters), but does not hold a regular size pencil.
>
> Mathematics: Monique consistently rote counts to 5 and can count to 10 when provided manipulatives. When shown groups of items and asked which group has more or less, she identifies the correct group. Monique recognizes the numerals 1-5 at 100% accuracy, but only correctly names the numerals 6 through 9 at 50% of opportunity.

Sample 5 provides specific information that clearly describes Monique's performance on the identified skill. The statements contain sufficient data that IEP teams could use as a baseline description and write measurable Annual Goals.

Writing Present Levels (Functional Performance)

The next two examples of present level statements are nonacademic, focusing on skills generally classified as functional in nature. As you will see, the target behaviors are described using information obtained through direct observation because there are no commercially prepared CBMs for these skills. Both examples address skills that are important for the success of these individuals in the community (as emphasized by IDEA 04). The IEP team should still develop present level statements describing academic skills for these students, but recognize that the skill may be at a different level than that of peers without disabilities.

Sample 6 (Functional, self-help)

> Miguel is at the beginning of the self-initiated stage of toileting where he indicates a need for elimination. On average, he indicates the need to use the restroom (urination) three times per day, but is already wet by the time he indicates a toileting need. He is compliant and cooperates during toileting and changing activities.
>
> During meal or snack, Miguel consistently uses a spoon to eat semi-solid food, such as pudding or jello without spilling. When eating more liquefied foods, such as soup or cereal with milk, he spills about half of the contents before getting the spoon to his mouth. He is beginning to use the fork to spear pre-cut food and consistently gets the food into his mouth without spilling. He consistently drinks liquid from a weighted cup with two handles, using both hands, without spilling when the cup is less than half full.

Sample 6 provides a simple description of behaviors related to eating and toileting. The descriptions contain enough detail to allow an IEP team could to use them as a baseline measure of performance when determining Annual Goals and associated Short-Term Objectives.

Sample 7 (Functional, behavior)

Vinnie experiences difficulty getting along with peers on the playground and in the classroom. When interacting with peers on the playground, he gets into verbal altercations three to four times per week. These altercations generally take place on either the basketball or foursquare courts and begin with his cussing at other students when he misses a shot but insists that he made the shot or point. If a peer disagrees with him, then Vinnie may either throw the ball at the peer or push the peer and leave the game. This happens at least three times per week. In the classroom, when assigned to work on small group academic activities, he fails to participate and lays his head on the desk while the others complete the task. When offered, a leadership role completing an activity involving tasks that he has already mastered, he regularly participates in the activity at a level similar to that of his peers.

When given a direction by an adult to complete an academic task independently, he generally delays following the direction until asked a third time or just refuses to complete the task. This behavior is rarely exhibited in math or science class unless he is required to write an answer to a question.

Sample 7 certainly addressed behavioral skills that would be important for a student to master in order to be successful in school, make friends, and that may ultimately be required in the workplace. These important skills should be addressed in the IEP. The behavioral descriptions also imply that writing is a source of difficulty.

Summary of Present Levels

We hope that the differences in information provided in the first three poor examples and the last four acceptable examples were obvious. The first three provided little, if any, useful information that would assist in developing educational goals, and any data presented was simply not helpful. The last four provided specific information regarding student performance that could be used to guide IEP teams. It would be an allowable and good practice for a special education teacher to come to an IEP meeting with present level statements drafted, and team members could provide additional input for inclusion in the present levels statements. It is important that present levels statements describe a child's competencies and not simply focus on challenges or difficulties. (Imagine how you would feel if a team of professionals met to discuss your child's performance and only focused on difficulties or concerns. We bet you would find IEP meetings aversive and question how the faculty actually views your child.) Should the IEP team believe that a Functional Behavioral Assessment (FBA) be conducted to provide necessary information for developing a proactive plan for dealing with behavior and helping support the student with difficult learning tasks, then the team could develop goals and objectives, and develop a plan or timeline for conducting the FBA as well as provide the necessary notice and obtain consent (further discussed in Chapters 6 and 7). Once completed, the IEP team could reconvene to review the findings, re-write or modify goals and objectives as needed, and develop a Behavior Intervention Plan (BIP). (This could be a viable option for sample 7 where Vinnie's behavior appears to deteriorate when he is required to complete writing tasks.)

On the IEP form we provided, the final legal requirement for present level statements is included as a separate statement. That requirement is a description of how the child's disability impacts his or her ability to participate in the regular education curriculum, or for preschool children, how the disability affects performance in other activities. The regulations don't limit the impact of the disability to the curricular goals identified in the official curriculum. One could also discuss the child's performance in the unofficial curriculum, such as communication, social skills, or other behaviors for which there is no official curriculum. Teams should feel empowered to address these needs of the child. In an interesting case that recognized the broad scope of curriculum, a school's practice of placing a child with a disability in a climate controlled cubicle within the classroom was challenged and repudiated. The court specifically noted that the regular education curriculum encompasses more than academic content: "Full social interaction is an important part of today's educational curriculum . . ." Espino v. Besterio (1981). Once descriptive, data-based present levels statements are written, the IEP team is ready to begin writing Annual Goals and Short-Term Objectives.

Annual Goals and Short-Term Objectives

While Short-Term Objectives are not required in the IEPs of all children by federal law, states may choose to require them for all or only certain subgroups of children. You will need to check to determine the policy in your state to see if your IEPs must include both Annual Goals and Short-Term Objectives. However federal law does require that anytime alternative assessments are used that are aligned to alternative achievement standards Annual Goals must be broken down into Short-Term Objectives or Benchmarks (we will discuss the difference between Benchmarks and Short-Term Objectives later in this chapter). Often we see this to be the case for our youngest students with an IEP since many states have developed an alternative "preschool" assessment based on alternative standards and rarely include this population in state-wide assessment programs. The requirement to include STOs would also apply to any goal for a functional skill since functional skills and functional performance are not aligned with achievement standards.

As you now know, present levels are statements that provide succinct descriptions of a child's performance on target academic and/or functional skills that include enough detail to develop measurable Annual Goals and/or Short-Term Objectives. Since goals and objectives must be measurable, it follows that the present levels must be data based as we have described in the previous section. Figure 4-1 presented earlier depicts the relationship between present levels and Annual Goals with Short-Term Objectives derived from the Annual Goals. As we noted, when identifying Annual Goals, IEP teams must decide the amount of progress that can be reasonably expected of the student during the calendar year and the goals must be related to the general education curriculum whenever possible. Sometimes, teams may question how a child with a severe disability could possible access the general education curriculum. It is important to consider downward extensions of skills when appropriate. For example, communication skills are addressed in the general education curriculum, but maybe exhibited differently by some students. So, whether a student is completing grade level writing tasks or using eye gaze to communicate, the behaviors are related to the communication skill requirement in the general education curriculum.

An Annual Goal is simply a statement describing the child's expected skill level within one calendar year, using the present levels as the baseline or starting point. Even though there is no guarantee that a child will achieve the Annual Goal, IEP teams should develop Annual Goals that are meaningful and have a reasonable probability of being achieved before the next IEP is due. Should the child achieve the goal before the end of the year, then the IEP team can reconvene, celebrate the achievement, and develop a new goal that would cover the time remaining on the current IEP. Should the child not achieve the Annual Goal when developing the new IEP at the annual review, the team should discuss possible reasons for the child's not achieving the goal and either replace the goal or make reasonable modifications. The annual IEP should not simply be a re-write of the same Annual Goals not met year after year. Doing so could be considered an indication that the child is not progressing because the school is not providing a meaningful education, which is a denial of FAPE. It is of utmost importance that the school provides the student with a meaningful education, even if the actual Annual Goal is not achieved.

Writing Annual Goals and Short-Term Objectives requires very similar skills. Before differentiating between the two, we will discuss common components and provide a basic structure for writing both. Once you understand the basic components, you can easily make additions that may be required by the school district, and we will discuss a couple of likely additions. This is not a creative writing task; rather, it should be a very consistent and predictable approach that is very easy for teachers, parents, and other IEP team members to understand. Since school personnel are very busy, the more precise and user-friendly a document is written, the more likely it will be followed. But first, some foundational rules:

(1) As we have noted, but want to emphasize, the Annual Goals are derived from the present levels and Short-Term Objectives are intermediate steps that follow a logical progression leading from the present levels to the Annual Goals.

(2) Annual Goals and Short-Term Objectives are only written for areas in which the student will receive specially designed instruction.

(3) The targeted behavior must be measurable. If you can't measure it, no matter how important you may consider the behavior, then you can't write a goal or objective for it.

(4) The Annual Goal and/or Short-Term Objective should pass the "stranger test" meaning that anyone could read and understand them. Avoid jargon that parents wouldn't likely understand or if a jargon term is required, explain it.

(5) Keep them simple and understandable. We will present a single-sentence format that should be written so clearly that you could close your eyes and accurately envision the child completing the task.

(6) Annual Goals are not lesson plan objectives; rather they represent major learning outcomes and should be written to include skills that are critical or important for the student to know. You don't need to write a goal or objective for every skill that a student will learn during the year.

You should write goals for critical functional skills such as those that someone would have to do for the student if he or she could not complete the task (such as dressing) and important skills that represent foundational academic or behavioral skills (such as reading fluency or responding to peers). If a skill isn't critical or foundational, don't be compelled to include it in the IEP or you could end up with an incredibly long and unwieldy IEP. The length of the IEP will be the responsibility of the IEP team, but it shouldn't be longer than needed to meet the unique needs of the child.

(7) Annual Goals and Short-Term Objectives should address the need to increase skills not simply remove skills. Do not write Annual Goals or Short-Term Objectives consisting of behaviors that a dead man could do. This means that you do not write Short-Term Objective for a task such as "sitting quietly with hands in lap" because a dead man could demonstrate that skill flawlessly. Rather identify a replacement behavior and write a Short-Term Objective to teach a replacement behavior that would make the problem behavior unnecessary.

(8) Short-Term Objectives should be written for only one student, the student with the IEP. While it may seem obvious, be sure to use the student's proper name in the objective. The authors have reviewed IEPs where the teacher failed to use the child's name, simply referring to "the student." This is a very impersonal approach, and we wondered what message this may have conveyed to parents.

(9) If writing Short-Term Objectives, write at least two for each Annual goal. We recommend the following formula for writing Annual Goals and Short-Term Objectives, with the exception that the fourth step is not always included in

Annual Goal statements, but there would be nothing wrong with including all four components in an Annual Goal. *First*, state the conditions under which the behavior should occur (we use the term to refer to academic behaviors as well as social, communicative, motor, and self-help behaviors *Second*, describe the behavior in clear, observable, and measurable terms. *Third*, identify the criteria or how well the student should perform the behavior, and *fourth*, identify how many times the child must demonstrate the behavior.

Annual Goals and Short-Term Objectives that you write will generally conform to the requirements above if they can (1) pass the "stranger test," (2) don't violate the "dead man rule," and (3) can pass a "so what" test. Passing the "stranger test" means that the goal or objective is written so clearly that a stranger who knew nothing of the student would understand what was to be accomplished. The "dead man rule" refers to the fact that goals and objectives should not be written for a skill that a dead man could do, such as sitting quietly. Remember, the purpose of education is to teach new skills, including replacement skills. Finally, the "so what" test helps determine whether the goals and objectives are written for critical skills. If it isn't a critical skill, then it may be nice to know, but wouldn't be so important that it would of such priority to be included on an IEP.

We will continue our discussion by describing each of the components in our four step formula with a focus on Short-Term Objectives. We will then compare the Short-Term Objective with the Annual Goal. Even though Annual Goals are first in the IEP, we are starting with Short-Term Objectives because that will allow us to present all four steps that are included in Short-Term Objectives whereas Annual Goals may not always incorporate the fourth step.

Conditions

You can think of the conditions statement as a description of either the antecedent event that will prompt the behavior or the materials that will be presented to the child for task completion. Consider the following sample Short-Term Objective for John that we provided in the last chapter. The bold words represent the condition. In this specific case, they indicate the materials and a directive will be provided to John. Remember, when writing Short-Term Objectives, you want them to be concise.

> **Given a worksheet with 30 single digit addition problems (0-9) and a direction to complete it,** John will write the correct answer to 29 problems within 60 seconds on three consecutive opportunities.

Following is a second example that we will discuss as we review writing Short-Term Objective. This objective focuses on the behavior rather than academic output as in the previous example. Let us assume that the present levels indicate that Maria does not consistently makes choices and when presented with two items, she looks back and forth, from object to object. This lack of focus on a single item makes it difficult to determine whether she has a preference for either item. The actual challenge of selecting appropriate items for her to select and teaching her to make that selection will be up to the teaching staff, but the success of the intervention will be measured by performance on the objective. On this example, the bolded item is the condition. Notice that it doesn't state that the teacher is asking her to make a choice. This is a more inclusive condition as it could be the teacher asking, but it could also the server in the lunch room or a peer during a play or academic activity. Of course, the teacher might be required to teach Maria's peers or lunch room staff to implement the strategy.

> **When shown a two different items and asked to choose one,** Maria will look at one item and maintain her gaze on that object for 2 seconds on three opportunities per day for three consecutive days.

Behavior

The second component of the objective is a description of the behavior that will be measured. If the objectives are to be measured, then the behavior must be clearly described in terms that anyone can understand and that can be measured. It is useful to keep the parent in mind when considering who the "anyone" might be. Alberto and Troutman (2013) stressed, the use of an "operational definition" of a behavior meaning that the behavior is described in a manner that eliminates ambiguity and ensures that everyone working with the student is viewing the behavior in a consistent manner. Lack of clarity in defining behavior is a frequent cause of mismeasurement and can lead to misunderstandings when working with students. (This idea of operationally defining behavior will also be a crucial component of the Functional Behavioral Assessment and Behavior Intervention Plan that will be discussed in a later chapter).

Properly written and meaningful objectives identify what the child will do, not what the child will be able to do. In fact, we really aren't concerned with what the child will be able to do, because we can't measure "able to" and it really isn't an acceptable learning outcome. An acceptable learning outcome is indicated by a measured change in behavior including academic behaviors. To illustrate our point, let's assume that we have a student who swears and hits other students on the playground. While we may want him to "be able" to play without swearing or hitting, just "being able" isn't enough. The student may be perfectly able to play appropriately on the playground but chooses to swear and hit. If our objective was "ability" then that child would have achieved the objective—he is able to play without swearing or hitting, but the meaningful objective is for him to actually play without swearing or hitting not just be "able to." We could measure the play behavior, but we cannot measure "able to."

It would behoove you to begin thinking of behaviors in clearly observable and operationally defined terms. Table 4-1 that we presented earlier contains a sample listing of observable behaviors and unobservable attributes. We think the differences are obvious and striking, but we guarantee that you will see IEPs with objectives that violate this simple tenant.

If we refer back to the example Short-Term Objectives presented for John and Maria, you will find that the items in bold type indicate the specific behavior that each child will complete.

In our next section, we will discuss the criteria used to determine whether the behavior has been demonstrated at an acceptable level.

> Given a worksheet with 30 single digit addition problems (0-9), **John will write** the correct answer to 29 problems within 60 seconds on three consecutive opportunities.

> When shown a two different items and asked to choose one**, Maria will look at one item** and maintain her gaze on that object for 2 seconds on three opportunities per day for three consecutive days.

Criteria

Criteria refer to a description of how well the student is expected to perform the target skill or behavior. Selecting criteria can be a challenging activity for an IEP team, because it requires that the team have an understanding of typical behavior, academic standards, behavioral expectations, and types of self-help skills needed. All of this must be considered in light of the individual student and his or her learning needs. The criteria selected must describe the level of performance that the IEP team expects the child to achieve for the year if we are considering an Annual Goal or before moving to the next Short-Term Objective if writing objectives. In addition, the criteria must be reasonable. In all likelihood, you will encounter IEPs that have had either unreasonably low expectations (e.g., Answer 1 of 2 questions correctly) or excessively high expectations, much higher than those of students without disabilities (e.g., Follow teacher directions 100% of the time). So, one of the tasks of the IEP team is to determine the appropriate standard or a criterion which is yet another reason that it is important for regular education teachers to participate in development of the IEP. When considering the criteria for a task, it is important to consider what is acceptable for students without disabilities and use that as a guideline. You will find many IEPs written with 80% or 85% accuracy criterion as if that was an unstated rule. There is **NO** such rule. Rather, it is important to determine the criteria on an individual basis and based on the consequence for not completing the skill accurately. For example, one might develop a reading objective, based on a GOM, that a student would read 60 words per minute with two or fewer errors. You might have decided that 100% accuracy, or reading with absolutely no errors, was not necessary before advancement to the next objective. However, if you were teaching a child to look both ways and check for traffic before entering the crosswalk, your criteria would have to be 100%. Failure to check for traffic and enter the crosswalk only when safe could result in a student getting hit by a car and being seriously injured or killed, so an 80% criterion would not be acceptable for such a critical skill.

Alberto and Troutman (2013) identified four fundamental ways to consider criteria: *accuracy, frequency, duration, and latency*. The type of criteria used will depend upon the specified target skill and how the skill can be measured. In some cases, you will find it helpful to combine the measures. We will discuss each of these measurement options in the following paragraphs followed by some examples and additional discussion regarding the development of Annual Goals and Short-Term Objectives. As you consider these measurement options, you may think of times when the objective may contain a combination of measurements, and you would be correct. We will address that, but first, we want to discuss the items separately.

Accuracy measures, how well a student completes a task and is commonly presented as a percentage. It can also be presented numerically without the use of a percentage, and sometimes that is an easier way to express the criteria. This type of measurement is useful with academic skills and other behaviors that lend themselves to this manner of measurement. Sometimes accuracy is the appropriate measure, for example:

> Write answer to 20 single-digit addition problems at 100% accuracy
>
> Or
>
> Correctly answer 20 of 20 single-digit addition problems (indicates 100% accuracy)
>
> Or
>
> Correctly answer 18 of 20 single-digit addition problems (indicates 90% accuracy if our ultimate goal was for him to answer all 20 problems correctly)

Other times, accuracy makes absolutely no sense because the skill is not measured in that manner. We have seen objectives stating that a student would sweep a floor at 100% accuracy. Now, ask yourself, what is 100% accuracy of floor sweeping? How would it be measured? We hope you understand that this measurement is simply not reasonable and would therefore be inappropriate for this task. In fact, sweeping the floor is likely not a critical skill that should not have been included in an IEP. You will likely see objectives that would require a student to make appropriate eye contact 100% of the time. As with the prior example, there is no way to measure this behavior. We could certainly write an objective for a child to make eye contact for a specified time in a specific and culturally appropriate manner, but the example we provided gave no guidance on what would be appropriate eye contact or how long the student would be required to demonstrate that behavior. Eye contact is an important skill in mainstream American culture and we might need to teach that behavior, but using a percentage is not an appropriate measure.

Frequency measures simply refer to how often a student completes a particular skill or behavior and is a useful metric with many behaviors that don't lend themselves to accuracy measurements. Many of the behaviors measured using a criteria based on frequency are those that are either exhibited or not exhibited. For example, consider a child who is at the beginning stage of toileting and learning to indicate the need to use the restroom. Stating that the child will indicate the need to use the restroom with 100% accuracy really doesn't make sense as a method of measurement. This is something that the child either does or does not do—there is no way to measure that he or she indicated the need to use the restroom at 50% accuracy. What would that behavior look like? Would he indicate the need to toilet 50% of the time or just complete 50% of the chain of behaviors that comprise "indicating the need to toilet?" Now assume you were working with a child who, according to baseline information included in the present levels statement, had an average of three wet accidents per day. You might have an Annual Goal for independent toileting, but a Short-Term Objective that might make sense could be that the child would indicate the need to use the restroom 2 of 3 opportunities.

Duration and *Latency* measures are third and fourth ways to measure behavior and are both related to time periods. *Duration* refers to how long a child exhibits a behavior and *latency* refers to how much time elapses after the direction or prompt before the student begins the behavior. These measures are used for skills that cannot be adequately measured using percentage or frequency. Following are a couple of simple examples to demonstrate the use of these measures. Assume that you are working with a young child who does not play in proximity of other children and regularly refuses to play within two feet of her peers for more than 10 seconds. Instead of playing, she gets up and goes to another place where she can play alone. The IEP team may decide to write an objective that uses a criterion related to duration, such as having her play within 2 foot proximity of other students for 3 minutes. Note that the criteria didn't try to place any percentage measure on play behavior. We have seen objectives stating that a child will play with 100% accuracy—this makes absolutely no sense whatsoever because there is no agreed upon definition of playing accurately. An example of a criterion statement using a latency measurement is to have a child respond to a verbal initiation from a peer within 3 seconds.

Now that we have covered the different methods of describing criteria for objectives, we will return to the objectives for John and Maria. The first objective for John is related to accuracy. He is required to answer 29 of 30 problems correctly which is a 96% overall accuracy rate. We could have stated 96% in the objective, but 29 or 30 problems is much easier for busy teachers to use, because it removes the step of determining 96% of 30. We also added a duration component by allowing him only 60 seconds to complete the task. Adding the time component can be an important consideration when teaching skills where a goal is to obtain automaticity and speed. Without that time requirement, John could take 5 hours to answer the problems and still meet the criteria of correctly answering 29 problems, but that would not be a satisfactory level of performance. For the second objective with Maria, it would make absolutely no sense to state that she would look at an object with 100% accuracy. The goal on this objective is for her to look at an object long enough to indicate her preference and 2 seconds was an appropriate time for her. The criterion for each objective is in bold font.

> Given a worksheet with 30 single digit addition problems (0-9), John will write the **correct answer to 29 problems within 60 seconds** on three consecutive opportunities.

> When shown a two different items and asked to choose one, Maria will look at one item and **maintain her gaze on that object for 2 seconds** on three opportunities per day for three consecutive days.

Number of Times to Meet Criteria

The fourth component of the objective (rarely included in an Annual Goal) is the number of times that the student must demonstrate the target behavior under the specified conditions and at criterion. Absent this statement, a student could technically complete the target behavior only once and be rated as having achieved the objective. Specifying the number of times to exhibit the behavior is no guarantee that the student has generalized the behavior or will maintain the behavior for an extended period of time, so teachers should periodically conduct probes to determine if a student has maintained a particular behavior and provide opportunities for skill generalization. If the student didn't pass a probe measure, then the skill should be retaught. We complete this section using the sample objectives for John and Maria. As indicated in bold font, John's objective required that he complete the task on three consecutive opportunities. The term opportunities does not necessarily mean days. It would be possible for him to have multiple opportunities to compete the task in one day, and he could technically complete the objective on that day. However, we know that such an approach would not be consistent with effective teaching practice. It would be much better for him to complete the task once per day across several days, whether they are consecutive or not. Either way, the teacher should still conduct probe measures and reteach if necessary.

This requirement was specified a bit differently for Maria. She was required to complete the skill three times per day across three consecutive days. For our purposes, we can safely assume that this means three consecutive school days, but it does require that the teacher ensure there are at least three opportunities for her to make a choice during the school day.

> Given a worksheet with 30 single digit addition problems (0-9), John will write the correct answer to 29 problems within 60 seconds on **three consecutive opportunities.**

> When shown a two different items and asked to choose one, Maria will look at one item and maintain her gaze on that object for 2 seconds **on three opportunities per day for three consecutive days.**

Concluding Comments on Short-Term Objectives

In the prior chapter, we noted that Short-Term Objectives are required on the IEPs of children who will be participating in alternative assessment procedures rather than the standard state or district mandated assessment with or without adaptations and modifications. However, we agree with Bateman and Linden (2012) who made the case that Short-Term Objectives should be included on the IEPs of all students with disabilities, because the Short-Term Objectives identify measurable intermediary steps that help determine whether the child is on track to meet the Annual Goal. Short-Term Objectives also make sense and must be written for skills where there is no official curriculum or benchmarking of skill, and thus there is no formal assessment administered by the district or state. Examples of these skills include eating, toileting, verbal communication, playing, social skills, following directions, and there are numerous other skills that are important for a particular child yet not included the state or district assessments mandated by No Child Left Behind (2001).

The regulations do allow the use of benchmarks in lieu of Short-Term Objective. The two items are similar in that they represent steps toward the Annual Goal. They differ in the fact that Short-Term Objectives are individually developed for each student whereas benchmarks are generally taken directly from a district curriculum and specify which skills a student should have acquired by a particular time, generally academic quarters or semesters. Some benchmarks may be stated in relatively broad and ambiguous terms making them difficult or impossible to measure, and therefore, not useful on an IEP. The more useful benchmarks are related directly to specific academic skills or GOM, such as oral reading fluency and can be readily presented as measurable Short-Term Objective. If using benchmarks, either ensure that they are measurable and comply with the guidelines for writing Short-Term Objectives or re-write the benchmarks to include the required measurable components.

Finally, it is important to emphasize that the IEP should identify the major learning targets for the child, not every item that the child will learn during the school year. A checklist for use when developing Short-Term Objectives is contained in Table 4-2. In the following section, we present a three selected Short-Term Objectives from some actual IEPs followed by a brief critique based on the criteria listed in the Short-Term Objective Checklist. These three really are poor examples and do not even approach a level of acceptability. We present them without the accompanying Annual Goals which were also poorly written.

TABLE 4-2. Short-Term Objective (STO) Checklist

1. Is the STO aligned with the AG?
2. Are there at least two STO for each AG?
3. Does the STO follow a logical sequence of skill acquisition leading from present level to AG?
4. Does the STO contain the following items in this order?
1. Condition under which the behavior will occur.
2. Clear description of observable, measurable behavior.
3. Criteria that would accurately measure the behavior.
4. The number of times the child must perform the skill at the specified criteria.
5. Is the STO written in clear, jargon free language that anyone could understand? (Does it pass the "stranger test?")
6. Is the STO written for a critical or otherwise important skill? (Does it pass the "so what" test?)
7. Is the STO written to increase desired behavior rather than merely remove undesired behavior? (Does it pass the "dead man test?)
8. Was the STO written for only one student?
9. Does the STO contain the name of the student?
10. If the child transferred to another school, would the receiving teacher know exactly what skills to address?

Our purpose here is to simply critique some poorly written Short-Term Objectives before reviewing some well-written Short-Term Objectives and associated Annual Goals. Despite the order in which we present these items, remember that a Short-Term Objective cannot stand alone, unconnected to an Annual Goal. Short-Term Objectives must be directly related to the Annual Goal.

Poorly Written Short-Term Objectives

Short-Term Objective Nonexample 1

To recognize sight vocabulary

This example does not contain any of the required components (condition, behavior, criteria, and number of times to meet criteria) for a Short-Term Objective. "Sight vocabulary" is presented as if there was a universal understanding of what constitutes sight vocabulary and which words the child will be working on.

Short-Term Objective Nonexample 2

Marty will spell 10 out of 15 words correctly during the school year.

Example 2 does not include the condition, and the behavior is not clearly presented. It is unknown whether he would spell the words orally, written, or some other format. More importantly, since it is written for the entire school year, the statement appears to more closely resemble an Annual Goal than a Short-Term Objective. An IEP is written for a calendar year and rarely written on the first day of school, which means the vast majority of IEPs span part of two different school years and this example statement is written for a school year, which is a highly unlikely timeframe. The only requirement for meeting this objective is for the student to learn 10 new words during the school year. This was originally written for a student who could have learned to spell considerably more than 10 words, so the objective probably fails to meet the requirement for meaningful learning. The actual Annual Goal listed on the IEP was the same as this objective with just the following minor wording differences. "Marty will improve his spelling ability by spelling correctly 10 out of 15 words given throughout the school year." If the Annual Goal and Short-Term Objective cover the exact same material, then there is no reason for the Short-Term Objective.

Short-Term Objective NonExample 3

When entering or leaving, Brittany will say hello or goodbye.

Nonexample 3 has numerous problems. The teacher attempted to provide a condition and did describe the behavior, but there is no criterion. Even though this example contained a couple more components than the prior nonexamples, the objective simply makes no sense. Does the condition refer to the "entering or leaving" behavior of Brittany or some other person? Does she say "hello or goodbye" or does she say "hello" when entering and "good bye" when leaving? Without further specific information, it is impossible to determine whether this is even a socially appropriate behavior. It certainly wouldn't be acceptable for Brittany or any other student to enter a classroom late and interrupt the class by saying "hello." You could imagine a whole range of activities that could comply with this objective, yet surely not be the intent of the writer. For instance, Brittany could be in the restroom stall sitting on the toilet when another person enters, and Brittney blurts out "hello." That would certainly be an inappropriate behavior, yet it would meet the guidelines of the objective.

These three Short-Term Objectives were poorly written and unmeasurable. As we have stated numerous times, measurability is a requirement of IDEA and failure to provide measurable outcomes may result in a court finding that a district failed to provide FAPE. We trust that you will find the following Annual Goals and Short-Term Objectives to be sufficient to provide the teacher with the information needed to work with the student while the previous three objectives were essentially worthless. Should a student move to your school with a poorly written IEP, then you should feel empowered to reconvene the IEP and write a document that is meaningful and will confer educational benefit.

Well Written Annual Goals and Short-Term Objectives

An Annual Goal is simply a statement of the skills the IEP team anticipates that the student will complete by the date the IEP ends. It must be measurable, and the starting point for development of the Annual Goal is the data provided in the present level statement. If a child achieves an Annual Goal sooner than anticipated, then the team should reconvene, celebrate the successes and update the goal.

We will present four examples of measurable Annual Goals and associated Short-Term Objectives that were developed for each. The first is for John. Throughout this chapter, we provided his present levels, and reviewed components of his IEP. This sample provides a clear example of an Annual Goal with the skills broken down in the associated Short-Term Objective.

Example 1 (mathematics)

The following Annual Goal notes that John will complete a worksheet containing mixed addition and subtraction problems. Completion of this goal requires that he is able to perform Short-Term Objectives 1 and 2 in addition to mixing the problems thereby requiring that John accurately discriminate addition from subtraction problems. The Short-Term Objectives progress from easier (addition) to more difficult (subtraction) in a logical manner that leads to completion of the Annual Goal.

> **Measurable Annual Goal** When presented with 50 single digit, mixed addition and subtraction problems using numerals (0-9), John will write the correct answer to 48 problems within 60 seconds.

> *Short-Term Objective 1:* Given a worksheet with 30 single digit addition problems (0-9) and a direction to complete it, John will write the correct answer to 29 problems within 60 seconds on three consecutive opportunities.

Short-Term Objective 2: Given a worksheet with 30 single digit subtraction problems (0-9) and a direction to complete it, John will write the correct answer to 29 problems within 60 seconds on three consecutive opportunities.

Example 2 (reading)

The second example uses a GOM to gauge student performance rather than listing every different skill that is necessary for proficient reading. The only difference between the objectives and the Annual Goal is the number of words per minute that the student will be required to read.

Measurable Annual Goal When presented with a 300 word third grade level reading passage, Manny will read 90 words per minute with fewer than 3 errors on two consecutive opportunities.

Short-Term Objective 1: When presented with a 300 word third grade level reading passage and asked to read aloud, Manny will read 70 words per minute with fewer than 3 errors on two consecutive opportunities.

Short-Term Objective 2: When presented with a 300 word third grade level reading passage and asked to read aloud, Manny will read 80 words per minute with fewer than 3 errors on two consecutive opportunities.

Example 3 (mobility)

The third example was included to demonstrate how gross motor skills could be addressed using functional, meaningful, and reinforcing activities for the student. Past practice for working with motor skill commonly consisted of removing the student from the general education setting and teaching the skill in an isolated setting that provided little opportunity for the student to actually exhibit the skill in a meaningful manner. You might have seen IEP objectives written to have a student stand on one foot for 90 seconds on three different occasions. The problem with this type of objective is that standing on one foot has no educational relevance unless it is incorporated into a meaningful activity. The following presents a meaningful motor skill that can be worked on during meaningful times during the day and concludes with naturally occurring reinforcement.

Measurable Annual Goal When going to the lunchroom, Ibrahim will independently walk from the classroom to the lunchroom (approximately 300 feet) within 90 seconds without stopping, falling, or leaning on the wall.

Short-Term Objective 1: When going to the lunchroom and assisted by his walker, Ibrahim will walk from the classroom to the lunchroom (300 feet) within 90 seconds without stopping, falling, or leaning on the wall on 3 consecutive days.

Short-Term Objective 2: When going to the lunchroom and assisted by his cane, Ibrahim will walk from the classroom to the lunchroom within (300 feet) 90 seconds without stopping, falling, or leaning on the wall on 3 consecutive days.

Example 4 (functional skills)

The fourth example was included to demonstrate a way to in teach critical skills within a functional activity. Rather than just recognizing colored flash cards, the student is required to identify the colors when shown items she encounters in her daily life activities. Teachers who understand behavioral learning principles understand the importance of programming for maintenance and generalization, especially for children with cognitive delays who experience difficulty with maintenance and generalization of skills. These objectives were written in a manner that would promote such instructional programming. In addition, this example demonstrates how to make color recognition a critical skill. In American culture, the colors red, yellow, and green have many important meanings that facilitate safety and community access. So, rather than just writing a goal for the student to recognize colors, the critical colors were specified which also helps when considering the "so what" rule as well as the stranger test.

> **Measurable Annual Goal** When asked to do so, Connie will correctly identify three colors (red, yellow, and green) 80% of opportunities.
>
> *Short-Term Objective 1:* When shown a color 8 × 10 photo of 10 common packaged food items and asked "Show me red" Connie will touch the one red item 8 of 10 times on each of three successive days.
>
> *Short-Term Objective 2:* When shown a color 8 × 10 photo of 10 children and asked "Show me red. Now show me yellow." Connie will first touch the child dressed in red and then touch the child dressed in yellow 8 of 10 times on three successive days.
>
> *Short-Term Objective 3:* When presented with 10 small toys, each a different color, and asked "Give me the red toy. Now give me the yellow toy. Now give me the green toy." Connie will do so 8 of 10 times on each of three successive days.

Chapter Summary

In this chapter, we have seen how an accurate and understandable statement of the present levels of performance in important academic and functional areas is the starting point for the IEP. It is only from a clear understanding of where the student is now that we can make a reasonably informed judgment of the specific need areas that must be addressed in the IEP. For each area where there is a significant need we must develop, first, an objective measurable statement of where we expect the student to be after one year of instruction. These Annual Goals then become the guiding focus of our instruction and provision of related services.

We have also seen that while it may not always be a requirement to include them in the IEP, it is important to conceptualize the path to the Annual Goal as consisting of a series of steps from the present level statements to the accomplished or mastered Annual Goals. These are the Short-Term Objectives that guide our daily and weekly activities as we move the student from where we find him or her to where we want him or her to be in a year. For those students who get alternative assessments that are aligned to alternative achievement standards or for whose IEPs include functional skills not aligned to standards we must break down each Annual Goal into a series of Short-Term Objectives and include them in the IEP document. In a real sense, these Short-Term Objectives are what our daily and weekly lesson plans should be designed to address. Does this mean that our curriculum in the general education classroom must be designed around the IEPs of the few students who have them? Certainly not. But, just as for all other students, it should be flexible enough to allow us to address important goals and instructional objectives for the student with an IEP. We will say more about how to do that in a following chapter.

In sum, taken together goal and objectives are the heart and soul of the IEP. They are clearly written and are derived from equally clearly stated present levels. Everything else that it is in the IEP is related to them. The activities that follow will help you practice principles and concepts introduced in this chapter.

Chapter Activities

Activity 1. Use the Short-Term Objective Checklist to evaluate the following objectives (most came from actual IEPs). Identify which meet the criteria and which do not. For those that do not meet the criteria, determine whether the content would be appropriate for inclusion on an IEP. For those you deem appropriate for an IEP, re-write them according to the guidelines on the Short-Term Objective Checklist. Since you don't have present level statements for the following objectives, you will need to make assumptions regarding the skill level of the students.

Once you have written Short-Term Objectives, exchange them with a classmate and rate each other's objectives using the checklist and provide constructive feedback.

1. With 80% or better accuracy according to teachers' observations, grades, assessments, and the student's work. Alex will know and use word analysis skills to comprehend new words.

2. Recognize an increased number of high-frequency words.

3. Marty will work one-to one with art personnel to develop artistic skills, art projects, and bulletin boards at 90% accuracy throughout the school year.

4. In a classroom setting, Stacey will reduce talking out in class by 50% of achieving a criteria of 4 out of 5 trials as implemented by special education and general education teacher.

5. Marcia will report to all scheduled classes on time during the school year 85% of the time.

6. When given a topic sentence, Marcus will write a four sentence paragraph with correct beginning and ending punctuation on 3 consecutive opportunities.

7. Given a topic sentence, Antonio will write a four sentence paragraph with subject and verb agreement on each sentence on three consecutive assignments.

8. When shown colored flashcards (red, green, and yellow) and asked to identify one of the colors, Tyrell will point to the correct card at 100% accuracy on 4 opportunities per day for 3 consecutive days.

9. OBJ1: Becky will be able to apply computational procedures with fluency to addition, subtraction, multiplication, and division problems.
   Criterion: When given 4 computational problems commonly found in textbooks, Becky will compute the correct answer for at least 3 of the 4 problems.

10. OBJ2: When presented with word problems commonly introduced in math textbooks, Becky will compute the correct answer.
    Criterion: Becky will compute the correct answer for at least 1 of 2 problems.

Activity 2: Following are present level statements that were provided in the chapter. For each student, write at least one Annual Goal and two Short-Term Objectives for each Annual Goal. Then exchange them with a classmate and rate each other's goals and objectives using the checklist and provide constructive feedback.

(1) Monique

Reading and writing: Monique names all upper and lowercase letters without error. She recognizes her own name in print and says the letter sound for the consonants (b, c, d, and f). She holds a primary pencil with a pincer grasp and copies her name in large (approx. 3 inch letters), but does not hold a regular size pencil.

Mathematics: Monique consistently rote counts to 5 and can count to 10 when provided manipulatives. When shown groups of items and asked which group has more or less, she identifies the correct group. Monique recognizes the numerals 1–5 at 100% accuracy, but only correctly names the numerals 6–9 at 50% of opportunity.

(2) Miguel

Miguel is at the beginning of the self-initiated stage of toileting. On average, he indicates the need to use the restroom (urination) three times per day but is already wet by the time he indicates a toileting need. He is compliant and cooperates during toileting and changing activities.

During meal or snack, Miguel consistently uses a spoon to eat semi-solid food, such as pudding or jello without spilling. When eating more liquefied foods, such as soup or cereal with milk, he spills about half of the contents before getting the spoon to his mouth. He is beginning to use the fork to spear pre-cut food and consistently gets the food into his mouth without spilling. He consistently drinks liquid from a weighted cup with two handles, using both hands, without spilling when the cup is less than half full.

(3) Vinnie

Vinnie experiences difficulty getting along with peers on the playground and in the classroom. When interacting with peers on the playground, he gets into verbal altercations three to four times per week. These altercations generally take place on either the basketball or foursquare courts and begin with his cussing at other students when he misses a shot but insists that he made the shot or point. If a peer disagrees with him, then Vinnie may either throw the ball at the peer or push the peer and leave the game. This happens at least three times per week. In the classroom, when assigned to work on small group academic activities, he fails to participate and lays his head on the desk while the others complete the task. When offered a leadership role completing an activity involving tasks that he has already mastered, he regularly participates in the activity at a level similar to that of his peers.

When given a direction by an adult to complete an academic task independently, he generally delays following the direction until asked a third time or just refuses to complete the task. This behavior is rarely exhibited in math or science class unless he is required to write an answer to a question.

Chapter 5

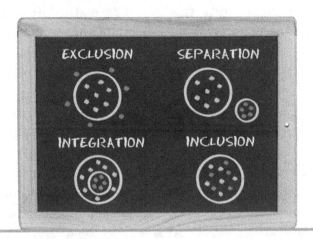

Least Restrictive Environment

Chapter Overview

In the past few chapters, we have provided a considerable amount of information that will help you to be a more active participant in IEP meetings and help the team develop educationally relevant IEPs. We discussed a wide range of topics including historical perspectives, the use of people-first language, the referral and eligibility process, including RtI, and procedures commonly used with preschool age children, as well as procedural issues such as Prior Written Notice and Informed Parental Consent. We also provided a comprehensive review of the IEP and instruction on writing data-based Present Level Statements, Annual Goals, and Short-Term Objectives. If you mastered that content, you have a solid foundation that will enable you to be a productive member of an IEP team without feeling intimidated by the process.

However, there is still crucial information that you must understand in order to develop IEPs that live up to the letter and intent of the law. In the next few chapters, we will provide you with information needed to make the IEP process complete. Specifically, in this chapter, we will discuss the Least Restrictive Environment (LRE) provision of IDEA. It is a crucial component and violating the LRE protections could adversely impact the civil rights of students with disabilities, specifically the First Amendment right to freedom of association. As we will discuss, a school can remove a child from the regular education setting if needed to provide FAPE and for some disciplinary reasons, but should do so with caution and provide legally sound justifications for any such removal (Turnbull et al., 2007). Given the interrelated nature of the different sections of the LRE provision, it is difficult to discuss the LRE in a completely linear manner, so there will be some overlap and repetition of very important concepts, but that should help you develop a solid understanding of LRE. In the first part of the chapter, we will provide a review of LRE relevant for all teachers. At the end of the chapter, we will discuss special applications of LRE particularly relevant for teachers of preschool children, secondary age students, and those receiving ESY. In subsequent chapters, we will review disciplinary procedures including Functional Behavioral Assessment and Behavior Intervention Plans, provide a brief overview of the Procedural Safeguards afforded parents, and describe some effective strategies for working with children with disabilities in inclusive educational settings. Upon completion of these remaining chapters, you will have an advanced understanding of the IEP process and be well equipped to develop relevant IEPs that include parental input and live up to the intent of the law. We fully understand that we will not have and could not possibly have addressed every conceivable issue, but then we are writing about Individualized Education Programs. In our opinion, the term "Individualized" represents the creative and fun process in which you tailor instruction and supports to meet the unique needs of a child. Since all children are different and may require different supports, our intent has been to provide you with a sound framework from which to develop legally compliant and educationally meaningful IEPs.

The concept of Least Restrictive Environment (LRE) has been a key component of special education law since its initial authorization in 1975 and the wording in the law and accompanying regulations remains essentially the same. However, nearly 40 years since the passage of federal special education law, the concept of LRE remains one of the most contentious sections of the law (Danile, 1997; Turnbull et al., 2007; Hyatt & Filler, 2011). In Chapter 1, we provided a brief synopsis of the history of services to individuals with disabilities and supplied references to authors who have written comprehensive descriptions. That historical background has had important influences on the development of the LRE policy and its inclusion in special education law. A thorough discussion of the evolution of LRE is beyond the scope of this text, but we will discuss the current legal interpretation of LRE as well as describe the basic assumptions underlying terms associated with LRE that are indicative of the evolution of the terms: mainstreaming, integration, and inclusion.

Mainstreaming, Integration, and Inclusion

Mainstreaming, integration, and inclusion are terms commonly used in education but often used erroneously (Filler, 1996). It is important that you understand the differences among the terms, because imprecise and faulty understandings can result in inequitable programming for students with disabilities and may even diminish your credibility. The terms are not synonymous; rather, they represent significant differences in the interpretation and application of the LRE mandate (Villa & Thousand, 2003). There are certainly variations to the definitions we will provide, but these descriptions represent the general theme for each of the practices.

The term "mainstreaming" generally referred to a process where a student with a mild disability (such as a learning disability) would leave the regular classroom to receive specially designed instruction (special education) in a separate area. (When IDEA was first passed, these separate areas were commonly makeshift classrooms in school basements or storage rooms.) Once the student was able to complete grade level work with little or no need for additional supports or modifications, the student was allowed to "earn" or "learn" his or her way back into the classroom and participate in activities with typically developing peers. Mind you, no other groups of students who experienced learning difficulty were systematically removed from the regular class and required to "earn" or "learn" their way back into the classroom. However, that was deemed an acceptable practice by some professionals and special education was viewed as a place where students went to get "fixed." Mainstreaming was commonly viewed as a "sink" or "swim" approach, because the child either succeeded in the regular classroom without any extra support or just failed.

In the 1980s, parents and advocates of students with more severe disabilities who were receiving services in special education schools began pursuing a practice called "integration." At a very basic level, "integration" required moving these students from the special schools and educating them in self-contained special education classrooms located on regular school campuses. The rationale was that the students would have an opportunity to interact with typically developing peers during nonacademic classes and activities, such as music, PE, art, lunch, and recess. However, special education was still viewed as a place and students with severe disabilities who were schooled under an integration model received their special education in a separate place. Few were ever afforded the opportunity to "earn" or "learn" their way into a regular education classroom.

The 1990s brought about the interpretation of LRE to favor "inclusion." Inclusive practices represented a drastic departure from both "mainstreaming" and "integration." Inclusion represented an underlying philosophical belief that all children belong in the regular class and do not have to "earn" or "learn" their way into the regular classroom. The necessary specially designed instruction and supports should be provided in the regular education setting and special education was now viewed as a service that follows children, not as a place where children were sent. A major tenant was that the schools should reflect the heterogeneous population and if 10% of the population had a disability, then 10% of students in a classroom should be expected to have a disability, and students with disabilities should be included in classrooms that are chronologically age-appropriate. While inclusion was framed around the needs of individuals with disabilities, the philosophy of belonging and acceptance while meeting individual needs applied to all children, regardless of learning needs.

Least Restrictive Environment (300.114)

IDEA does not require mainstreaming, integration, or inclusion. In fact none of these terms are even mentioned in the law. You might read of the "mainstreaming mandate", but that phraseology simply refers to the LRE mandate, and IDEA does require that all IEP teams comply with the LRE requirements clearly articulated in the law and in sections §300.114 through §300.120 of the regulations. To review the specific LRE requirements, we will present the regulatory language and discuss major components with a special focus on sections 300.114 through 300.117. The first section, §300.114, provides the following language defining LRE and identifies each state's responsibility for ensuring that effective policies are in place:

§300.114 Least Restrictive Environment

(a) General.
(1) Except as provided in §300.324(d)(2) (regarding children with disabilities in adult prisons), the State must have in effect policies and procedures to ensure that public agencies in the State meet the LRE requirements of this section and §§300.115 through 300.120.

(2) Each public agency must ensure that—

(i) To the maximum extent appropriate, children with disabilities, including children in public or private institutions or other care facilities, are educated with children who are nondisabled; and
(ii) Special classes, separate schooling, or other removal of children with disabilities from the regular educational environment occurs only if the nature or severity of the disability is such that education in regular classes with the use of supplementary aids and services cannot be achieved satisfactorily.

Paragraph (a)(1) of §300.114 clearly notes that states are responsible for ensuring compliance with all LRE provisions with one exception. It does relieve the state of its responsibilities regarding LRE for students with disabilities who are incarcerated in adult prisons.

The primary purpose of IDEA is to ensure the provision of FAPE to eligible children with disabilities, but the provision of service must be in the Least Restrictive Environment to the maximum extent appropriate. The issue of what comprises LRE has been a contentious issue (Danile, 1997; Turnbull et al., 2007). Some claim that the LRE is different for different children (Fuchs & Fuchs 1994; Kauffman, 1995; Kauffman & Hallahan, 2005) or even changes for children over time (Heward, 2006). While others have presented legal, philosophical, and programmatic rationales supporting the case that the LRE for all children is the regular education environment and that there are not different LREs for different children (Hyatt & Filler, 2011; Sailor et al., 1989), and the regulatory language in paragraph (2)(ii) of §300.114 clearly states that the LRE is the regular education setting with the use of supplementary aids and supports. However, simply placing students in the regular education environment without ensuring participation in typical activities may not live up to the goal of least restrictive (Hamre-Nietupski & Nietupski, 2008), and educators must guard against marginalization of students (Petrou, Angelides, & Leigh, 2009) by ensuring meaningful participation and facilitating group membership.

To consider the regular education setting to be the LRE is clearly aligned with the law and the congressional intent that the presumed placement for all children is the regular education environment with supplementary aids and services as needed. Special education should be viewed as a service that follows the child, not a place where a child is sent. Lest there be any question of intent, Congress made the following statements in the preamble to IDEA '04 (Public Law 108-446):

> 601(c)(1): Disability is a natural part of the human experience and in no way diminishes the right of individuals to participate in or contribute to society. Improving educational results for children with disabilities is an essential element of our national policy of ensuring equality of opportunity, full participation independent living, and economic self-sufficiency for individuals with disabilities.

> 601(c)(5): Almost 30 years of research and experience has demonstrated that the education of children with disabilities can be made more effective by:

> (A) having high expectations for such children and ensuring their access to the general education in the regular classroom, to the maximum extent appropriate;

> (B) ... families of children to have meaningful opportunities to participate in the education of their children;

> (C) ... special education can become a service for such children rather than a place where such children are sent;

> (D) providing appropriate special education and related services, and aids and supports in the regular classroom, to such children, whenever appropriate; and

> (E) supporting high-quality, intensive preservice preparation and professional development for all personnel who work with children with disabilities.

This leads us to a review of foundational information provided in paragraphs 2(i) and 2(ii) of §300.114, the LRE definition. Paragraph 2(i) clearly identifies state responsibility for ensuring that children with disabilities are educated with typically developing peers to the maximum extent appropriate. This responsibility extends to students that may have been placed in highly restrictive residential facilities, even if those facilities are located in a different state.

In other words, sending a student to a 24 hour residential treatment facility located in a different state would not absolve the student's home state of responsibility for ensuring compliance with LRE regulations. Paragraph 2(ii) provides the unequivocal presumption that children with disabilities be educated in the regular education environment to the maximum extent appropriate with the use of necessary supplementary aids and services. It does not require placement of all children with disabilities in the regular education environment, but as we shall see, it identifies the regular education environment as the presumed and least restrictive placement option for children with disabilities. So, while regular education placement is clearly the presumed placement for all children, it may not be the appropriate placement for all children, and we will discuss placement options when we review §300.115, the Continuum of Alternative Placements.

In our experience, many of our university students shake their heads affirmatively when considering whether the regular education environment is where children with disabilities should be educated. However, when those same students were asked the question with a slightly different twist—"Where should a student with a severe disability should be educated?"—many who had just seconds earlier affirmed regular education placement for all children, indicate that children with severe disabilities should be educated in self-contained, pull-out special education classrooms (a much more restrictive placement than the regular education setting). This response highlights the importance of IEP committees understanding the requirements of the LRE, lest they inappropriately infringe upon an individual student's civil rights by placing him or her in a setting that is more restrictive than needed to receive FAPE or place a child in a particular setting or program due solely to disability label—a practice negated in the landmark decision in *Mills v. District of Columbia Board of Education* (1972). It also indicates that we have considerable work yet to do before we have truly inclusive classroom and school settings where all students are welcomed and valued members of the community. Turnbull et al. (2007) noted that discrimination in numerous aspects of life is related to stigma, and that the meaningful enactment of the LRE principle provides "the only truly effective method of addressing stigma for persons with disabilities: familiarity" (p. 209). So, while placement in the regular education environment is a beginning, it is no panacea to all that ails public education, but it is likely a necessary precondition for ensuring that students with disabilities have the least possible restriction placed upon their education and their freedom to associate (Hyatt & Filler, 2011).

Continuum of Alternative Placements (§300.115)

In the previous section, we began discussing LRE and making the case that the LRE is the regular education setting for all children. However, the regular education setting is just one setting along the continuum of alternative placements that we will be discussing. Due to the potential for infringements on civil liberties from unnecessary segregation, we will discuss the controversies surrounding the continuum, hoping that this discussion may prompt thoughtful consideration before any decision is made to remove a child from the regular education environment. With that in mind, we note that the regular education setting may not be appropriate for all children all of the time. The regulations include the following guidelines regarding the Continuum of Alternative Placements that must be available.

§300.115 Continuum of Alternative Placements

(a) Each public agency must ensure that a continuum of alternative placements is available to meet the needs of children with disabilities for special education and related services.

(b) The continuum required in paragraph (a) of this section must—

(1) Include the alternative placements listed in the definition of special education under §300.38 (instruction in regular classes, special classes, special schools, home instruction, and instruction in hospitals and institutions); and

(2) Make provision for supplementary services (such as resource room or itinerant instruction) to be provided in conjunction with regular class placement.

Lake and Norlin (2006) noted that if regular education placement is not appropriate for a particular student and he or she must be moved to an alternative placement to receive FAPE, that new placement should have the least amount of segregation from typically developing peers and the community. As we continue our discussion of the LRE components of the law, you will find that the comment by Lake and Norlin cuts right to the heart of the matter. When schools start restricting the access students with disabilities have to the activities and individuals that are readily available to children without disabilities, then their placement has become more restrictive. All such removals or restrictions must be justified by the IEP team, and if the team decides that a student must be removed from the regular education environment in order to receive FAPE, the team must consider the next least restrictive placement along the continuum of alternative placements. It is important to emphasize that the team is required to place the child in the least restrictive placement in which he or she would receive FAPE. Placing a child in an unnecessarily restrictive placement could be considered a denial of FAPE.

At the end of our discussion of the LRE regulations in this chapter, we will review different Circuit Court decisions that provided guidelines for IEP teams to consider when making placement decisions, but we want to be clear that a particularly relevant component of FAPE is that the child receive meaningful educational benefit. So, if a child was receiving meaningful educational benefit in the regular education environment, the IEP team could not justify removal from the regular education environment to a more restrictive placement along the continuum simply because the child would receive more benefit in a segregated setting (*Roncker v. Walter, 1983*). The law requires that schools develop IEPs and provide services that are reasonably calculated to confer educational benefit, not provide the best possible benefit as the U. S. Supreme Court determined in *Hudson v. Rowley* (1982). In addition as noted in *Espino v. Bestiero* (1981) and again in *Sacramento v. Holland* (1994), there are many important things, such as social skills, taught in the regular education setting that may not be part of the official curriculum but do positively impact a child's ability to be a productive member of society.

As will be discussed further, some children with disabilities might be removed from the regular education setting if required to provide FAPE but removal does have costs. In addition to the loss of access to peers without disabilities, an inherent cost in removing children from the regular education classroom is the possible reduction in access to the regular education curriculum due to both scheduling decisions and to the actual removal from the class.

For example, if a child is removed for reading, is that child always removed during reading time or is the child taken out during social studies or other classes; thereby limiting his or her access to the regular education curriculum? If removed during reading, does the child miss out on important grade level readings and stories, thereby limiting his or her access to the grade level material? If the IEP team determined that removal was necessary for reading instruction, then it is incumbent on the school team to schedule the timing of the removal so it has the least possible negative impact on the child's access to the regular curriculum and not simply schedule removal for administrative convenience. We will continue to emphasize that decisions to remove a child from the regular education setting should not be taken lightly, as any removal has the potential of negatively impacting the educational experience. In a later chapter, we will provide some helpful strategies for supporting children with disabilities in the regular education setting.

Turnbull et al. (2007) noted that the concept of LRE and the associated continuum was built upon the constitutionally based concept of Least Restrictive Alternative (LRA). Simply stated, LRA requires that the least intrusive or restrictive treatment option be used by the government when providing rehabilitative services. This requirement has a direct application to placement decisions. If a child is removed from the LRE to receive FAPE, then the movement along the continuum (from least to most) must be as little as needed to achieve FAPE. Remember, removal from the regular education setting (LRE) is allowable only when the child cannot receive meaningful educational benefit even with the use of supplementary aids and services in the regular education setting. So, services and aids provided in the regular education setting would likely be considered a Least Restrictive Alternative (LRA) when compared with removing the child from the regular education setting and providing those services in a segregated setting. The point is that numerous alternative supports and services can be provided in the regular education setting that will enable many children with disabilities to receive FAPE without being removed from their peers. To emphasize the importance of LRA, Turnbull, Stowe, and Huerta (2007) referred to a commonly used and illustrative metaphor by Chambers (1972), recognizing that the LRA mandate means that the state cannot use a bazooka to kill a fly if a swatter will do. Thus, IEP teams and schools should view movement to more restrictive placements with caution and be sure that any decisions comply with the principle of LRA.

The concept of the continuum has not been without criticism with some advocating for its use (Kauffman, 1995), while others have argued against it (Biklen, 1982; Taylor, 1988). In 2001, Taylor reemphasized that his numerous concerns about the continuum expressed in 1988 remain relevant more than a decade later. Among those concerns is an inherent assumption that individuals with disabilities will be separated from individuals without disabilities; it is just a matter of those without disabilities determining how segregated the setting will be. Second, the use of the continuum confuses the intensity of service with intensity of segregation. The model assumes that the most intensive services automatically require the most segregated placement, and it assumes that those who work in more segregated settings have specific training and use specialized techniques that cannot be replicated in the regular education setting. We know that is an erroneous assumption and schools across the country have experienced success providing intensive supports in a wide range of settings, including the regular education setting as well as in the home and community. A third dangerous assumption commonly associated with the continuum is the idea that children must "earn" or "learn" their way back into the regular education setting. We have previously addressed problems associated with this readiness model, but want to emphasize that the IEP team has great power to employ the services and supports that will ensure that the school and classroom are "ready" to provide meaningful learning opportunities for children with disabilities. (Remember that one of the related services that can be included on an IEP is training for the teacher.)

Paragraph (b)(1) of §300.115 (Continuum of Alternative Placements) lists the placement options from least restrictive (regular classroom) to most restrictive (institution). If you consider the placement options as they move from the regular class to institutions, you will notice that the options get progressively more restrictive and provide for less access to typically developing peers or activities until there is essentially no opportunity for contact or participation. Even so, remember that according to §300.114 (Least Restrictive Environment), states are required to ensure that all children with disabilities, including children educated in institutions, are educated in the regular education environment to the maximum extent appropriate. So, if a district placed a child in a residential treatment facility in another state, that facility must provide service aligned with the LRE mandate. This can be a difficult balancing act, but the requirements emphasize the importance afforded the LRE, the constitutional foundation upon which it is built, and recognize the real possibility that civil liberties may be violated via improper programming or restriction of rights to associate.

Earlier, we had mentioned that some people claim that there are different Least Restrictive Environments for different children, but we contend that such a view tends to confuse LRE with placement along the continuum. The regulations do not identify a continuum of LREs, rather they contain a section called the Continuum of Alternative Placements which lists placements from the LRE (regular classroom) to the most restrictive (institutions). As previously noted, if children with disabilities are removed from the regular education environment, then they must be moved to the placement that will provide FAPE while having minimum impact on their access to typically developing peers, i.e., placement must comply with the LRA requirement. So, when a child is removed from the LRE, he or she must be placed in the Least Restrictive Placement along the continuum that will allow for the provision of FAPE.

The practice of calling a segregated placement the LRE for a particular child is not an accurate portrayal. If, for example, you have ever visited a residential psychiatric facility, you likely noticed that the setting was very restrictive and not typical of an environment where you would find a typically developing child. We are not implying that psychiatric hospitalization may not be necessary for a particular child, rather we are saying that it should not be considered the child's LRE. In fact, a psychiatric setting is a very restrictive environment. The LRE for that child is still the regular education classroom, but the hospitalization may represent the *least restrictive placement* along the continuum in which the child can receive FAPE at that time. Still the ultimate goal is to provide the supports necessary to ensure that the child will receive FAPE in the regular education setting and not keep the child in what some consider his LRE, a psychiatric hospital.

Labeling different placements as "the LRE" for a particular child may predispose the IEP team to the illegal and indefensible prospect of predetermining placement for a child before the IEP is even completed (Hyatt & Filler, 2011). As you will see in regulatory language yet to be provided, the placement determination is based on the child's IEP. That means that the team must have identified the goals, objectives, related services, and considered any supplementary aids and services that will allow the child to be educated in the regular education setting. This requirement is true even for children who are in segregated placements when the IEP is written. The regular education placement is the presumed placement and the IEP team must begin developing an IEP with the assumption that the child will be educated in the regular education setting, because IEPs are written to reflect a child's needs not a particular placement. Only if the needs cannot be met in the regular education setting can an alternative placement be considered. Predetermination continues to happen in IEP meetings, and Courts may find that a school's predetermination of placement resulted in denial of FAPE, because it could indicate a denial of parents' right to participation (*Spielberg v. Henrico County Pub. Sch., 1988*).

You will likely encounter IEP meetings in which participants approach the development of the IEP by trying to describe why a child should not be in the regular education setting. You will know that is happening when you hear phrases, such as, "we can't do that in the classroom" or "he needs to go to ..." before or during the development of goals and objectives. Instead of continuing with similar statements, you could help ensure compliance with LRE by refocusing the IEP team to change the line of reasoning with questions such as, "What supports can be provided in the classroom or to the teacher that will enable Emily to meet this goal in the regular education setting?" This second line of inquiry is clearly in line with the congressional presumption that children with disabilities will be educated in the regular setting and the requirement that IEP teams seriously consider provision of what ancillary supports and services can be provided to enable the child to succeed in the regular education environment.

While there is a strong legal presumption favoring placement in the regular education setting, nothing in the law requires that an IEP team place a child in the regular education setting and be allowed to fail before considering a more restrictive placement. However, the IEP team must have seriously considered options to keep the child in the regular education setting before moving to a restrictive placement. Neither does the law require that a child's placement move along the continuum in a step-by-step manner, with the child demonstrating a lack of benefit in successively restrictive placements. For example, if a child had AIDS and her immune system was compromised and she could easily catch any virus in the regular

The authors have been in IEP meetings where the condition section on an objective began with the statement, "In the special education classroom." That statement clearly indicates a predetermined placement. When challenged, the school personnel stated that the computerized IEP form required that the field be completed. They ultimately found a way to remove that terminology, but this experience just demonstrates that bad habits exist in the field and you may need to work with the team to ensure that placement decisions are not predetermined, but are made after the IEP is fully developed. Decisions regarding the placement should reflect not only the need to meet goals and objectives in a timely fashion, but should also reflect an awareness of the educational value of having needs met in the general education setting. Most would agree that accessing the general education curriculum is an easier task to accomplish when the attempt to do so is made in the general education setting.

education classroom, her placement would likely be in a hospital setting (moving directly from regular education classroom to the most restrictive placement along the continuum). However, she would be placed back in the regular education setting as soon as her health allowed. She would not have to move back down the continuum from hospital, to special school, to special class, etc.

The last paragraph (b)(2) of §300.115 (Continuum of Alternative Placement) provides clear guidance that the IEP team consider supplementary aids and services that can be used in conjunction with the regular education setting to keep the child in the LRE. For those of you who have some familiarity with special education, it may be surprising to learn that the regulations allow a resource room to be considered a supplementary aid or service rather than a placement along the continuum. The term "resource room" typically refers to a traditional pull-out, special class that children with disabilities attend for specialized instruction, and in such case, that would represent a movement along the continuum and a more restrictive placement. If the resource room was a service rather than a placement, it could be presented as an option, such as a place to take an exam if a longer time was allowed for test taking or if a quiet setting was required. It may also be a place where a student could go to calm down if upset. In those cases, it is used to support the student in the regular class and not as a primary instructional environment as if it was a placement.

Placement Determination (§300.116)

The next section of the LRE provision provides guidance regarding placement determinations. We have already alluded to parts of the following section, so our remaining discussion of this section will be relatively brief.

§300.116 Placements.

In determining the educational placement of a child with a disability, including a preschool child with a disability, each public agency must ensure that—

(a) The placement decision—

(1) Is made by a group of persons, including the parents, and other persons knowledgeable about the child, the meaning of the evaluation data, and the placement options; and
(2) Is made in conformity with the LRE provisions of this subpart, including §§300.114 through 300.118; (b) The child's placement—

(1) Is determined at least annually;

(2) Is based on the child's IEP; and

(3) Is as close as possible to the child's home;

(c) Unless the IEP of a child with a disability requires some other arrangement, the child is educated in the school that he or she would attend if nondisabled;

(d) In selecting the LRE, consideration is given to any potential harmful effect on the child or on the quality of services that he or she needs; and

(e) A child with a disability is not removed from education in age appropriate regular classrooms solely because of needed modifications in the regular education curriculum.

As required by the regulations, the placement decision (where along the continuum of alternative placements the child will receive service) must be made on an annual basis, include parental input, and be based on the IEP. This provides the regulatory support to our prior statements that the decision must be made at the end of the annual IEP, that is, after all the goals and objectives are written and the IEP team has considered what supplementary aids and services might be provided to allow the child to benefit from placement in the regular education setting. The requirement that parents be fully informed and involved in the decision should prevent the school IEP team from predetermining placement based on label.

In spite of these long-standing regulations, the authors have consulted with numerous parents who were provided with completed IEPs that included segregated placements for their children at the very beginning of the IEP meeting before a meaningful discussion with parents was even attempted. This was clearly an illegal practice by school staff and often required a considerable amount of effort on the part of the parents to remediate. This is but one type of school practice that can seriously undermine the relationship between parents and the school resulting in IEP meetings that have more of an adversarial than cooperative atmosphere. Fortunately, this isn't the case in all IEP meetings—many schools implement exemplary practice in which teachers and others advocate for children with disabilities and comply with the legal requirements in the law. We are confident that anyone reading this text would want the school to follow the law when working with their children.

The regulations also indicate a preference that the placement should be as close to the child's home as possible and in the school he or she would attend if nondisabled. However, this requirement does not reach the same level of scrutiny as an LRE placement (Yell, 2006). In fact, the regulations provide some recognition that if a child required a special class or special school placement, that the physical location may not be the neighborhood school. However, if the child was moved from his or her home school to a different school to meet special education needs, it should be the closest program to the child's home.

Recently one author received a call from a parent whose child had Down syndrome and would be transitioning from kindergarten to first grade. Upon arrival to the IEP meeting, she was presented with a completed IEP that identified the child's placement in a self-contained classroom at a school other than the neighborhood school. This parent appealed to the principal with no luck and only reached a resolution once she met with the superintendent and stated that she planned to file for a due process hearing. The district did concede their error, reconvened the IEP meeting, developed it with the parent, and placed the child in the regular education first grade classroom with supplementary aids and services.

In another case, when one of the authors worked at a public school, he was approached by a district representative who requested to attend an IEP meeting for a young child with a vision impairment. The representative wanted to move the child from the regular classroom at his neighborhood school to a self-contained classroom at a school several miles away. When asked the reason for the proposal, the representative, who did not know the student and was not involved in his education in any way, stated that they had specialized equipment at the special school and full-time teachers. He was reminded that any necessary equipment could be located on the current campus, that the child was benefitting from his current placement, and that the school also had full-time teachers. The district representative was not invited to the IEP meeting. A short time later, what appeared to be the likely reason for the suggested placement of this child in a self-contained classroom became apparent. The self-contained program the district representative wanted to place the child in had a full-time teacher, full-time assistant, three students, and needed additional students to keep from being consolidated with other programs. In this case it appeared that the administrative needs of the district nearly took precedence over the requirement to educate in the LRE.

The notes accompanying the regulations do recognize that children with hearing impairments, in particular, should be afforded an opportunity to be placed in settings where they can communicate with other peers with hearing impairments. Paragraphs (c)–(e) of §300.116 (Placements) are relatively straightforward. Similar to the assumption that the child will be educated in the regular education setting, paragraph (c) recognizes that, barring some other arrangement, the child would attend the same school as if he or she did not have a disability. This provides some flexibility in school attendance that may be important, especially if the district provides options such as magnet schools or charter schools. Rather than requiring the child to attend the neighborhood school, the child could also attend those schools. It also reinforces the presumption that the child will be educated on a regular education campus as opposed to a special school or institution.

Paragraph (d) requires the consideration of potential harmful effects of placement in different settings. That is an important requirement, especially when considering moving a student to a more restrictive setting where there may be a disconnect from the regular education curriculum, a lack of access to typically developing peers, lack of role models, and stigmatization, just to list a few drawbacks to segregated placement. That, however, does not mean that the regular education classroom may not have negative impacts without the use of appropriate supports and training. A child can be segregated and excluded in a regular education classroom, so appropriate interventions and academic supports must be provided to facilitate successful inclusive programming. This should not be read to imply that a child should be moved because he or she might be teased, a commonly expressed concern. If teasing is an issue, there are more effective ways to deal with the issue than segregating the victim. The teacher and school have the responsibility of setting an accepting tone in the school, and can minimize teasing and provide instruction on how to deal with teasing. Finally, paragraph (e) simply prohibits removing a child from a chronologically age-appropriate classroom solely due to the need for modifications to the regular education curriculum.

There are four remaining regulatory portions on the LRE section of the regulations, §300.117 through §300.120. We won't provide you with the regulatory language for §300.118, §300.119 or §300.120 because those sections provide directions to states and don't directly impact the IEP process. However, we will provide a summarization of those duties required of the states detailed in these sections. Please note that the language regarding the state duties specifically references the first section of the regulatory LRE language, §300.114, which clearly specified that students with disabilities should be educated in the regular education setting with the use of supplementary aids and supports and that any removal from the regular education setting could only happen if the child's needs could not be met with the use of supplementary aids and services.

The simple fact that the regulations contain three separate sections specifically addressing implementation of §300.114 lends considerable credence to the importance Congress placed on the LRE provision of the law. The regulations at §300.118 specify that states are responsible for ensuring LRE provisions in §300.114 are made available for students placed in public or private institutions, except those incarcerated in adult prisons. Section 300.119 requires that states provide training to ensure that all teachers and administrators in public agencies are aware of their responsibilities for complying with §300.114. Finally, Section §300.120 requires that states develop monitoring procedures to ensure that the requirements of §300.114 are implemented correctly.

Section 300.117 (Nonacademic Settings) does have direct applicability to IEP teams, however. As stated in the regulatory language to be provided following this paragraph, it extends the responsibility for ensuring access to the regular education classroom to nonacademic times and extracurricular activities. Consider the numerous after-hours extracurricular activities carried on at preschool and elementary schools, such as talent shows, bike safety demonstrations, or carnivals and note that the school must ensure that the supports needed to ensure that the child participate in those activities are provided. We will discuss issues commonly encountered in secondary schools in Chapter 7. But we stress that schools must ensure that students with disabilities are afforded equitable access and not discriminated against or prohibited from participation solely on the basis of disability.

§300.117 Nonacademic settings.

In providing or arranging for the provision of nonacademic and extracurricular services and activities, including meals, recess periods, and the services and activities set forth in §300.107, each public agency must ensure that each child with a disability participates with nondisabled children in the extracurricular services and activities to the maximum extent appropriate to the needs of that child. The public agency must ensure that each child with a disability has the supplementary aids and services determined by the child's IEP Team to be appropriate and necessary for the child to participate in nonacademic settings.

Summary of LRE Regulations

The actual definition of LRE continues to be a source of controversy. We have presented a case for considering the LRE as the regular education environment and acknowledged that others have maintained that there are different LREs for different children. A possible unintended consequence of considering a restrictive placement to be a child's LRE is that IEP teams may inadvertently begin an IEP with an incorrect and legally erroneous assumption, that the child who is currently in a segregated setting will continue to be educated in that setting because it has already been determined to be his or her LRE, rather than beginning the IEP with the required presumption of regular class placement and justifying any removal based on §300.114. Regardless of which view you hold, treating the regular education setting (which could include community settings) as the presumed placement at every IEP meeting and recognizing that any movement away from that setting represents a

One of the authors worked as a school psychologist at an elementary school that housed self-contained programs for students with behavioral problems. The principal had attempted to keep students in those programs from going to lunch and recess with typically developing peers simply because they might have some behavioral problems—as if none of the students without disabilities ever had behavioral problems at recess time. This practice was clearly in direct conflict with the regulations and could be seen as a violation of the civil rights—the children were being discriminated against solely on the basis of disability (this is an example of the intersection of Section 504 discussed in chapter 1 and IDEA). When the issue was discussed and the principal assured that any disciplinary issues would be dealt with accordingly, she changed her position.

more restrictive placement because it limits the child's access to typically developing peers and activities will help you live up to the intent of the law. This understanding represents a basic familiarity with the core concept behind LRE, and that any infringement upon individual liberty for the provision of FAPE must be the Least Restrictive Alternative that would result in meaningful educational benefit.

In essence, the IEP team must begin with the assumption that the child will be educated in the regular education environment, including both academic and nonacademic classes as well as extracurricular activities. The team must consider what supports and services can be provided to keep the child in the general education environment. The regular class may not be the appropriate placement for all children, but removal must be justified and based upon the inability to meet the child's IEP goals and objectives in the regular education environment, so the placement decision can only be made at the end of the IEP. In Chapter 3, we discussed Prior Written Notice and want to remind you that if the IEP team changes the placement of a child, the parent must be provided PWN (even though the parent was at the IEP meeting where the placement decision was made). In the next section, we briefly review some prominent court decisions regarding LRE.

Key Circuit Court Decisions on LRE

Since LRE has been a source of controversy, it was inevitable that the controversy would find its way to the courts. The U. S. Supreme Court has not heard an LRE case, but there are important guiding decisions from four Circuit Courts that provide judicial standards that must be followed in the states constituting their respective jurisdictions. Absent a Supreme Court decision, this group of Circuit Court decisions represents the guiding authority and will likely provide considerable precedent should an LRE case be considered in other courts. We offer a brief review of the cases and the considerations the courts provided when making decisions regarding the LRE standard. There are still Circuit Courts that have not officially adopted a standard or test for use when LRE decisions are challenged, so we encourage you to inquire within your district to determine which standard it is employing. Following is a brief review of the four Circuit Court Decisions regarding LRE that provided the following four tests: 1) Roncker Portability Test, 2) Daniel Two-Part Test, 3) The Rachel H. Four Factor Test, and 4) The Hartmann Three-Part Test. We encourage you to read the Court decisions for yourself as they are very informative and provide factual information regarding the cases that we don't include in our synopses. Through the previous review of the regulations and summaries of the following court decisions, you will have insights into how the LRE provision has been applied, and your understandings will assist you in helping the IEP team comply with the LRE provision.

Roncker Portability Test

One of the earliest decisions that dealt with LRE, *Roncker v. Walter* (1983), was decided by the Sixth Circuit Court of Appeals. **http://openjurist.org/700/f2d/1058/roncker-roncker-v-b-walter-n** This case involved Neill Roncker, a 9 year-old student identified as having mental retardation. The district wanted to place Neill in a special school. The parents disagreed and wanted him educated in a special education classroom at a regular school where he would have opportunities for integrated activities with peers without disabilities. The Circuit Court ruled in favor of the parents and stated:

> In a case where the segregated facility is considered superior, the court should determine whether the services which make the placement superior could feasibly be provided in a nonsegregated setting. If they can, the placement in the segregated school would be inappropriate under the Act. (Roncker, p. 1063).

The Roncker case was really not about regular classroom placement, but about whether placement in a segregated school setting was necessary to provide FAPE. The Court developed a two-part test, commonly referred to as the Portability Test, to assist in making the decision. An affirmative answer to the first question would require the district to make necessary modifications and provide the services in a nonsegregated setting. The two-part test follows:

(1)   Can the educational services that make a segregated placement superior be feasibly provided in an unsegregated setting?

(2)   If so, the placement in the segregated setting is inappropriate.

Daniel Two-Part Test

Daniel R. R. v. State Board of Education, the second major LRE case, was decided by the Fifth Circuit in 1989. The case involved Daniel, a 6 year-old student with a disability who was placed half day in regular pre-kindergarten and half day in an early childhood special education class. Daniel's pre-k teacher reported that he was not participating in class, was failing to master any skills taught, and required almost constant teacher attention. The district claimed that Daniel was not receiving meaningful educational benefit and his presence was detrimental to the other children, because he required an inordinate amount of teacher time. He was removed from the pre-kindergarten class and attended only the early childhood special education class with opportunities to integrate with typically developing peers during lunch and recess. Parents challenged the district's change in placement and the Circuit Court ruled in favor of the school.

The Fifth Circuit Court considered the Roncker test to be excessively intrusive into the practice of local school districts and decided to use the statutory language in the LRE requirements to develop a test evaluating school compliance with the LRE mandate. The Court reasoned that the appropriate test was to determine if the school followed the statutory requirements (Yell, 2006). The two questions in the Daniel Two-Part Test are:

(1) Can education in the general education classroom with supplementary aids and services be achieved satisfactorily?

(2) If a student is placed in a more restrictive setting, is the student integrated to the maximum extent appropriate?

If the school complies with both parts of the test, then the district has satisfied the LRE mandate. **http://openjurist.org/874/f2d/1036/daniel-rr-v-state-board-of-education** The Daniel Two-Part Test was subsequently adopted by the Third and Eleventh Circuit Courts (Yell, 2006).

The Rachel H. Four Factor Test

Sacramento City School District v. Rachel H. (1994) was a Ninth Circuit Court decision that provided guidance on placement in regular education settings. Rachel was a 9 year-old girl who attended Sacramento City Schools. The district proposed placing her in a self-contained program with opportunities for integration in nonacademic activities and the parents challenged the placement requesting that she be educated in the regular education setting. The district refused, so the parents placed her in a private school and challenged the district's decision. (This was an interesting case considering that the district lost at the due process level, at district court level, at the Circuit Court level, and was denied a review by the U. S. Supreme Court. The State of California even submitted a brief on behalf of the Hollands; yet, for some reason, the district spent a considerable amount of money trying to defend the segregated placement.) The District Court developed a Four Factor Test (Holland Standard) for determining whether regular education placement or special education placement was the appropriate setting. Upon appeal by the district, the Ninth Circuit Court adopted The Holland Standard which includes the following considerations:

(1) The educational benefits of placement in the regular class;

(2) The nonacademic benefits of such placement;

(3) The effect of the student's presence on the teacher and on other students in the classroom.

(4) The cost of mainstreaming.

The court found that Rachel received educational benefit in regular class placement. In fact, during court testimony, the teacher from the private school indicated that Rachel received both academic and nonacademic benefit from placement in the regular education class. The Court also found that Rachel's presence did not have a detrimental impact on the teacher or other students, and Sacramento was unable to convince the Court that the cost of including Rachel in the regular education classroom was prohibitive. **http:// openjurist.org/14/f3d/1398/sacramento-city-unified-school-district-board-of-education-v-rachel-h-holland** In *Clyde K. v. Puyallup* (1994), the Ninth Circuit Court used the Holland Standard and sided with the district by ruling that the regular education setting was not the appropriate placement for a child because he was not receiving a meaningful education despite the significant behavioral supports that the district had provided. **http://openjurist.org/35/f3d/1396/ clyde-v-puyallup-school-district-no-clyde-k**

The Hartmann Three-Part Test

In 1997, the Fourth Circuit Court, which had previously applied the Roncker standard, developed a Three-Part Test in *Hartmann v. Loudoun County Board of Education*. Mark Hartmann was an 11 year-old student with a disability who was in the regular education classroom and received a considerable amount of support including: a full-time aide, specialized training for the teacher and assistant, speech therapy, in-service training for the entire school staff, and behavioral supports. Despite these supports, he exhibited aggressive behavior, and the IEP team determined that he was not benefitting from placement in the regular classroom setting and decided to move him to a self-contained special education class. The parents disagreed with the IEP and challenged the placement decision. (These cases often seem so simple, but for information sake, in this case, the parents challenged the IEP and lost at the Due Process hearing. They subsequently filed an appeal with the District Court which overruled the Due Process hearing officer's decisions and ruled for the parents. The District Court decision was appealed by the school district to the Fourth Circuit Court and the ruling of the District Court was overruled which resulted in a finding supporting the school district.) **http://openjurist. org/118/f3d/996/hartmann-hartmann-v-loudoun-county-board-of-education-b**

The Hartmann Three-Factor Test consists of the following considerations:
Mainstreaming not required when:

(1) A student with a disability would not receive educational benefit from mainstreaming in a general education class.

(2) Any marginal benefit from mainstreaming would be significantly outweighed by benefits that could feasibly be obtained only in a separate instructional setting.

(3) The student is a disruptive force in the general education classroom.

LRE Issues for Preschool, ESY, and Secondary Students

In this concluding section on LRE, there are three remaining issues to address: contrasting Part C with Part B requirements, LRE for preschool children, and ESY. As noted in Chapter 3, Part C does not contain an LRE provision; rather it requires that services be included in "natural environments" to the maximum extent and defined "natural environments" to include the home and other settings where you would find the typically developing peer infants and toddlers. We mention this because parents of children transitioning from Part C to Part B services may not have a thorough understanding of the difference and school staff may be required to assist parents in understanding the different requirements. Since the IFSP requires a transition plan, it is reasonable to expect that such preparation has (or will) occur prior to the actual movement from a Part C program. This leads directly to the issue of providing services to preschool children with disabilities. The regulations require that the continuum of services be available to preschool children; however, if a school does not provide preschool services to children without disabilities, the district is not required to develop new programming to comply with the LRE requirement. Rather, the district can find other options to provide preschool children with services with typically developing peers (Letter to Grether, 1994). For example, schools could contract with Head Start or community-based preschools and provide special education services in those settings. If a preschool is offered by a religious organization, then state law must be referenced to determine if provision of services on sectarian property is allowable.

As discussed in Chapter 3, Extended School Year or ESY is a continuation of the provision of special education services beyond the typical school calendar, whether that be longer instructional days, instruction on weekends, or additional instructional days during breaks and vacations. The decision of whether to provide ESY is the responsibility of the IEP team and that team must be familiar with state eligibility requirements for ESY. The determination is commonly based upon recoupment and regression of skills, but states have flexibility in determining the specific criteria that will be used to determine ESY eligibility (71 Fed. Reg. 46582, 2006). ESY is commonly offered during the summer, but is not the same as summer school; rather, it is a continuation of the special education services provided at no cost to the parents. LRE requirements may still apply for ESY, but if a district does not offer summer school programs or other extended programs to students without disabilities, it is not required to start new programs in order to meet the LRE requirements (San Francisco Unified School District, 2009). The district could meet the LRE requirements through alternative means when it is determined that the child must have interactions with typically developing peers (Letter to Myers, 1989).

So, while the application of LRE may be somewhat different for preschool children and those receiving ESY service, the only option a district has for disregarding the LRE mandate is for students incarcerated in adult prisons. We have spent a considerable amount of time on issues related to LRE and believe that time was warranted, because it impacts a child's First Amendment rights to freedom of association and any restriction automatically invokes the due protection clause (Turnbull et al., 2007). As will be further discussed in Chapter 7, the LRE issue for older students may presuppose that those students who are receiving educational services in community settings should be receiving those services in typical settings. In other words, LRE would support a student receiving vocational training at a local business that employs typically developing adults rather than at a sheltered workshop or small group that consists only of individuals with disabilities.

Chapter Summary

LRE is a particularly important issue in special education and including children in the general education classroom is second only to FAPE. If a child requires a more restrictive placement to receive FAPE, then the team can make that justification. However, the team should seriously consider what supports can be provided in the regular education setting to facilitate the child's education. An often quoted statement by Judge Gerry in the District Court decision in *Oberti I* (1992) that "Inclusion is a right not a privilege for a select few" represents an important value statement based in legal principles. Most parents want their children to be valued and included members of the school and larger community. So having the same goal for children with disabilities in the school setting is consistent with the desires that parents of children without disabilities have for their children. It does not represent a different standard, rather challenges schools to develop different approaches based on the unique needs of the child.

The court decisions we reviewed did not always rule in favor of inclusive placements. We encourage you read those cases and consider the facts presented. There are a couple of important comments to make regarding the findings. First, Lake and Norlin (2006) recognized that even though cost has been a consideration taken up by the courts, it has not been found to be a factor precluding placement in the regular education classroom. In Sacramento v. Holland, the Circuit Court strongly rejected the district's contention that providing support was too expensive.

The cases and tests reviewed also included a consideration of disruptive behavior as a condition for removal from the regular education setting and placed in a more restrictive setting. Except for special cases that will be discussed in the disciplinary section, the change in placement due to behavior is not simply finding that a child is disruptive and using that as a justification for removal. It is incumbent upon the school and IEP team to have developed a plan to address the behaviors of concern. If a child requires behavioral supports, then it is reasonable to expect that the IEP contain behavioral goals and objectives and possibly a behavior support plan. (We will briefly discuss behavior support plans later.)

Chapter Activities

1. Review an IEP and separately apply each of the four tests (Roncker, Daniel R.R., Holland, and Hartmann). Using the guidance provided by the courts, did the IEP team decision comply with each of the tests, or did you notice a difference among the outcome when applying each of the tests?

2. Find the standard, if any, that is followed in your state. How might you incorporate that legal requirement in the IEP process?

3. Conduct an internet search to find inclusion resources.

4. Brainstorm how you might select materials for your classroom that support inclusive values; consider items such as books and action figures that include people with disabilities.

5. Consider the curriculum, school-wide disciplinary practices, school motto, etc., and describe how you might develop a school that supports inclusive practices.

6. Read the following article describing how a school proceeded through the process of becoming an inclusive setting. If your school hasn't adopted an inclusive model yet, would the process described in this article support that change? **http://journals.cec .sped.org/tecplus/vol1/iss3/art2/**

Chapter 6

© Constantin Stanciu/Shutterstock.com

Disciplinary Issues, Harassment, and Bullying

Chapter Overview

We approach the topics of this chapter a bit differently than we did when discussing other aspects of the IEP. First, the IEP team is not involved in all disciplinary procedures, but it is important that the team understands the procedures as well as its responsibilities in order to make informed decisions when required. For example, involvement of the IEP team is not needed for suspensions of 10 or fewer days during a school year, but the IEP team is involved in disciplinary actions that result in a change of placement. So we will spend a considerable amount of time describing or clarifying the procedures required by the regulations and explaining the role of the IEP team. Second, while conducting a Functional Behavioral Assessment (FBA) or developing a Behavior Intervention Plan (BIP), as required by the regulations under certain conditions, the specific actions or components required of each are not specified in the regulations. (As a side note, when searching the literature, you may find the BIP referred to by other names, such as Positive Behavior Support Plan, but we will use BIP as it is the term used in the regulations.) There are several different models for conducting quality FBAs and developing BIPs. Instead of trying to teach you how to use a particular model, we will outline a general approach with the underlying assumption that conducting meaningful FBAs and developing effective BIPs requires a greater understanding of behavioral and instructional principles than we could provide in this chapter. In fact, there are entire books written on the topics and we will provide references to those sources. In essence, this chapter will be focused on providing you with necessary information regarding disciplinary requirements that will enable you to fulfill the duties of an informed IEP team member, provide you with information necessary to prevent you from inadvertently infringing on a child's rights, and provide you with a very basic understanding of an FBA and a BIP. Following our discussion of disciplinary issues, we will differentiate between disability based bullying. Both can significantly impact the well-being of victims, and schools must respond in a responsible manner to continue to contain these potential threats to the civil rights of students who are being harassed, bullied, or both.

Background Information: Discipline

Since children with disabilities were routinely excluded from schools and denied access to educational opportunities, the initial special education law (P.L. 94-142) provided them with certain safeguards that were not available to other children. The initial legislation, however, did not contain guidance regarding disciplinary actions. In their 1988 decision in *Honig v. Doe*, **http://laws.findlaw.com/us/484/305.html** the U. S. Supreme Court issued a ruling on disciplinary procedures as applied to children with disabilities who exhibited dangerous or violent behavior. The Honig ruling made clear that students with disabilities can be disciplined, but the school must ensure that the specific rights identified in *Goss v. Lopez* (1975) **http://laws.findlaw.com/us/419/565.html** be afforded to children with disabilities and that districts comply with the procedural requirements of IDEA. In *Goss v. Lopez*, the U. S. Supreme Court recognized that compulsory attendance laws resulted in education being considered a property right. Therefore, it is protected by the 14th Amendment which effectively prohibits a state from depriving an individual of property rights without providing due process of law. For short-term suspensions (10 days or less), the court noted that the due process rights that must be afforded a student are relatively minor and consist of three items: 1) a student must receive oral or written notice of the charges, 2) the student must be provided an explanation of the reasons for the suspension, and 3) the student must be provided an opportunity to present his or her side of the case. In *Honig v. Doe*, the Court reaffirmed the applicability of this decision to all students and also noted that the 10 day removal would allow districts an opportunity to work with parents to change the placement of a child with a disability or, alternatively, seek assistance from the courts to order an alternative placement if needed to ensure safety.

In Honig, the district argued that Congress had not intended to limit the ability of school districts to exclude students. The Supreme Court contradicted the school district's claim and recognized that the Congressional intent was to strip districts of their power to unilaterally exclude students with disabilities from school, but not at the expense of providing safe school environments conducive to learning (Yell, 2006).

The regulatory language specifically related to disciplinary procedures is contained in Table 6-1. As you read the regulations, you will note there is considerable cross-referencing which requires that you consult different sections to ensure disciplinary actions are aligned with the regulations. If you will read the regulatory language before proceeding in this chapter, you will be better prepared for the discussion to follow. As the regulations can appear somewhat convoluted and confusing, we also encourage you to refer back to Table 6-1 as you read the following text.

TABLE 6-1. Discipline Procedures

§ 300.530 Authority of school personnel
(a) Case-by-case determination. School personnel may consider any unique circumstances on a case-by-case basis when determining whether a change in placement, consistent with the other requirements of this section, is appropriate for a child with a disability who violates a code of student conduct.
(b) General. (1) School personnel under this section may remove a child with a disability who violates a code of student conduct from his or her current placement to an appropriate interim alternative educational setting, another setting, or suspension, for not more than 10 consecutive school days (to the extent those alternatives are applied to children without disabilities), and for additional removals of not more than 10 consecutive school days in that same school year for separate incidents of misconduct (as long as those removals do not constitute a change of placement under § 300.536).
(2) After a child with a disability has been removed from his or her current placement for 10 school days in the same school year, during any subsequent days of removal the public agency must provide services to the extent required under paragraph (d) of this section.
(c) Additional authority. For disciplinary changes in placement that would exceed 10 consecutive school days, if the behavior that gave rise to the violation of the school code is determined not to be a manifestation of the child's disability pursuant to paragraph (e) of this section, school personnel may apply the relevant disciplinary procedures to children with disabilities in the same manner and for the same duration as the procedures would be applied to children without disabilities, except as provided in paragraph (d) of this section.
(d) Services. (1) A child with a disability who is removed from the child's current placement pursuant to paragraphs (c), or (g) of this section must—
(i) Continue to receive educational services, as provided in § 300.101
(a), so as to enable the child to continue to participate in the general education curriculum, although in another setting, and to progress toward meeting the goals set out in the child's IEP; and
(ii) Receive, as appropriate, a functional behavioral assessment, and behavioral intervention services and modifications, that are designed to address the behavior violation so that it does not recur.
(2) The services required by paragraph (d)(1), (d)(3), (d)(4), and (d)(5) of this section may be provided in an interim alternative educational setting.
(3) A public agency is only required to provide services during periods of removal to a child with a disability who has been removed from his or her current placement for 10 school days or less in that school year, if it provides services to a child without disabilities who is similarly removed.
(4) After a child with a disability has been removed from his or her current placement for 10 school days in the same school year, if the current removal is for not more than 10 consecutive school days and is not a change of placement under § 300.536, school personnel, in consultation with at least one of the child's teachers, determine the extent to which services are needed, as provided in § 300.101(a), so as to enable the child to continue to participate in the general education curriculum, although in another setting, and to progress toward meeting the goals set out in the child's IEP.

continued

§ 300.530 Authority of school personnel
(5) If the removal is a change of placement under § 300.536, the child's IEP Team determines appropriate services under paragraph (d)(1) of this section.
(e) Manifestation determination. (1) Within 10 school days of any decision to change the placement of a child with a disability because of a violation of a code of student conduct, the LEA, the parent, and relevant members of the child's IEP Team (as determined by the parent and the LEA) must review all relevant information in the student's file, including the child's IEP, any teacher observations, and any relevant information provided by the parents to determine— (i) If the conduct in question was caused by, or had a direct and substantial relationship to, the child's disability; or (ii) If the conduct in question was the direct result of the LEA's failure to implement the IEP. (2) The conduct must be determined to be a manifestation of the child's disability if the LEA, the parent, and relevant members of the child's IEP Team determine that a condition in either paragraph (e)(1)(i) or (1)(ii) of this section was met. (3) If the LEA, the parent, and relevant members of the child's IEP Team determine the condition described in paragraph (e)(1)(ii) of this section was met, the LEA must take immediate steps to remedy those deficiencies.
(f) Determination that behavior was a manifestation. If the LEA, the parent, and relevant members of the IEP Team make the determination that the conduct was a manifestation of the child's disability, the IEP Team must— (1) Either — (i) Conduct a functional behavioral assessment, unless the LEA had conducted a functional behavioral assessment before the behavior that resulted in the change of placement occurred, and implement a behavioral intervention plan for the child; or (ii) If a behavioral intervention plan already has been developed, review the behavioral intervention plan, and modify it, as necessary, to address the behavior; and (2) Except as provided in paragraph (g) of this section, return the child to the placement from which the child was removed, unless the parent and the LEA agree to a change of placement as part of the modification of the behavioral intervention plan.
(g) Special circumstances. School personnel may remove a student to an interim alternative educational setting for not more than 45 school days without regard to whether the behavior is determined to be a manifestation of the child's disability, if the child— (1) Carries a weapon to or possesses a weapon at school, on school premises, or to or at a school function under the jurisdiction of an SEA or an LEA; (2) Knowingly possesses or uses illegal drugs, or sells or solicits the sale of a controlled substance, while at school, on school premises, or at a school function under the jurisdiction of an SEA or an LEA; or (3) Has inflicted serious bodily injury upon another person while at school, on school premises, or at a school function under the jurisdiction of an SEA or an LEA.
(h) Notification. On the date on which the decision is made to make a removal that constitutes a change of placement of a child with a disability because of a violation of a code of student conduct, the LEA must notify the parents of that decision, and provide the parents the procedural safeguards notice described in § 300.504. (i) Definitions. For purposes of this section, the following definitions apply: (1) Controlled substance means a drug or other substance identified under schedules I, II, III, IV, or V in section 202(c) of the Controlled Substances Act (21 U.S.C. 812(c)).

§ 300.530 Authority of school personnel
(2) Illegal drug means a controlled substance; but does not include a controlled substance that is legally possessed or used under the supervision of a licensed health-care professional or that is legally possessed or used under any other authority under that Act or under any other provision of Federal law.
(3) Serious bodily injury has the meaning given the term "serious bodily injury" under paragraph (3) of subsection (h) of section 1365 of title 18, United States Code.
(4) Weapon has the meaning given the term "dangerous weapon" under paragraph (2) of the first subsection (g) of section 930 of title 18, United States Code. (Authority: 20 U.S.C. 1415(k)(1) and (7))
§ 300.531 Determination of setting
The child's IEP Team determines the interim alternative educational setting for services under § 300.530(c), (d)(5), and (g).
§ 300.532 Appeal
(a) General. The parent of a child with a disability who disagrees with any decision regarding placement under §§ 300.530 and 300.531, or the manifestation determination under § 300.530(e), or an LEA that believes that maintaining the current placement of the child is substantially likely to result in injury to the child or others, may appeal the decision by requesting a hearing. The hearing is requested by filing a complaint pursuant to §§ 300.507 and 300.508(a) and (b).
(b) Authority of hearing officer. (1) A hearing officer under § 300.511 hears, and makes a determination regarding an appeal under paragraph (a) of this section.
(2) In making the determination under paragraph (b)(1) of this section, the hearing officer may—
(i) Return the child with a disability to the placement from which the child was removed if the hearing officer determines that the removal was a violation of § 300.530 or that the child's behavior was a manifestation of the child's disability; or
(ii) Order a change of placement of the child with a disability to an appropriate interim alternative educational setting for not more than 45 school days if the hearing officer determines that maintaining the current placement of the child is substantially likely to result in injury to the child or to others.
(3) The procedures under paragraphs (a) and (b)(1) and (2) of this section may be repeated, if the LEA believes that returning the child to the original placement is substantially likely to result in injury to the child or to others.
(c) Expedited due process hearing
(1) Whenever a hearing is requested under paragraph (a) of this section, the parents or the LEA involved in the dispute must have an opportunity for an impartial due process hearing consistent with the requirements of §§ 300.507 and 300.508(a) through (c) and §§ 300.510 through 300.514, except as provided in paragraph (c)(2) through (4) of this section.
(2) The SEA or LEA is responsible for arranging the expedited due process hearing, which must occur within 20 school days of the date the complaint requesting the hearing is filed. The hearing officer must make a determination within 10 school days after the hearing.
(3) Unless the parents and LEA agree in writing to waive the resolution meeting described in paragraph (c)(3)(i) of this section, or agree to use the mediation process described in § 300.506—
(i) A resolution meeting must occur within seven days of receiving notice of the due process complaint; and (ii) The due process hearing may proceed unless the matter has been resolved to the satisfaction of both parties within 15 days of the receipt of the due process complaint.

continued

§ 300.532 Appeal
(4) A State may establish different State-imposed procedural rules for expedited due process hearings conducted under this section than it has established for other due process hearings, but, except for the timelines as modified in paragraph (c)(3) of this section, the State must ensure that the requirements in §§ 300.510 through 300.514 are met.
(5) The decisions on expedited due process hearings are appealable consistent with § 300.514.
§ 300.533 Placement during appeals. When an appeal under § 300.532 has been made by either the parent or the LEA, the child must remain in the interim alternative educational setting pending the decision of the hearing officer or until the expiration of the time period specified in §A300.530(c) or (g), whichever occurs first, unless the parent and the SEA or LEA agree otherwise.
§ 300.534 Protections for children not determined eligible for special education and related services
(a) General. A child who has not been determined to be eligible for special education and related services under this part and who has engaged in behavior that violated a code of student conduct, may assert any of the protections provided for in this part if the public agency had knowledge (as determined in accordance with paragraph (b) of this section) that the child was a child with a disability before the behavior that precipitated the disciplinary action occurred.
(b) Basis of knowledge. A public agency must be deemed to have knowledge that a child is a child with a disability if before the behavior that precipitated the disciplinary action occurred—   (1) The parent of the child expressed concern in writing to supervisory or administrative personnel of the appropriate educational agency, or a teacher of the child, that the child is in need of special education and related services;   (2) The parent of the child requested an evaluation of the child pursuant to §§ 300.300 through 300.311; or   (3) The teacher of the child, or other personnel of the LEA, expressed specific concerns about a pattern of behavior demonstrated by the child directly to the director of special education of the agency or to other supervisory personnel of the agency.
(c) Exception. A public agency would not be deemed to have knowledge under paragraph (b) of this section if—   (1) The parent of the child—   (i) Has not allowed an evaluation of the child pursuant to §§ 300.300 through 300.311; or (ii) Has refused services under this part; or   (2) The child has been evaluated in accordance with §§ 300.300 through 300.311 and determined to not be a child with a disability under this part.
(d) Conditions that apply if no basis of knowledge.   (1) If a public agency does not have knowledge that a child is a child with a disability (in accordance with paragraphs (b) and (c) of this section) prior to taking disciplinary measures against the child, the child may be subject(c) Exception. A public agency would not be deemed to have knowledge under paragraph (b) of this section if—   (1) The parent of the child—   (i) Has not allowed an evaluation of the child pursuant to §§ 300.300 through 300.311; or   (ii) Has refused services under this part; or   (2) The child has been evaluated in accordance with §§ 300.300 through 300.311 and determined to not be a child with a disability under this part.

§ 300.534 Protections for children not determined eligible for special education and related services
(d) Conditions that apply if no basis of knowledge.
(1) If a public agency does not have knowledge that a child is a child with a disability (in accordance with paragraphs (b) and (c) of this section) prior to taking disciplinary measures against the child, the child may be subjected to the disciplinary measures applied to children without disabilities who engage in comparable behaviors consistent with paragraph (d)(2) of this section.
(2)(i) If a request is made for an evaluation of a child during the time period in which the child is subjected to disciplinary measures under § 300.530, the evaluation must be conducted in an expedited manner.
(ii) Until the evaluation is completed, the child remains in the educational placement determined by school authorities, which can include suspension or expulsion without educational services.
(iii) If the child is determined to be a child with a disability, taking into consideration information from the evaluation conducted by the agency and information provided by the parents, the agency must provide special education and related services in accordance with this part, including the requirements of §§ 300.530 through 300.536 and section 612(a)(1)(A) of the Act.
§ 300.535 Referral to and action by law enforcement and judicial authorities
(a) Rule of construction. Nothing in this part prohibits an agency from reporting a crime committed by a child with a disability to appropriate authorities or prevents State law enforcement and judicial authorities from exercising their responsibilities with regard to the application of Federal and State law to crimes committed by a child with a disability.
(b) Transmittal of records.
(1) An agency reporting a crime committed by a child with a disability must ensure that copies of the special education and disciplinary records of the child are transmitted for consideration by the appropriate authorities to whom the agency reports the crime.
(2) An agency reporting a crime under this section may transmit copies of the child's special education and disciplinary records only to the extent that the transmission is permitted by the Family Educational Rights and Privacy Act.
§ 300.536 Change of placement because of disciplinary removals
(a) For purposes of removals of a child with a disability from the child's current educational placement under §§ 300.530 through 300.535, a change of placement occurs if—
(1) The removal is for more than 10 consecutive school days; or
(2) The child has been subjected to a series of removals that constitute a pattern—
(i) Because the series of removals total more than 10 school days in a school year;
(ii) Because the child's behavior is substantially similar to the child's behavior in previous incidents that resulted in the series of removals; and
(iii) Because of such additional factors as the length of each removal, the total amount of time the child has been removed, and the proximity of the removals to one another.
(b)(1) The public agency determines on a case-by-case basis whether a pattern of removals constitutes a change of placement.
(2) This determination is subject to review through due process and judicial proceedings.

A major issue that informs discipline of students with disabilities is whether there has been a change of placement as a result of disciplinary action. Remember from the chapter on LRE that placement refers to placement of the child's program along the continuum of alternative placements as opposed to location. Location is the physical surrounding, such as a specific classroom, unless a change in location is also deemed to be a substantial change in program (Fed. Reg. 71, 46588, 2006).

When determining the placement of students at the end of an IEP, the action is relatively easy to understand—if the child can't receive FAPE in the regular education setting with the us of supplementary aids and services, then the IEP team could justify removal to a more restrictive placement. However, determining whether a disciplinary removal has resulted in a change of placement can present more of a challenge. Zirkel (2006) and Kubick (2008) noted that the disciplinary procedures in IDEA have and continue to be controversial, often lacking specificity, which makes it even more important that school teams use a thoughtful, informed, and data-based decision-making process when dealing with disciplinary concerns.

Some of the lack of specificity is intentional to allow districts to determine on a case-by-case basis whether some removals constitute a change of placement (§300.530(a)). This decision can be a source of disagreement and under such conditions it is likely that some parents will challenge the disciplinary decisions of a school via the due process procedure (discussed in a later chapter). We mention this to point out that there could be disagreements, not to cause undue concern about due process hearings, but to note that the best thing that a school could do to try and avoid an unnecessary due process hearing is to follow the regulations and 1) develop appropriate IEPs, 2) implement all provisions on the IEP, 3) collect data and use it to inform actions to meet the goals and objectives in a timely fashion, and 4) work collaboratively and proactively with parents. Our goal here is to provide you with an overview of the disciplinary procedures that will be easy to follow and minimize the likelihood that you make procedural errors while increasing the likelihood that you will make decisions that benefit children requiring behavioral supports. To accomplish this goal, we will discuss salient aspects of the regulations presented in Table 6-1.

Short-Term Suspensions (10 days or less)

A student with a disability can be suspended or removed to an alternative placement for up to 10 days in a school year for a violation of the code of conduct (school rules), as long as that same consequence would be applied to students without disabilities. If the school does not provide educational services to children without disabilities during short-term suspensions or removals, then it would not be required to provide services to children with disabilities (during those first 10 days of suspension). The guiding condition is that the disciplinary procedures must not discriminate against students with disabilities. As long as the school is not discriminating against children with disabilities, the regulations do not require any special practice, and a suspension or removal of 10 days is not considered a change in placement, so it does not trigger procedural safeguards under IDEA. Please note that while an IEP is good for a calender year, the disciplinary guidelines refer to a school year.

In School Suspensions and Bus Suspension

The use of In School Suspension (ISS) is not specifically addressed in the regulatory language; however, it is mentioned in the notes accompanying the regulations. The Department of Education policy has been that ISS would not be considered short-term suspensions or removals specified in §300.530 as long as the child: 1) was afforded the opportunity to continue to appropriately participate in the general curriculum, 2) continued to receive the services specified in the IEP, and 3) continued to participate with nondisabled children to the same extent prior to the ISS. (Fed. Reg. 71, 46715, 2006). However, portions of a school day that a child is removed may still be considered as a removal if there is a pattern of removal. So, if a child was continually sent to ISS rather than allowed to attend math class, the case may be made that the pattern of removal from math class resulted in a change of placement thereby triggering specific safeguards.

Like ISS, bus suspension is not specifically mentioned in the regulations, but clarifying commentary is provided in the accompanying notes (Fed. Reg. 71, 46715, 2006). If bus transportation is included on a child's IEP because it is needed to ensure FAPE and the child is removed from the bus, effectively prohibiting school attendance, then that bus suspension would count as a disciplinary suspension. The only way the district could avoid having this count as a suspension would be to provide an alternate form of transportation, such as taxi, to and from school thereby enabling the child to continue his or her education in the current placement. If bus transportation is not included on the child's IEP, then the consequence of being suspended from the bus would be the same as it would be for any other child. In that case, it would be up to the child and his or her parents to arrange for alternate transportation, and any school missed would be counted as an absence but not as a day of suspension or removal.

However, if behavior on the bus is a concern, then the school would be wise to consider whether special education support should be provided on the bus, even if the child did not receive transportation as a related service. The IEP team should also remember that the LRE provision applies to transportation and the team should consider providing service on the regular bus rather than automatically removing a child to a "short bus."

Multiple Short-Term Suspensions (10 days or less)

As previously stated, the regulations allow for the removal of children with disabilities for 10 days in a school year without imposing any additional requirements on the school. The regulations (300.530(b)(1)) also permit additional suspensions for 10 days or less in a school year for separate incidents of misconduct without activating procedural safeguards, unless those additional removals constitute a change of placement as described in §300.536; we discuss guidelines regarding change of placement in the following section. However, beginning on day 11, the child must receive special education services regardless of whether the removal is considered a change of placement.

Change of Placement

A school can make a change of placement in several different ways, as discussed in this section (§300.536). Of course, a hearing officer or court could order a removal from the current placement if the district made a suitable case in a due process hearing, but we will focus on four options for removals conducted at the school level. Remember that a change of placement requires that the school provide the parent or guardian with PWN. If a change of placement is made for disciplinary issues, then the parents must also be provided a copy of the Procedural Safeguards. In addition, it may also require that an evaluation be conducted if a substantial change in placement is made, but that is determined on an individual basis (71 Fed. Reg. 46588, 2006).

A change of placement does require that the school authorities perform certain actions and follow a specific time line, so it is important that school personnel be familiar with their responsibilities, track disciplinary issues, and act accordingly. We will discuss school responsibilities following a change in placement in a later section of this chapter, but first we provide general guideline on when a change of placement occurs.

First, the parent/guardian and school could agree to change the child's placement through the IEP process. Based on information presented in previous chapters, you know that the IEP team can remove a child from his or her current placement to a more restrictive placement along the continuum if needed to provide FAPE. However, if a child is exhibiting behavioral difficulties, then the IEP team need not wait until the child has had a change of placement to review the IEP. In fact, it would be consistent with best practice and the intent of the law for the team to act proactively and try to remediate behavioral disruptions and support the child before considering a change of placement. The approach may include developing/reviewing behavioral goals and objectives, ensuring use of instructional strategies/materials that provide meaningful academic success, maintaining an environment conductive to learning, and actively promoting practices that recognize the importance of each individual by honoring differences and recognizing contributions. The IEP team could also conduct a Functional Behavioral Assessment (FBA) and develop a Behavior Intervention Plan (BIP) as a proactive approach to avoiding an escalation of problematic behavior by teaching the child acceptable alternative behaviors and supporting his or her success in the school setting before a BIP is legally required.

Second, if the child was removed from his or her current placement for more than 10 consecutive school days, that automatically constitutes a change in placement. The district must follow the appropriate procedures which include provision of education services that will allow the child to participate in the regular curriculum and work toward meeting IEP goals beginning on day 11, providing PWN as well as a copy of procedural safeguards, and possibly conducting an evaluation.

A third way in which a child's placement could be changed is one that is decided on a case-by-case basis which requires careful analysis on the part of the district. The regulations allowed multiple short-term removals of less than 10 days each but cumulating to more than 10 days in a school year without automatically resulting in a change in placement. This is not a loophole intended to allow districts to circumvent their responsibilities to students by continually excluding students with challenging behavior from the educational system. Rather, it is included to provide school districts with flexibility that may be needed to work with individual students. (We are not weighing in on the efficacy of suspension or removals, but that is a worthy topic that you may want to research.) The multiple short-term removals could be considered a change of placement if those removals constituted a pattern of exclusion, because the behavior for which the student was removed was substantially similar to behavior that resulted in prior removals and because of additional factors such as the length of removals, proximity of removals to one another, and the total number of days removed (§300.536).

Consider the following examples. If a child was suspended for three days in September for cussing at a teacher, three days in January for destruction of school property, and five days in May for fighting for a total of 11 school days, that would likely not be a change in placement. The days totaled more than 10, but the behaviors were very different and spread across the entire school year. However, if a child was suspended for three days in September for swearing at a teacher, another three days in September for swearing at classmates, and five days in September for fighting, for a total of 11 school days, one could make the case that this was a change in placement due to the proximity of suspensions and to the similarity of behaviors. This pattern of exclusion may imply that the strategy for dealing with misbehavior employed by the district was exclusion from school rather than implementation of educational interventions and supports that would have increased the likelihood of that student learning. Some cases may not always be so clear and may ultimately be decided in due process hearings or the courts.

It is important to stress that tracking the number of days suspended/removed is recorded for a school year regardless of the number of schools a student may attend. The count does not start over if a student transfers to a different school. So, if a student transferred to your school, and his records indicated an accumulation of suspension days, you may want to reconvene the IEP and try to develop effective interventions. Don't simply assume that if a prior school faculty experienced difficulty that you will also experience difficulty supporting the child. Consider the information from the prior school carefully, but it is certainly possible that their program was poorly implemented and may have contributed to the difficulties encountered by the child. It is also possible that there are other unidentified variables in play and the change in environment may have a dramatic effect on the child's behavior.

The fourth way a district could remove a child to a different placement is due to something called "special circumstances". A school district could, but is not required, to unilaterally change a child's placement for up to 45 school days if the child commits any of the following specific behaviors while at school, on school premises, or at an activity sponsored by the school or state educational agency: 1) possesses a weapon at school, or a school function; 2) knowingly possesses or uses illegal drugs, or sells or solicits the sale of a controlled substance; or 3) inflicts serious bodily injury upon another person. If a district does decide to remove a child for 45 school days because of special circumstances, then on the day of the decision to remove the child, the district must provide parents/guardians with PWN and notice of procedural safeguards. The disciplinary procedures allowed for "special circumstances" do not preclude a school from referring a student to law enforcement, as will be discussed later in this chapter.

As noted in 71 Fed. Reg. 46,723 (2006) the law does not contain unique definitions of dangerous weapons, serious bodily injury, or controlled substance because the terms are defined in other legislation and if that legislation were to change, then the references to these terms in special education law would need to be revised. However, the notes to the regulations do include the statutory definitions assigned to weapons and serious bodily injury that were in effect when the law was written. The specific definition of controlled substance was not included in the notes, because the definition is lengthy and subject to frequent changes. However, it was noted that controlled substance means a drug or other substance identified under schedules I, II, III, IV or V in section 202 (c) of the Controlled Substances Act (21 U.S.C. 812 (c)). **http://www.gpo.gov/fdsys/pkg/USCODE-2010-title21/pdf/USCODE-2010-title21-chap13-subchapl-partB-sec812.pdf.**

The definition of serious bodily injury does not include minor injuries that may result from a physical fight or threatening behavior. Rather, the term refers to injuries that most would consider very severe. The definition from section 1365(h)(3) of title 18, United States Code follows:

The term serious bodily injury means bodily injury that involves—

(1)   A substantial risk of death;

(2)   Extreme physical pain;

(3)   Protracted and obvious disfigurement; or

(4)   Protracted loss or impairment of the function of a bodily member, organ, or mental faculty.

The definition of dangerous weapon was taken from section 930(g)(2) of title 18, United States Code. As defined in the code, dangerous weapon means:

A weapon, device, instrument, material, or substance, animate or inanimate, that is used for, or is readily capable of, causing death or serious bodily injury, except that such term does not include a pocket knife with a blade of less than 2 ½ inches in length.

Schools must be vigilant in tracking student removals or suspensions, because whenever a student is removed for more than 10 days during the year, he or she must begin receiving special education supports on day 11. Additionally, when the removals result in a change of placement, certain procedures must be followed. The school must conduct a manifestation determination (next section) when there is a change of placement due to disciplinary actions including: 1) removal for more than 10 consecutive days, 2) removals for "special circumstances" if longer than 10 days, and 3) a series of short-term removals of less than 10 days but cumulating in more than 10 days if they constituted a change in placement because of the pattern length removals, proximity of removals, frequency of removals, and similarity of behaviors that resulted in removal.

Before moving to the manifestation determination, it is important to note that the zero tolerance policies adopted by many school districts cannot usurp federal law regarding the discipline of children with disabilities. State and school policies may increase the rights afforded students with disabilities under federal laws but cannot infringe upon those rights. An excellent source of information regarding the questionable efficacy of exclusionary disciplinary practices is the National Association of School Psychologists (NASP). The following link is to a NASP document that discusses the inherent dangers with the zero reject policies, recognizes the inequity in suspension among different groups of children, and also notes the generally poor outcomes associated with these practices. **http://www.nasponline.org/publications/ cq/mocq375zerotolerance.aspx** NASP provides many useful publications and position statements describing evidence based practices, many of which are available on line.

Manifestation Determination

The regulations regarding disciplinary procedures were initially developed for IDEA '97, but were significantly changed with the passage of IDEA '04. For the most part, the new guidelines regarding manifestation determinations leave less to interpretation than the IDEA '97 regulations and are fairly straightforward, but that should not be read to mean the regulations have not been the source of controversy.

The regulations require that within 10 days of a decision to change placement as a result of a violation of the code of conduct the school, parents, and relevant members of the IEP team must meet for a manifestation determination. At this meeting, they are required to determine if the behavior of question was 1) caused by or had a direct and substantial direct relationship to the child's disability or 2) a result of the school's failure to implement the IEP. If either was affirmed, then the team must find that the behavior of concern was a manifestation of the disability. To make this decision, the team must review all relevant information in the student's file including the current IEP, disciplinary records, communication methods, teacher observations, parental input, etc. Unfortunately, there is a relative lack of empirical or legal guidance to assist teams in making the manifestation determination (Osborne & Russo, 2009; Zirkel, 2006), but the following procedures may provide a beginning structure for effective team functioning.

For the team to reach an affirmative decision to the first issue, it is clear that the disability must have had a causal or substantially direct relationship to the behavior. Osborne and Russo (2009) suggest that the team carefully consider the current IEP to see if it indicates concerns with behavior, such as statements in the Present Levels, the inclusion of behavioral goals or objectives, or the existence of a behavior intervention plan. They also recommend that the team consider any commentary in the most recent evaluations that may have suggested behavioral concerns. In addition, the team may want to consider the eligibility category, but should not assume that behavior is only an issue for students identified as eligible due to behavioral concerns. Students with learning disabilities or communication problems may also present behavioral issues. The point is that it be a clear relationship and documentation of behavioral concerns in the child's record may help the team make an informed decision.

The team must also determine if the behavior was a result of the district's failure to implement the IEP. There are no specific guidelines for making such a determination, but the team could assemble the available data and consider the following questions:

(1)   Were the support services specified in the IEP provided?

(2)   Were the goals and objectives addressed?

(3)   Was the placement decision identified in the IEP followed?

(4)   If there was a BIP, was it implemented as specified?

A negative response to any of these questions may indicate failure to implement the IEP and require the team to determine that the behavior was a manifestation of the disability. Of course, there could be numerous other considerations, depending upon the IEP and the child. An important point is that school personnel should maintain adequate records and performance data to demonstrate that the IEP was implemented as written.

The regulations state that when making a determination of whether a change in placement for disciplinary purposes is appropriate for a particular student, factors such as disciplinary history, ability to understand consequences, and expression of remorse are examples of issues that may be considered. In addition, we would add communicative skill and intent. Most people have some familiarity with the story of Helen Keller, an incredibly bright person who could neither see nor hear. When young, she exhibited behavioral outbursts related to her difficulty to communicate and make her needs known. Rather than punishing students who communicate in a unique manner, the team should develop an appropriate communication system and provide the necessary supports, thereby enabling the child to make his or her needs known and interact successfully with others. This instructional intervention may resolve many of the behavioral concerns while providing valuable communicative opportunities/skills to the child. We would also add that the team should consider whether the student could control the behavior. For example, if a student had Tourette syndrome and exhibited corprolalia (involuntary swearing), then suspending the child for swearing (a behavior he or she could not control) would be inappropriate and have no educational merit. (It would be akin to suspending a child with diabetes whose blood sugar spiked. The suspension certainly wouldn't help the child better metabolize glucose.) Rather, the team should develop a supportive intervention that could include ignoring as well as providing the child with a designated private area to release tic energy.

If the team determines that the behavior was not a manifestation of the child's disability, then the school can apply appropriate consequences, provided it would do the same to a child without a disability. However, as previously mentioned, the district must still provide services that will allow the child to participate in the general education curriculum and progress toward meeting IEP goals and objectives beginning on the 11th day of suspension during an academic year, but the district is not required to provide exactly the same services as the child received prior to the disciplinary removal.

If the team determines that the behavior was a manifestation of the disability because either 1) it was caused by or had a direct and substantial direct relationship to the child's disability, or 2) it was a result of the school's failure to implement the IEP, then the child must be immediately returned to the placement from which he or she was removed, with two exceptions. First, if the child's placement was changed because the district and parent determined that a different placement was necessary to provide FAPE, then the child would stay in the newly agreed upon placement. Second, if the district made a unilateral decision to remove the child to an alternative placement due to "special circumstances" (dangerous weapons, controlled substance, serious bodily injury), then the child would stay in the alternative placement. However, parents would have the right to challenge the district's decision using rights afforded them in the procedural safeguards.

If the behavior was a manifestation of the disability, then the IEP team must either: 1) conduct an FBA then develop and implement a BIP, or 2) if an FBA was already conducted and a behavior plan existed before the change in placement, review and revise the BIP as needed. If an FBA existed, it may also be prudent for the team to review the hypotheses that had been generated to determine the validity of the assumptions made regarding the purpose(s) of the behavior. If the conclusions drawn from the FBA appear to be inaccurate, then the team could certainly conduct an additional FBA and modify the BIP. (See more about FBA and BIP later in this chapter.)

Interim Alternative Educational Setting

If a student's placement is changed due to disciplinary procedures, then the child may be placed in an Interim Alternative Education Setting (IAE). As noted in the regulation (§300.531), the IEP team determines the IAE setting under the following three conditions. First, if the child was removed for more than 10 days for a behavior that was not a manifestation of the disability, then the team determines the IAE where special education services that must begin on day eleven will be provided (§300.530 (c)). Second, §300.530 (d)(5) requires the IEP team to determine the IAE if the child's placement changed as a result of a series of short-term removals (less than 10 days each) totaling more than 10 days during the school year. Third, the IEP team also determines the IAE if the child is removed due to "special circumstances." The district must consider a variety of options for IAE and cannot have home based service as the only option. It certainly can be one option, but other options could also include an alternative school, a public library, school district offices, etc.

Appeal (§300.532)

We won't delve into the legal aspects of the due process rights as they can be complicated and are best addressed by an attorney who is versed in procedural aspects of the law, but we will provide a brief overview in a Chapter 8. It is helpful for teachers to have at least a rudimentary understanding of the procedures available to parents and schools. During your career, you may even find yourself in a position to support your building principal's compliance with disciplinary requirements, because as Yell (2006) noted, many school administrators erroneously believe that children with disabilities are exempt from disciplinary rules. You know that is not true, but it is true that children with disabilities may be afforded different procedures and protections. The appeal process is a very specific procedure and, rather than going through it in detail, we will refer you to the regulations (§300.532-300.533) and again encourage you to contact your district counsel for guidance should parents decide to appeal decisions regarding the manifestation decision or alternative placement.

In cases where a child has been removed to an IAE and the district believes that returning the child to the prior placement is substantially likely to result in injury to the child or others, the district can file due process and request that the Hearing Officer order that the child remain in the IAE for a longer period of time. According to §300.533, when there is an appeal made under §300.532, the child remains in the IAE pending the decision of the hearing officer or expiration of time assigned unless the parents and district agree to something different.

Referral to Law Enforcement (§300.535)

Earlier we noted that the disciplinary procedures for "special circumstances" should not be interpreted to prevent a school from reporting criminal activity to the appropriate authorities. Fortunately, criminal activity is an uncommon behavior for most students of any age, but it is important to have an understanding of the regulatory requirements requiring reporting and provision of confidential information, such as special education records. According to §300.535(b)(1)-(2), the agency reporting a crime committed by a student with a disability must ensure that the disciplinary records and special education records are provided to authorities as allowed by the Family Educational Rights and Privacy Act (FERPA) **http://www2. ed.gov/policy/gen/guid/fpco/ferpa/index.html** FERPA (34 CFR § 99.31) does allow release of student records to State and local authorities, within a juvenile justice system, pursuant to specific State law. Before releasing records without written parental consent, we strongly encourage you to check with district counsel for any changes that may have been made to FERPA or state law as they are in a position to keep abreast of any changes.

Protections for Children Not Deemed Eligible for Special Education (§300.534)

If a child who has not yet formally been evaluated and determined to be eligible for special education and related services (but is suspected to be eligible) is subjected to disciplinary procedures, he or she should be afforded the same protections as if the district had knowledge that the child was a child who is eligible. A district would be assumed to know that the child had a disability and might reasonably be expected to be eligible if: 1) the parent expressed concern in writing that the child was in need of special education, 2) the parent requested an evaluation for special education, or 3) a teacher or other district employee expressed a concern about a pattern of behavior to either the special education director or another supervisor.

The district would be considered to not have knowledge that the child was a child with an eligible disability if 1) the parent had not allowed the child to be evaluated or 2) the child was evaluated and found ineligible. In either of these cases, the district could implement the same disciplinary procedures used with children without disabilities. If during this disciplinary process, an eligibility evaluation was requested, then the district must complete the evaluation in an expedited manner, and the child would stay in the current placement determined by the administration. If the child was found eligible, then an appropriate IEP would be developed.

Summary of Disciplinary Procedures

Thus far we have provided a basic review of the disciplinary procedures as described in IDEA '04 and the accompanying regulations. There is certainly much more to the development of effective disciplinary practices and procedures than what is covered in the regulations. In our opinion, rather than focusing on helping children develop appropriate social and coping skills, discipline is often viewed as a punishing reaction to the undesired behavior of students. We encourage teams to consider that effective classroom management is a result of many components, some of which include a challenging and interesting curriculum, an environment conducive to learning, effective teaching and learning strategies, proper instructional planning, and the effective use of reinforcement strategies. Covering all of these areas would be beyond the authority and scope of the regulations but should not be an overlooked aspect of your professional practice and they may be components considered in the development of an FBA and a BIP.

Functional Behavior Assessment and Behavior Intervention Plans

The requirement for conducting an FBA was first included in IDEA '97, and the law only requires its use in limited instances, i.e., when a child's placement is changed due to disciplinary actions. Nevertheless, nothing in the law or regulations prevents an IEP team from behaving in a proactive manner and conducting an FBA if it is evident that a child is experiencing behavioral difficulties that will likely impede his or her education or social-emotional development.

The regulations do not describe the procedure for conducting an FBA or identify what should be included in the assessment. However, a high quality FBA that will likely provide the necessary information to develop truly effective interventions can be time intensive, whereas, the time invested in conducting a poorly developed FBA is generally wasted and results in frustration and failure on the part of all involved. A quality FBA which leads to the development of a positive BIP might provide the necessary supports that will enable a child to succeed without a disciplinary change in placement or reduce the amount of time a child is removed from the regular classroom setting. An FBA is considered an evaluation, not for eligibility purposes, but to help determine the special education supports and services that will be provided to the child (Letter to Christiansen, 2007). In accordance with the regulations, parents should be provided with PWN and informed written consent should be obtained before conducting the evaluation.

As noted, we are purposefully providing an extremely brief review of FBA and BIP, because effective development of both requires a sound understanding in applied behavior analysis, effective collaborative skills, and skill in selecting and developing effective interventions which is well beyond the scope of this text. Our intention is only to orient you to the process, so in the following discussion, we will identify and describe the major components. However, we will provide you with references that provide detailed information for conducting FBA and providing positive behavioral supports at both the individual and school-wide levels. Before proceeding, we do want to note that more than three decades of research supports the development of interventions based on an understanding of the function of the target behavior(s), a finding that is consistent across disabilities and behaviors (Steege & Watson, 2008).

A basic assumption in FBA is that most behavior serves a purpose and that all behavior has a cause and an effect that, once identified can be the basis for change. (However, there are some behaviors that may have a neurological basis like myoclonic contractions of the long muscles during a seizure that is not purposeful and is not "controllable." Those behaviors should be identified in an FBA and appropriate supports identified in the BIP.) Once that purpose of a behavior is reliably identified, then the team can develop a BIP or Positive Behavior Support Plan (PBS) to help the individual obtain the desired outcomes without exhibiting the undesired target behavior. O'Neill et al. (1997) identified the following 6 major outcomes of FBA:

(1) *Provide a clear, operant description of the student's problem behavior(s).* This requires that the behaviors be described in observable terms that could be reliably identified from the description. There really isn't room for sloppy descriptions of behavior, because poor descriptions will not lead to reliable measures when trying to determine the occurrence of the behavior before, during, or after the intervention. For example, "fights with peers" would not be an acceptable operant description, because "fights" could have many different meanings across observers. Some might consider it to include physical fights only, whereas others may consider verbal altercations to also be considered "fight" behaviors. A better description would be "kicks and punches peers." Another nonexample may be "acts out to get attention." As you can probably imagine, "acts out" is open to many different interpretations and may even be influenced by the mood of the teacher. For example, a teacher who is rested and refreshed on a Monday morning might not consider a particular behavior as "acting out" but by Friday, that same teacher may be tired, have less patience, and consider that behavior as an incident of "acting out." So, just as with writing IEP objectives, clearly specifying the behavior

will result in better measurement. If rather than "acting out," the behavior was specified as "sticks tongue out, yells, or spits at other students," then the teacher or other observer could identify the behaviors on Monday or Friday, regardless of personal physical state.

(2) *Identification of consequence conditions that maintain the problem behavior.* The basic assumption is that behavior does not occur in a vacuum; rather, behavior occurs for a purpose. Research into operant conditioning has shown that behavior occurs because the individual either gets something or avoids something after exhibiting the behavior (also known as positive and negative reinforcement). However, there may be health related issues contributing to some behaviors and that should be considered.

(3) *Identification of antecedent events that "trigger" the behavior.* At this point, the focus is generally on identifying the immediate or proximal antecedent that occurs right before the behavior. For example, it is possible that a behavior might be more likely to occur after a student is asked to complete writing assignments. For those of you familiar with operant behavioral theory, you likely notice that we are simply describing the three contingency model of behavior.

Antecedent → Behavior → Consequence

(4) *Identification of setting events.* This provides an additional component to the three contingency model. Setting events are temporary conditions that alter the value of the reinforcing consequence that is maintaining the behavior. The existence of setting events may help explain why instruction goes well on some days and on other days, the child exhibits problematic behavior (Horner, Albin, Todd, Newton, & Sprague, 2011).

(5) *The FBA should result in the development of a testable hypothesis.* The team should consolidate the information obtained thus far and develop a reasonable hypothesis describing what consequence event(s) are maintaining the target behavior(s).

(6) *The hypothesis should be tested.* Once the hypothesis has been developed, direct observation should be conducted to confirm or disconfirm the hypothesis. If the hypothesis is not confirmed, the team should reconvene and conduct additional assessment. If the hypothesis is confirmed, the team can move to the development of a BIP.

We recognize that our description of an FBA is very limited and that there are other models for conducting an FBA. Our purpose was to provide you with the understanding that an FBA is a complex and multifaceted procedure. It really should be a more involved process than the IEP team sitting and making conjecture on what is maintaining a particular behavior of concern. As Watson and Steege (2003) aptly noted, interventions based on information obtained through comprehensive FBAs rather than opinion will likely achieve better out-comes for children.

Horner et al. (2011) provided an excellent example of conducting an FBA and tying that information directly to a BIP for two different students. Their examples take you through the entire process in sequential manner. Another source for obtaining quality information regarding FBA and PBS is the Office of Special Education Programs Center on Positive Behavior Interventions and Support **http://www.pbis.org/** This link also provides valuable guidelines for developing proactive school-wide positive behavioral supports which, when properly implemented, may reduce the number of disciplinary issues for students with and without disabilities. The Center for Effective Collaboration and Practice is another site that contains a considerable amount of useful information regarding both FBA and PBS. **http://cecp.air.org/center.asp.**

In and of itself an FBA does not identify the supports needed to help the child suc-ceed. It is, however, a necessary first step in the development of a comprehensive BIP. We want to remind you that the law and the regulations use the term BIP but in the field and in the literature, you will likely find the term Positive Behavioral Supports. There is a bit of difference, though. Depending on state law, you may find a BIP that includes the sys-tematic use, not just emergency use, of aversive interventions as part of a treatment pro-tocol—a treatment that you would not expect to find on most PBS plans. Those aversive interventions include mechanical restraint, physical restraint, and seclusionary time-out. The use of these procedures has been an area of considerable debate with movement in the Congress to regulate or abolish the use of the procedures. TASH, formerly The Associa-tion for Persons with Severe Handicaps, has taken a lead in advocating the abolishment of aversive practices **http://tash.org/tash-shows-%E2%80%98the-cost-of-waiting%E2%80%99-to-end-restraint-seclusion/** and in a U.S. Department of Education resource document on restraint and seclusion, Arne Duncan, U.S. Secretary of Education, stated, "Furthermore, there continues to be no evidence that using restraint or seclusion is effective in reducing the occurrence of the problem behaviors that frequently precipitate the use of such techniques (p. iii)." **http://www2.ed.gov/policy/seclusion/restraints-and-seclusion-resources.pdf.** Some states have regulations and/or prohibitions regarding the use of aversive, so be sure to consult state law before the use of any aversive theory.

Just as there are numerous models for conducting an FBA, there are also different ways to structure and develop a BIP. When discussing PBS Horner et al. (2011) noted, the plan must be contextually appropriate, meaning that those involved in implementing the plan should agree on the outcomes and implement the procedures across settings with fidelity. The best plan is absolutely no good if it is not used with consistency, so it is crucial that the development of the BIP be a collaborative team venture that addresses all behaviors of concern.

Horner et al. (2011) described a process for developing a plan based on an analysis of competing behaviors. In this model, the setting events and antecedent events are identi-fied. In addition, the problem behavior(s), desired behavior(s), or replacement behaviors(s) are specified, and consequences are recognized. The plan addresses all areas, and the team develops a specific plan that recognizes the setting events, the antecedent events and includes behavioral teaching strategies, and consequence strategies.

Background Information: Bullying and Harassment

As teachers or future teachers, we assume that you value the right of students to participate in school activities without fear and free from intimidation. Unfortunately, instances of bullying and harassment of students, reports or bullying and harassment, or both appear to have increased in recent years. The news has been replete with many cases that have resulted in psychological damage, physical insult, and even death.

There is considerable overlap between the responsibilities of school districts for a student who is either IDEA eligible or only receiving 504 supports and is victim of bullying/harassment. Both laws require that students with disabilities receive FAPE, and student with disabilities are protected from disability harassment. In the following sections, we will provide definitions of the two terms, examples of prohibited behaviors, and responsibilities of school personnel. We will also discuss the role of IEP teams in addressing the challenges of bullying and harassment.

Bullying and Harassment Defined

Bullying behaviors and harassment share some similarities and sometimes the terms are used interchangeably in the schools. At times, it can be difficult to tell the difference, because some bullying behaviors may also be considered harassment. We will provide the general descriptions of these terms and recognize that there may be overlap in instances where students may be subjected to both bullying and harassment at the same time. The key point is that regardless of how you categorize the behaviors, both must be addressed. According to a Dear Colleague Letter of 2013, the US Department of Education uses the following definitions:

> "Bullying is characterized by aggression used within a relationship where the aggressor(s) has more real or perceived power than the target, and the aggression is repeated, or has the potential to be repeated, over time. Bullying can involve overt physical behavior or verbal, emotional, or social behaviors (e.g., excluding someone from social activities, making threats, withdrawing attention, destroying someone's reputation) and can range from blatant aggression to far more subtle and covert behaviors. Cyberbullying, or bullying through electronic technology (e.g., cell phones, computers, online/social media), can include offensive text messages or e-mails, rumors or embarrassing photos posted on social networking sites, or fake online profiles."

Bullying can happen to any person and requires a real or perceived power differential. Harassment, however, is behavior directed toward students of specific groups at such severity that it creates a hostile environment that is encouraged, tolerated, not adequately addressed, or ignored by school employees (Dear Colleague Letter, 2010). Harassment is a violation of a student's civil rights and there are several laws prohibiting such behavior. The Office for Civil Rights (OCR) in the Department of Education has consistently held that districts must respond to instances of harassment of students in these specific groups. The following quotation from a Dear Colleague Letter (2010) provides some clarification and clearly demonstrates the seriousness with which OCR views the issue.

> The statutes that OCR enforces include Title VI of the Civil Rights Act of 1964 (Title VI), which prohibits discrimination on the basis of race, color, or national origin; Title IX of the Education Amendments of 1972 (Title IX), which prohibits discrimination on the basis of sex; Section 504 of the Rehabilitation Act of 1973 (Section 504); and Title II of the Americans with Disabilities Act of 1990 (Title II). Section 504 and Title II prohibit discrimination on the basis of disability. School districts may violate these civil rights statutes and the Department's implementing regulations when peer harassment based on race, color, national origin, sex, or disability is sufficiently serious that it creates a hostile environment and such harassment is encouraged, tolerated, not adequately addressed, or ignored by school employees.

According to OCR, disability harassment that is prohibited under Section 504 and Title II is intimidation or abusive behavior based on disability that is of such severity it creates a hostile environment. This is an environment that interferes with or denies the student from participating or benefiting in the services or opportunities of the school.

Following are examples of harassment that could create a hostile environment and school personnel must address the issues (Dear Colleague Letter, 2000):

- Several students continually remark out loud to other students during class that a student with a learning disability is "retarded" or "deaf and dumb" and does not belong in the class; as a result, the harassed student has difficulty doing work in class and her grades decline.

- A student repeatedly places classroom furniture or other objects in the path of a classmate who uses a wheelchairs, impeding the classmate's ability to enter the classroom.

- A school administrator repeatedly denies a student with a disability access to lunch, field trips, assemblies, and extracurricular activities as a punishment for taking time off from school for required.

In a Dear Colleague Letter dated October 21, 2014, OCR provided additional guidance and more in-depth examples. The questions OCR considers when analyzing complaints regarding bullying of a student with a disability are provided below. Following the discussion of those questions, we share excellent hypothetical examples of the following: A) Disability-based harassment and violation of FAPE, B) FAPE violation but no disability-based harassment, and C) No disability-based harassment and no FAPE violation. The questions and examples were taken directly from the letter which is available in its entirety at **http://www2.ed.gov/about/offices/list/ocr/letters/colleague-bullying-201410.pdf.**

How OCR Analyzes Complaints Involving Bullying of Students with Disabilities

When OCR evaluates complaints involving bullying and students with disabilities, it may open an investigation to determine whether there has been a disability-based harassment violation, a FAPE violation, both, or neither, depending on the facts and circumstances of a given complaint.

When investigating disability-based harassment, OCR considers several factors, including, but not limited to:

- Was a student with a disability bullied by one or more students based on the student's disability?
- Was the bullying conduct sufficiently serious to create a hostile environment?
- Did the school know or should it have known of the conduct?
- Did the school fail to take prompt and effective steps reasonably calculated to end the conduct, eliminate the hostile environment, prevent it from recurring, and, as appropriate, remedy its effects?

If the answer to each of these questions is "yes," then OCR would find a disability-based harassment violation under Section 504 and, if the student was receiving IDEA FAPE or Section 504 FAPE services, OCR would have a basis for investigating whether there was also a denial of FAPE under Section 504. Even if the answers to one or more of these questions is "no," for a student who was receiving IDEA FAPE or Section 504 FAPE services, OCR may still consider whether the bullying resulted in a denial of FAPE under Section 504.

When investigating whether a student receiving IDEA FAPE or Section 504 FAPE services who was bullied was denied FAPE under Section 504, OCR considers several factors, including, but not limited to:

- Did the school know or should it have known that the effects of the bullying may have affected the student's receipt of IDEA FAPE services or Section 504 FAPE services? For example, did the school know or should it have known about adverse changes in the student's academic performance or behavior indicating that the student may not be receiving FAPE? If the answer is "no," there would be no FAPE violation. If the answer is "yes," OCR would then consider:

- Did the school meet its ongoing obligation to ensure FAPE by promptly determining whether the student's educational needs were still being met, and if not, making changes, as necessary, to his or her IEP or Section 504 plan? If the answer is "no," and the student was not receiving FAPE, OCR would find that the school violated its obligation to provide FAPE.

Hypothetical Examples

The following hypothetical examples illustrate how OCR would analyze a complaint involving allegations of the bullying of a student with a disability who receives only 504 services.

A. Disability-Based Harassment Violation and FAPE Violation

At the start of the school year, a ten-year-old student with Attention Deficit Hyperactivity Disorder (ADHD) and a speech disability is fully participating in the classroom, interacting with his peers at lunch and recess, and regularly attending speech therapy twice a week. In addition to providing for speech services, the student's Section 504 plan also provides for behavior supports that call for all his teachers and other trained staff to supervise him during transition times, provide constructive feedback, and help him use preventative strategies to anticipate and address problems with peers.

Because of the student's disabilities, he makes impulsive remarks, speaks in a high-pitched voice, and has difficulty reading social cues. Three months into the school year, students in his P.E. class begin to repeatedly taunt him by speaking in an exaggerated, high-pitched tone, calling him names, such as "weirdo" and "gay," and setting him up for social embarrassment by directing him to ask other students inappropriate personal questions. The P.E. teacher witnesses the taunting, but neither reports the conduct to the appropriate school official, nor applies the student's behavior supports specified in his 504 plan. Instead, she pulls the student aside and tells him that he needs to start focusing less on what kids have to say and more on getting his head in the game. As the taunting intensifies, the student begins to withdraw from interacting with other kids in P.E. and avoids other students at lunch and recess. As the student continues to withdraw over the course of a few weeks, he misses multiple sessions of speech therapy, but the speech therapist does not report his absences to the Section 504 team or another appropriate school official.

In this example, OCR would find a disability-based harassment violation. The student's peers were making fun of him because of behaviors related to his disability. For OCR's enforcement purposes, the taunting the student experienced, including other students impersonating him and calling him "weirdo" and "gay," was therefore based on his disability. The school knew about the bullying because the P.E. teacher witnessed the conduct. Yet upon witnessing the taunting, the P.E. teacher not only failed to provide the student behavior supports as required in the student's 504 plan, but also failed to report the conduct to an appropriate school official. Had she taken this step, the school could have conducted an investigation and found that the conduct created a hostile environment, because it interfered with the student's ability to benefit from the speech therapy services that he should have been receiving and negatively affected his ability to participate fully in P.E., lunch, and recess. The school's failure to appropriately respond to the bullying violated Section 504.

OCR would also find FAPE violations under Section 504. First, when the P.E. teacher failed to implement the behavior supports in the student's Section 504 plan, the school denied the student FAPE under Section 504. In addition, and independent of the failure to provide behavior supports, because the bullying impacted the student's receipt of Section 504 FAPE, the school should have addressed the student's changed needs; by failing to do so, the student was denied Section 504 FAPE. The school should have known about the missed Section 504 services and related changes in behavior. The P.E. teacher knew about the bullying but did nothing to report the student's behavioral changes (e.g., the student's increasing efforts to isolate himself from other students) to the Section 504 team members or other appropriate school official. Similarly, the speech therapist knew that the student was missing speech therapy but did not report this to the 504 team or to an appropriate school official. By failing to address the adverse effects of the bullying on FAPE, the school did not make necessary changes to ensure the student was provided FAPE under Section 504. If, upon concluding its investigation, OCR and the district were to enter into a resolution agreement, OCR could require, for example, that the district (1) ensure that FAPE is provided to the student by convening the Section 504 team to determine if the student needs different or additional services (including compensatory services) and, if so, providing them; (2) offer counseling to the student to remedy the harm that the school allowed to persist; (3) monitor whether bullying persists for the student and take corrective action to ensure the bullying ceases; (4) develop and implement a school-wide bullying prevention strategy based on positive-behavior supports; (5) devise a voluntary school climate survey for students and parents to assess the presence and effect of bullying based on disability and to respond to issues that arise in the survey; (6) revise the district's anti-bullying policies to develop staff protocols in order to improve the district's response to bullying; (7) train staff and parent volunteers, such as those who monitor lunch and recess or chaperone field trips, on the district's anti-bullying policies, including how to recognize and report instances of bullying on any basis; and (8) provide continuing education to students on the district's antibullying policies, including where to get help if a student either witnesses or experiences bullying conduct of any kind.

B. FAPE Violation, No Disability-Based Harassment Violation

A thirteen-year-old student with depression and Post-Traumatic Stress Disorder (PTSD) who receives counseling as part of her Section 504 services is often mocked by her peers for being poor and living in a homeless shelter. Having maintained an A average for the first half of the academic year, she is now getting Bs and Cs, neglecting to turn in her assignments, and regularly missing counseling sessions. When asked by her counselor why she is no longer attending scheduled sessions, she says that she feels that nothing is helping and that no one cares about her. The student tells the counselor that she no longer wants to attend counseling services and misses her next two scheduled sessions. The counselor informs the principal that the student has missed several counseling sessions and that the student feels the sessions are not helping.

Around the same time, the student's teachers inform the principal that she has begun to struggle academically. The principal asks the teachers and counselor to keep her apprised if the student's academic performance worsens, but does not schedule a Section 504 meeting.

In this example, whether or not the school knew or should have known about the bullying, OCR would not find a disability-based harassment violation under Section 504, because the bullying incidents were based on the student's socio-economic status, not her disability. Independent of the basis for the bullying and regardless of whether school officials knew or should have known about the bullying, the school district still had an ongoing obligation under Section 504 to ensure that this student with a disability was receiving an education appropriate to her needs. Here, the student's sudden decline in grades, coupled with changes in her behavior (missing counseling sessions), should have indicated to the school that her needs were not being met. In this example, OCR would find that these adverse changes were sufficient to put the school on notice of its obligation to promptly convene the Section 504 team to determine the extent of the FAPE-related problems and to make any necessary changes to her services, or, if necessary, reevaluate her, in order to ensure that she continues to receive FAPE. By failing to do more than keep track of the student's academic performance, the school failed to meet this obligation, which violated Section 504.31

C. No Disability-Based Harassment Violation, No FAPE Violation

A seven-year-old student with a food allergy to peanuts has a Section 504 plan that provides for meal accommodations, the administration of epinephrine if the student is exposed to peanuts, access to a peanut-free table in the cafeteria, and the prohibition of peanut products in the student's classroom. In advance of the upcoming Halloween party, the teacher reminds the class that candy with peanuts is prohibited in the classroom at all times, including Halloween. That afternoon, while on the bus, a classmate grabs the student's water bottle out of the student's backpack, drinks from it, and says, "I had a peanut butter sandwich for lunch today, and I just finished it." The following day, while having lunch at the peanut-free table in the lunchroom with some friends, a classmate who had been sitting at another table sneaks up behind her and waves an open candy bar with peanuts in front of her face, yelling, "Time to eat peanuts!" Though the candy bar does not touch her, a few other classmates nearby begin chanting, "Time to eat peanuts," and the student leaves the lunchroom crying. When the student goes back to her classroom and tells her teacher what happened at lunch and on the bus, the teacher asks her whether she came into contact with the candy bar and what happened to the water bottle. The student confirms that the candy bar did not touch her and that she never got the water bottle back from the classmate who took it, but says that she is scared to go back into the lunchroom and to ride the bus. The teacher promptly informs the principal of the incidents, and the peers who taunted the student on the bus and in the lunchroom are removed from the lunchroom, interviewed by the assistant principal, and required to meet with the counselor during recess to discuss the seriousness of their conduct. That same week, the school holds a Section 504 meeting to address whether any changes were needed to the student's services in light of the bullying. The principal also meets with the school counselor, and they decide that a segment on the bullying of students with disabilities, including students with food allergies, would be added to the counselor's presentation to students on the school's antibullying policy scheduled in the next 2 weeks. Furthermore, in light of the young age of the students, the counselor offers to incorporate a puppet show into the segment to help illustrate principles that might otherwise be too abstract for such a young audience. In the weeks that follow, the student shows no adverse changes in academic performance or behavior, and when asked by her teacher and the school counselor about how she is doing, she indicates that the bullying has stopped.

In this example, based on the school's appropriate response to the incidents of bullying, OCR would not find a disability-based harassment violation under Section 504. The bullying of the student on account of her food allergy to peanuts was based on the student's disability. Moreover, the physically threatening and humiliating conduct directed at her was sufficiently serious to create a hostile environment by limiting her ability to participate in and benefit from the school's education program when she was near the classmates who bullied her in the lunchroom and on the bus. School personnel, however, did not tolerate the conduct and acted quickly to investigate the incidents, address the behavior of the classmates involved in the conduct, ensure that there were no residual effects on the student, and coordinate to promote greater awareness among students about the school's anti-bullying policy. By taking prompt and reasonable steps to address the hostile environment, eliminate its effects, and prevent it from recurring, the school met its obligations under Section 504.

OCR also would not find a FAPE violation under Section 504 on these facts. Once the school became aware that the student feared attending lunch and riding the bus as a result of the bullying she was experiencing, the school was on notice that the effects of the bullying may have affected her receipt of FAPE. This was sufficient to trigger the school's additional obligation to determine whether, and to what extent, the bullying affected the student's access to FAPE and take any actions, including addressing the bullying and providing new or different services, required to ensure the student continued receiving FAPE. By promptly holding a Section 504 meeting to assess whether the school should consider any changes to the student's services in light of the bullying, the school met its independent legal obligation to provide FAPE under Section 504.

Thus far, we have described the difference between bullying and harassment based on disability status. We have also noted that the federal laws require that districts act appropriately when there are issues of bullying or harassment that result in a denial of FAPE. In the next section, we will describe the responsibilities of the IEP team.

IEP Team Responsibilities

If the instigator of the bullying or harassing behavior is a student with a disability, then the IEP team should reconvene, review the IEP, and determine whether the IEP contains appropriate Annual Goals and Short-Term Objectives designed to facilitate prosocial interactions.

The team should also consider whether appropriate instructional activities and/or supports and, if needed, assistive technologies are being provided to the student. If deemed necessary, the team could require that a Functional Behavior Assessment (FBA) be conducted in order to get at the root cause of the bullying/harassing behavior. Upon completion of the FBA, the team may determine that environmental modifications and social skill instruction would be useful strategies to help the student develop and exhibit prosocial skills that preclude bullying and harassing behavior. In this case, for example, it would be entirely acceptable for an IEP team to develop a Behavior Intervention Plan.

If the victim of the bullying or harassing behavior is a student with a disability, then the IEP team should reconvene and develop an anti-bullying plan to be included in the IEP. In a Dear Colleague Letter (2013), the Office of Special Education Programs noted changes in student behavior that might trigger a district to reconvene an IEP may include a decline in grades, increased behavioral outbursts, and increased number of absences. Districts were cautioned that changing the placement of the victim should not be the first choice for dealing with bullying. Districts are still responsible for providing services in the Least Restrictive setting in which the student's special education needs can be met, and the student's placement should be changed only if he or she cannot be provide FAPE in the current setting.

There is no "one size fits all" response to bullying and harassment. The Pacer Center (pacer.org) contains a considerable amount of anti-bullying information including the following suggestions for items to include in the IEP of a student who is a victim of bullying:

- Identifying an adult in the school who the child can report to or seek assistance from.

- Determine how incidents will be documented.

- Hold trainings for staff and students about the effects of bullying and district policies regarding bullies.

- Making sure that the student who has been bullied is shadowed or consistently in view of an adult who would be able to intervene.

In addition, schools may find it helpful to implement a system of Positive Behavioral Supports that will promote the acquisition of prosocial skills, ensure that the school environment is supportive and welcoming for all, and create a truly inclusive environment. Some websites that offer a considerable amount of evidence-based practice on anti-bullying and anti-harassment programs include:

> www.stopbullying.gov
>
> www.pbis.org
>
> safesupportivelearning.ed.gov
>
> suicidepreventionlifeline.org

Chapter Summary

The regulations covering disciplinary practices and safeguards for students with disabilities have changed significantly since first included in the law in 1997. However, ambiguity is still present in some of the legislation, largely due to the allowance for decisions to be made on a case-by-case basis at the local level. This recognition that disciplinary concerns require the freedom to make individualized decisions based on the facts of the case is clearly in alignment with the tenets of IDEA. The flexibility associated with this practice requires that schools keep accurate records regarding any behavior incidents as well as data verifying the implementation of the IEP. A question and answer document that may provide valuable guidance covering disciplinary procedures was prepared by the Office of Special Education and Rehabilitation Services in 2009 and is available at **http://idea.ed.gov/explore/view/p/%2Croot%2Cdynamic%2CQaCorner%2C7%2C.**

This chapter had two primary focal points. The first related to the disciplinary removals that may require the attention the IEP team. The regulations don't contain specific guidance regarding the use of FBA and PBS, the truly effective practices, and we recommend that you receive training in effective use of behavioral supports as part of your professional development. Your ability to effectively provide behavioral supports to students with and without disabilities will make teaching a much more enjoyable activity for you and will provide students with meaningful opportunities for learning and succeeding in school.

The second area of emphasis covered issues related to disability harassment and bullying. We defined both terms and noted that schools must act pro-actively in cases where a student with a disability is the victim of harassment or bullying. Schools must also intervene in cases when the student with a disability is the perpetrator of harassment or bullying. The topics discussed in this chapter were complimentary, because they emphasize the responsibility of school staff to develop safe environments where proactive strategies are implemented and students are allowed to learn free from harassment and bullying.

Chapter Activities

1. Develop a flow chart of the different requirements for disciplinary procedures with any required time lines. The chart should be something that you could quickly reference to determine if you are responsible for additional actions. Compare your flow chart with one developed by a peer.

2. Review the websites referenced in this chapter. Identify specific prevention activities that you could implement in your classroom or school.

3. Review the websites to identify specific activities related to the development of FBA and PBS.

4. Read the documents from TASH and the Department of Education regarding the use of aversive interventions.

5. Read your state guidelines to determine if there are guidelines or prohibitions regarding the systematic use of aversive interventions. Based on information obtained by reading the documents in the previous item, what changes, if any, might you make to your state regulations regarding the use of aversive interventions?

6. Think of an instance(s) where you might have observed disability based harassment or bullying when you were in school. How would you recommend school personnel intervene in that situation?

7. Review the information on the anti-bullying and anti-harassment websites that were presented in this chapter. Develop an anti-bullying/anti-harassment resource guide for yourself as a teacher. Include lesson plan ideas, link to videos, curricular ideas.

Chapter 7

© Nelson Marques/Shutterstock.com

Postsecondary Transitions and Other Common Issues on Secondary Age IEPs

Chapter Overview

Most chapters in this text cover information relevant to the development of IEPs for all eligible students with disabilities attending public schools, regardless of age. We now take a bit of a departure and focus on issues that are more relevant when working with secondary age students.

The chapter begins with a brief review of the less than stellar postsecondary outcomes for students with disabilities. Hopefully, this information will highlight the importance of developing and implementing carefully planned postsecondary transition plans to better enable students to either overcome or minimize existing disadvantages they may encounter in securing equitable postsecondary opportunities. A description of postsecondary transition as defined in IDEA 04 follows as does a discussion of transition in the IEP. You will undoubtedly find that postsecondary transition is a topic much too broad to be covered adequately in one chapter, but there are numerous resources provided throughout this chapter where you can find additional information. Following our examination of postsecondary issues, we will discuss the following items that are either required activities or common considerations for IEP teams of secondary age students: (1) Summary of Performance (SOP), (2) extracurricular and nonacademic activities, (3) grading, (4) diploma and graduation, and (5) transfer of rights at age of majority.

Review of Postsecondary Outcomes

In the current educational milieu of the United States with the emphasis on scholastic testing, it can appear that the only valued goal of schooling is the acquisition of academic skills. There is no arguing that academic competence is important, but so is the development of nonacademic skills, such as the social skills which are integral to developing a foundation for success. The importance of addressing nonacademic skills has even been validated by the courts. For example, when chastising the Brownsville School District for placing a child in an air-conditioned cubicle rather than simply air conditioning the classroom, the court stated, "Full social interaction is an important part of today's educational curriculum . . . " (*Espino v Besterio*, 1983). While this decision was made prior to the mandated inclusion of transition services in the IEP, it meshes well with the current requirement to prepare a student for successful adulthood by developing transition goals that address the needs of the entire child without limiting goals to academics. The court's statement clearly recognizes that the general education curriculum is broader than academics and includes implied or hidden curricular areas, such as social skills.

While transition from secondary school to adult life can be a difficult activity for many youth, it may be a significantly more challenging process for students with disabilities (Neubert & Leconte, 2013). In the following paragraphs, we share some postsecondary education/training and employment outcome data for students with disabilities and emphasize that success in both education/training and employment are positively correlated with many of the outcomes teachers and families want for students, e.g. the skills necessary to lead productive and happy lives as members of a democracy. Unfortunately, the data indicate that a majority of students with disabilities are not succeeding at levels comparable to their peers without disabilities. Given the difficulties encountered by students with disabilities after leaving school, transition planning remains one of the most crucial experiences (Wehman, 2013).

As a group, students with disabilities have a higher rate of dropping out of school and increased risk of both under and unemployment. DePaoli, Fox, Ingram, Maushard, Bridgeland, and Balfanz (2015) reported that the 2013 average graduation rate for student with disabilities was 61.9%, which was approximately 20% lower than the rate for students without disabilities. Failure to graduate from high school results in greatly diminished earning power, education, and employment opportunities for students without disabilities and may have an even more dramatically negative impact among student with disabilities. While the following data are not broken down according to whether the students graduated or did not graduate, they do provide general information suggesting lower wage earnings and employment rates for youth with disabilities when compared with their typically developing peers.

The National Longitudinal Transition Study—2 (NTLS-2) (Sanford, Newman, Wagner, Cameto, Knokey, & Shaver, 2011) was a 10-year study that investigated the postsecondary experiences of a nationally representative sample of youth with disabilities age 13-16 who received special education in grade 7 or above on December 1, 2000 (**www.ntls2.org**). Some of the key findings included:

(1) Students with disabilities were less likely to have enrolled in postsecondary education than were their typically developing peers.

(2) Employment rates varied by disability category, ranging from 30% for students who had been identified as deaf/blind to 79% for those identified as having a learning disability.

(3) The hourly wage for individuals with disabilities averaged $9.40 compared to $13.40 earned by their typically developing peers. In addition, salary varied by disability category, ranging from $7.60 for individuals who had been identified as having intellectual delay to $9.60 for those identified as having a learning disability.

The Office of Disability Employment Policy in the United States Department of Labor, collaborated with other agencies and identified several "key points" regarding the relationship of disability to employment (**www.dol.gov/odep/pdf/20141022-KeyPoints.pdf**). The following are some of the points identified in that report:

(1) During 2010–2012 only one-third (32%) of working-age people with disabilities were employed compared to over two-thirds (72.7%) of people without disabilities.

(2) Employment rates among people with disabilities did not vary significantly by gender, but were particularly low among Black Americans and those with low-education levels.

(3) Employed people with disabilities are underrepresented in management and technical/professional jobs.

These data, although brief, do provide a representative summary of the findings in both reports, which we believe sufficient to make the case that postsecondary outcomes for students with disabilities are substandard. We encourage you to review these comprehensive reports in more detail and find additional information regarding areas of transition in which you have may a personal interest. Our goal was to simply demonstrate the need for an effective approach to transition planning.

Postsecondary Transition Services as Defined in IDEA

Williams-Diehm and Benz (2008), noted that participation in general education classrooms and earning a diploma increased the likelihood of successful postsecondary outcomes for students with disabilities. Similarly, a comprehensive meta-analysis conducted by Oh-Young and Filler (2015) demonstrated that 80 years of research has shown that both the academic and social outcomes of students with disabilities are significantly better when educated in more integrated settings than in less integrated and more restrictive settings. In a previous chapter, we recognized the importance of statutory language from the preamble to IDEA 04 when discussing Least Restrictive Environment (LRE) and access to the general education curriculum, but a closer look reveals its applicability to transition services as well. As can be gleaned from the following section of the preamble, Congress considered access to the regular curriculum in the general classroom necessary to prepare students for adult life.

(5)   Almost 30 years of research and experience has demonstrated that the education of children with disabilities can be made more effective by—

(A) having high expectations for such children and ensuring their access to the general education curriculum in the regular classroom, to the maximum extent possible, in order to—

(i)   meet developmental goals and, to the maximum extent possible, the challenging expectations that have been established for all children; and

(ii)   *be prepared to lead productive and independent adult lives* (italics added), to the maximum extent possible; (Public Law 108-446).

As noted throughout this text, access to the general education curriculum in the regular classroom is recognized as a fundamental starting point in the development of the IEP. Some students will be able to address transition requirements within the school setting and others may require community-based activities, as well. While LRE specifies the regular education environment as the default, a reasonable extension of the concept would ensure that students participating in community-based activities were doing so with typically developing adults to the maximum extent. In essence, high expectations, inclusive environments, and challenging expectations are viewed as crucial components of preparing students with disabilities to successfully transition to a productive life after school.

The reauthorization of IDEA 04 emphasized the importance of student outcomes not just legal procedural compliance (Turnbull, Stowe, & Huerta, 2007). For example, IDEA 04 requires that states report on 20 different Performance Indicators. We chose not to address each of the indicators; rather, we decided to include a short mention in this chapter to emphasize the importance afforded transition indicators specifically related to secondary age students (Indicators 1, 2, 13, and 14). A description of those indicators is included in Table 7-1. Of course, many of the remaining indicators deal specifically with the IEP and there are also indicators for Part C.

TABLE 7-1. State Performance Indicators Specifically Related to Secondary or Postsecondary Students

Indicator Number	Description
1	Percent of youth with individualized education programs (IEPs) graduating from high school with a regular diploma compared to percent of all youth in the State graduating with a regular diploma. 20 U.S.C. 1416 (a)(3)(A)
2	Percent of youth with IEPs dropping out of high school compared to the percent of all youth in the State dropping out of high school. 20 U.S.C. 1416 (a)(3)(A)

| 13 | Percent of youth aged 16 and above with an IEP that includes coordinated, measurable, annual IEP goals and transition services that will reasonably enable the child to meet the postsecondary goals. 20 U.S.C. 1416 (a)(3)(B) |
| 14 | Percent of youth who had IEPs, are no longer in secondary school and who have been competitively employed, enrolled in some type of postsecondary school, or both, within one year of leaving high school. 20 U.S.C. 1416 (a)(3)(B) |

Retrieved on August 17, 2015 from **http://www2.ed.gov/policy/speced/guid/idea/bapr/2008/5relstedrequirements081308.pdf.**

A description of all indicators as well as statutory and regulatory authority is available at **http://www2.ed.gov/policy/speced/guid/idea/bapr/2008/5relstedrequirements081308.pdf.**

If there was any concern that transition and secondary issues were not important, the fact that 4 of 20 (20%) of the Indicators that states must report are related to secondary-age students should remove any lingering doubt. Thus far, we have discussed postsecondary outcomes for students with disabilities and the importance of transition services. Following is the regulatory definition of transition services followed by a brief description of what those services encompass.

§300.43 Transition Services

(a) *Transition Services* means a coordinated set of activities for a child with a disability that

  (1) Is designed to be within a results-oriented process, that is focused on improving the academic and functional achievement of the child with a disability to facilitate the child's movement from school to post-school activities, including postsecondary education, vocational education, integrated employment (including supported employment), continuing and adult education, adult services, independent living, or community participation;

  (2) Is based on the individual child's needs, taking into account the child's strengths, preferences, and interests; and includes

   (i) Instruction;

   (ii) Related services;

   (iii) Community experiences;

   (iv) The development of employment and other post-school adult living objectives; and

   (v) If appropriate, acquisition of daily living skills and provision of a functional vocational evaluation.

(b) *Transition services* for children with disabilities may be special education, if provided as specially designed instruction, or a related service, if required to assist a child with a disability to benefit from special education.

So, transition services include a "coordinated set of activities" to prepare the student for transition from school to the postsecondary world including undertakings such as work, education, and independent living. The regulations just presented include a nonexhaustive listing of possible postschool activities to consider (§300.43 (a)(1)). These activities were not specifically described in the regulations, but the following definitions may help you gain an understanding of different available options and an appreciation for the degree of personal planning needed to help each student identify and develop appropriate individualized transition goals.

Postsecondary education: continued education in settings such as community colleges, four-year universities, trade schools.

Vocational education: participation in regular education vocational preparation programs and apprenticeships.

Integrated employment (including supported employment): The US Department of Labor has the following specific definition: *Integrated employment refers to jobs held by people with the most significant disabilities in typical workplace settings where the majority of persons employed are not persons with disabilities.* In these jobs, the individuals with disabilities earn wages consistent with wages paid workers without disabilities in the community performing the same or similar work; the individuals earn at least minimum wage, and they are paid directly by the employer **(http://www.dol.gov/odep/topics/IntegratedEmployment.htm 4-28-15)**.

Continuing and adult education: Adult education programs are typically provided to individuals over 16 years of age who are not being served by P-12 schools or attending college (Norlin, 2011), and continuing education commonly includes personal enrichment courses, such as weight training or meal planning, that do not focus on vocational training.

Adult services: A wide array of services may be available for adults with disabilities, and connection to agencies providing those services may help to facilitate a seamless transition from secondary school to postsecondary life. These agencies may have a career focus, such as vocational rehabilitation, or support services such as may be offered through state offices, for example, a Division on Developmental Disability.

Independent living: Consideration of living arrangements after leaving secondary school can be an important transitional activity and may include a wide array of supports or activities. Some students may live at home, others may live in supported living situations, while others may live independently.

Community participation: This appears to be a purposefully broad term that could include recreation and leisure activities as well as purpose functioned use of community transportation options.

As can be inferred from these brief descriptions, the range, types, and exact nature of services needed for students to successfully move from school to postsecondary settings are highly variable and dependent upon the individual student. It should also be clear that these options are not mutually exclusive and more than one activity may be appropriate for any particular individual.

Part two of the definition (§300.43 (a)(2)) requires that student interests, preferences, and needs be considered when identifying transition services (i.e., the coordinated set of activities). This requirement recognizes the particularly important aspect of student centered programming. In the recent past, a common practice was for professionals to make important life decisions for the person with a disability, particularly a severe disability, without carefully considering the individual's preferences, interests, or strengths (Taylor, 1988, 2001). Just imagine how unfair it would be for others to make decisions on where you would live, who would be your friends, whether you would get married, whether you would be employed, and in which recreation activities you would be allowed to participate. Our guess is that you would find it highly intrusive and a violation of your individual rights. However, that was an approach frequently taken with individuals with disabilities. It certainly still happens, but with greater organized advocacy on behalf of individuals with disabilities, greater societal support for person-centered planning and empowerment and improved methods of assessment and training, more individuals with disabilities can expect to have control over these important aspects of their lives. It should be remembered that at the age of majority (18 in most states) students with disabilities become adults with all of the associated rights and entitlements allowed by law. The fact that they may continue to receive special education and related services until the age of 22 years does not diminish rights of adulthood including control over the IEP.

The regulations further recognize that transition services can include instruction, related services, community activities, employment, and daily living skills. Notes to the regulations are more detailed and specify that transition services can address health and physical care, leisure, mobility, social skills, money management, etc. (Fed. Reg. 71, 46579, 2006). The important point here is that, just as Annual Goals and Short-Term Objectives on the IEP must be individualized, so must transition goals and planning be specific to the needs of each student.

Finally, in §300.43(b), the regulations specify that transition services can be considered to be "special education" if specially designed instruction is required. So it would be possible for transition services to be the only special education a student received. For example, consider a 20-year-old student who needs some specialized support on the work site to learn his or her job, manage finances, or control behavior when frustrated. It would be acceptable for the specially designed instruction to consist of only strategies designed to help meet these transition needs. In fact, it would be very possible that the special education be provided to the student at sites other than the school, such as the workplace and the local credit union or bank.

Thus far, we have reviewed the postsecondary outcomes for students with disabilities and found significant differences when compared to students without disabilities. Data clearly identified disadvantages encountered by individuals with disabilities and emphasized the importance of transition planning if students are to overcome these challenges. We also pointed out the importance of access to both the general education classroom and curriculum, as well as integrated community sites, crucial factors for increasing the likelihood of students with disabilities having productive and enriching lives. In addition, we noted the increased importance the Federal Government has placed on transition and discussed some possible transition activities. Given this background information, it is now appropriate to address the issue of transition and the IEP.

Transition Components and the IEP

Transition was first addressed in IDEA 90, which mandated that it be discussed beginning at age 14 with additional requirements at age 16; however, the regulations were somewhat ambiguous regarding the differences between transition planning at ages 14 and 16. IDEA 04 provided some clarification. Now, transition planning does not need to be conducted at age 14, but must be addressed in the IEP that is in effect when the student turns 16-years old. So, for most students, transition planning will be initially implemented when the child is 15-years old, because that IEP will likely be the IEP in effect when the child turns 16. If the IEP team decides to begin transition planning before the mandatory age, then all components of transition planning must be addressed. It is neither permissible nor is it appropriate to only address part of a transition plan simply because a student is younger than 16 years.

There is an exception to the transition requirement. For students incarcerated in adult prisons and whose expected prison release date will be after they age-out of special education eligibility, the IEP is not required to address transition (§300.324(d)(1)(ii). Whether that is a good idea or not is beyond the scope of this text, but it may be helpful to note that the law does not prohibit transition planning for those students, it just doesn't require it.

There is no particular format in which postsecondary transition must be presented on an IEP document and there is no federal requirement for a "transition IEP." IDEA 04 simply requires that the student's transition needs be addressed. States or districts may require that a particular format be followed when developing a transition plan, so you should consult your school district or state department of education to determine whether a specific format is required. Regardless of what IEP format is used by your district, there are specific components that must be included in order for the transition planning to be compliant according to Indicator 13 criteria. The National Technical Assistive Center on Transition (NTACT) has developed an Indicator 13 Checklist that can be used to determine whether transition planning for a student contains the required items and was conducted in a compliant manner. A copy of the Indicator 13 Checklist is contained in Appendix D, and you can refer to it as we discuss transition in the rest of the chapter. The Indicator 13 Checklist can also be accessed at the NTACT website (**www.transition.org**). The Information at this website is public domain, so it can be used by schools and districts at no cost. This site provides access to a considerable amount of additional information including lesson plans, resources, research syntheses, and evidence-based practices.

We included a sample of IEP form in the text, but for transition planning, we will refer you to sample plans written by the NTACT for several reasons. First, the site contains sample transition plans for students with a variety of different disabilities (see Table 7-2). This way, you can choose to review plans that may be similar to those you will develop for students with whom you work. Second, each of the plans provides a "right" and "wrong" way to address the required components with comprehensive explanations. Third, the plans address the transition components that must be met to ensure compliance and follow the Indicator 13 Checklist. Finally, a review of these comprehensive plans will assist you in obtaining a thorough understanding of transition planning requirements. We encourage you to consult one of those plans as we take you through the following 6-step process for postsecondary planning and see how the process works for students with different disabilities and levels of support.

TABLE 7-2. Postsecondary Transition Plans for Student with Varying Needs

The following links provide access to transition documents originally created by NSTTAC, now NTACT. Each document provides a comprehensive review of transition planning for each student. Included are examples, nonexamples, and explanations about the different components of each plan.

Student	Age/Disability/Link
Alex	17, autism http://transitionta.org/sites/default/files/dataanalysis/I13_Alex.pdf
Allison	18, learning disability http://transitionta.org/sites/default/files/dataanalysis/I13_Allison.pdf
Jamarreo	19, behavior, hearing http://transitionta.org/sites/default/files/dataanalysis/I13_Jamarreo.pdf
Jodi	17, mild intellectual disability http://transitionta.org/sites/default/files/dataanalysis/I13_Jodi.pdf
Kevin	18, significant intellectual disability http://transitionta.org/sites/default/files/dataanalysis/I13_Kevin.pdf
Paulo	18, mild intellectual disability and autism http://transitionta.org/sites/default/files/dataanalysis/I13_Paulo.pdf

Steps in Writing Postsecondary Transition Plans

There are six major steps or tasks involved to the development of a good a transition plan: (1) conduct an age appropriate transition assessment, (2) develop postsecondary goals, (3) identify transition services, (4) determine the course of study, (5) develop annual IEP goals, and (6) develop interagency collaborations. We will briefly address each of these steps in the following sections and have provided a graphic portrayal of the transition planning process in Figure 7-1 to serve as a concept map for you as you read the text. The graphic was developed at the Center for Change in Transition Services at Seattle University. You can find the graphic, training modules and other transition information at **https://www.seattleu.edu/ccts/about/**.

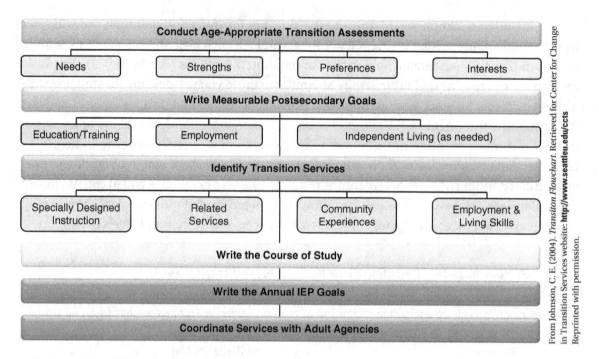

From Johnson, C. E. (2004). *Transition Flowchart*. Retrieved for Center for Change in Transition Services website: **http://www.seattleu.edu/ccts** Reprinted with permission.

FIGURE 7-1. Transition services flow chart.

Step 1: Age-Appropriate Transition Assessment

The first step involves the completion of an age-appropriate transition assessment that includes identification of student's strengths, interests, and preferences. Transition assessments can be formal or informal and need not be based on commercially prepared, norm-referenced instruments. The overarching purpose is to obtain information that will help identify meaningful postsecondary goals that will be addressed via the IEP.

When writing this chapter, we considered listing numerous web sites that deal with a variety of transition topics, including assessment. However, the Health Resource Center at the National Youth Transition Center **(http://heath.gwu.edu/directory-of-transition-websites)** and the Center for Change in Transition Services **(https://www.seattleu.edu/ccts/resources/)** are two organizations that have already developed portals to a wide variety of transition sites. Their listing are much more comprehensive than we could have provided and are nicely organized by topic. You are encouraged to view the sites to obtain a working familiarity with a variety of age-appropriate assessment instruments and other resources available to support students with postsecondary transition.

In an earlier chapter, we discussed the need for consent prior to conducting assessments. If transition assessment information will be used to determine eligibility for special education services then consent would certainly be required. However, there are conflicting interpretations regarding the need for consent when addressing transition. For example, Illinois has determined that consent is not required **(http://www.isbe.net/spec-ed/pdfs/parent_guide/**

ch8-secondary_transition.pdf), Virginia noted that consent requirements can vary by locale (http://www.doe.virginia.gov/special_ed/transition_svcs/transition_assessment.pdf), and Massachusetts stated that in some cases consent is required (http://www.doe.mass.edu/sped/advisories/2014-4ta.html). In Massachusetts, for example, consent is not required if the assessment is administered to all students or is part of an assignment or activity routinely conducted in the curriculum. Consent is needed if the assessment instrument or activity is not administered to all students, not part of routine classroom activities, or not simply an aspect of on-going progress monitoring. We tend to agree with the Massachusetts approach because the reasoning is aligned with the IDEA guiding principles of parental (or adult student) involvement. In spite of our preference, you are ultimately responsible for familiarizing yourself with the requirements in your state and complying with those procedures.

Step 2: Write Measurable Postsecondary Goals

Just as Annual Goals and Short-Term Objectives must be based on assessment results that are described in the Present Levels Statement, measurable postsecondary goals must be based on results from age appropriate assessment conducted in Step 1. For each student, the IEP must include measurable postsecondary goals related to (1) education/training and (2) employment. So, there must be two postsecondary goals, at a minimum. For some students, regardless of disability, there may also be goals for independent living if determined necessary by the IEP team.

There are differences between the Annual Goals and Short-Term Objectives discussed Chapter 4 and postsecondary goals. We stressed that if the Annual Goals and Short-Term Objectives were well written and appropriate special education/related services were provided, then the student would have different Annual Goals and Short-Term Objectives developed at the next annual IEP meeting. This makes sense because an "annual goal" is just that— a goal written for one year. These Annual Goals are very specific and mastery of the Annual Goals and Short-Term Objectives can be one factor in determining whether or not a student received a FAPE.

However, postsecondary goals may remain the same across several years. For example, if a student had a postsecondary transition goal related to attaining skills as a motorcycle technician, that goal could remain the same across numerous years. Still it is crucial that the postsecondary goals be revisited on an annual basis and updated or totally rewritten, if necessary. On a final note, providing postsecondary goals does not in any way imply that special education supports will be provided after the student graduates from high school with a regular diploma or ages out. Rather, they provide some focus for the IEP team to help support the student in achieving his or her postsecondary goals.

The format for writing Annual Goals and postsecondary goals also differs. We hope that you recall the formula we presented in Chapter 4: an Annual Goal should begin with the condition (or antecedent), followed by specific measureable behavior, and a criteria for determining success as indicated in the following diagram.

Condition   →   Behavior   →   Criteria

For writing postsecondary goals the following formula suggested by NTACT is appropriate,

_____   _____ will _____   _____
(After high school)   (Student's name)   (behavior)   (when and how)
(After graduation)
(Upon completion of high School)

For example, assume that we have a student, Julia, who would like to work part-time in a retail store, requires some job support/training assistance, and would also benefit from support for to meet her independent living desires. Applying the NTACT formula to develop postsecondary goals the IEP team could develop the following compliant postsecondary goals:

Employment:
After high school, Julia will work 20–30 hours per week as a cashier at a local retail store.

Education/Training:
After high school, Julia will work with a job coach to learn the job-specific social skills required at the retail store where she will be working.

Independent Living:
After high school, Julia will live in a supported living arrangement with a roommate, independently prepare her meals, and take the bus to/from work.

These postsecondary goals would be acceptable, because they will be completed after leaving high school, are measureable, and contain activities that can be achieved. Contrast these with the following goals that would not be acceptable. None of the following specify that the goal would be achieved upon completion of high school or contain measurable outcomes (liking and wanting are not behavioral outcomes).

Employment: Julia would like a job as a retail clerk.

Education/Training: Julia wants to take some cooking classes.

Independent Living: Julia likes watching movies, playing video games, and taking Zumba classes at the gym.

Step 3: Identify Transition Services

Transition services include those services that a student may need to meet postsecondary goals. As can be seen in Figure 7.1, transition services can be broadly categorized into the following groupings: (1) instructional services, (2) related services, (3) community services, and (4) employment, adult living, and daily living. Students may not need services in all of these areas for each postsecondary goal. For our hypothetical student Julia, the IEP team decided that she needs the following:

(1) Instructional services:

basic math and money skills

job-related social skills

reading bus schedules

(2) Related Services:

None

(3) Community Services

Meet with supported work providers and select provider

Using the bus to get to the gym and work

(4) Employment, Adult Living, and Daily Living

Apply for SSI

Part-time paid employment in retail store

Step 4: Plan of Study

The IEP should contain a plan of study that identifies the specific courses or general types of courses that the student will take in order to meet the postsecondary goals. The plan of study should not just be a statement that the student will complete courses needed to graduate. For Julia, her course of study for grade 12 and beyond includes the following:

Grade 12	Postgrade 12
Basic math and money	Community access
Community access	Independent living
Reading	Work experience/Job-related social skills

Step 5: Annual IEP Goals

The fifth step in transition planning is the development of Annual IEP Goals and associated Short-Term Objectives. Even though STO are not required, we take the position that STOs are always appropriate because they give specificity to the process and lessen the likelihood of confusion and resulting disagreements. At least one IEP Annual Goal should be written to address the skills the student needs to meet the postsecondary goals. It is likely that at least one Annual Goal would need to be written for each postsecondary goal. For example, an Annual Goal that might be written for Julia to help her achieve her postsecondary employment goal of working as a cashier in a retail store could be:

When role-playing as a cashier and presented a purchase ticket identifying the total amount due and either a $10, $20, or $50 bill to pay for the sale, Julia will make the correct change on 20 consecutive transactions.

Step 6: Develop Adult Agency Collaboration

The final step can be very important for helping to ensure effective transition. We will discuss the activity a bit more in the section on IEP team membership, but for now, recognize that the school must identify other agencies, if any, that may be involved in providing or paying for transition services during the current IEP. Those agencies may be invited to the IEP, but should only attend the part of the meeting clearly linked to transition planning. Agencies that provide services to adults with disabilities vary by locale, and may include organizations, such as Vocational Rehabilitation, Community Transition Services, or Division for Developmental Disabilities.

The need to invite possible providers can present a bit of a temporal conundrum for IEP teams because determination of which adult agency or agencies to invite should be made after transitional goals and needs are identified, which would occur well into the actual IEP meeting. To deal with potential issues, the IEP team does have several options which may include:

First, there are students who do not need transition services provided by an outside agency, so there would not be a need to invite anyone. For these students, it is still important that they be informed of adult agencies that would be available should they require supports in the future.

Second, prior to the IEP meeting, the team may deem it too early to identify the outside agencies that may need to be involved. Agencies could always be invited to a subsequent annual IEP meeting or an addendum meeting.

Third, the IEP team may have a good idea of the content of postsecondary goals that will be developed as well as the adult services a student may need. With prior planning, the school could be in a position to invite the appropriate agency before even developing postsecondary transition goals. For example, the IEP team may know that a student wants to participate in different job exploration activities and will require services from a supported employment agency to organize and provide those services. In this case, the specific goal may not have been developed, but the team may already know that this is an area for consideration at the IEP and have agreed that it will be addressed in the IEP.

In summary, transition planning is an especially important activity for youth with disabilities. Carefully developed plans and the provision of necessary services may substantially increase the likelihood of success. The essential components of transition planning have been discussed, and the following section describes additional notice requirements and information for the IEP team.

IEP Team Membership and Notice of When Transition is to be Discussed

When considering transition, there are some significant changes in the composition of the IEP team (§300.321) and some additional procedures that must be followed (§300.322). First, as with other IEP teams, the team must consist of the parent(s), district representative, general education teacher, and special education teacher unless a team member was excused following the procedures described in Chapter 3. This team composition should sound familiar, as the same people should attend other IEP meetings. As noted in our prior discussion and the following regulations, outside agencies that will be involved in providing or paying for transition services must also be invited. In addition, the child must be invited and parents must be informed that transition will be a topic of discussion in the IEP meeting.

§300.322 Parent Participation

For a child with a disability beginning not later than the first IEP to be in effect when the child turns 16, or younger if determined appropriate by the IEP team, the notice also must—

(i)   Indicate—

   (A)   That the purpose of the meeting will be the consideration of the post-secondary goals and transition services for the child, in accordance with §300.320(b); and

   (B)   That the agency will invite the student; and

(ii) Identify any other agency that will be invited to send a representative.

When inviting the student, prior to the child's reaching the age of majority, the district need not send written notice to the student. However, the written notice to the parents must indicate that the student will be invited to the meeting, even if the district knows that the parents may disagree. If the parents decide not to bring the minor student to the meeting, the district cannot override parental authority and compel the child's attendance. In that case, the district must take action to ensure that the minor student's interests, strengths, and preferences are considered when the team addresses transition.

As previously discussed, the district must, to the extent appropriate, "invite a representative of any participating agency that is likely to be responsible for providing or paying for transition services" (§300.321(b)(3)). Since personal and confidential material may be discussed at an IEP meeting, the district must receive written consent from the parents or student who has reached age of majority for agency representatives to attend the meeting. This consent must be obtained for every IEP to which the agency representative is invited. It cannot be blanket consent that lasts from age 16–21 as clarified by OSEP in the 2008 Letter to Gray.

If an agency agrees to provide a service but subsequently fails to do so, the district must make other arrangements for the student to receive the services. Remember, if it is in the IEP, then the district has ultimate responsibility for ensuring the student receives the specified service. This concludes our discussion of postsecondary transition, and we will proceed to the following issues that are either required or commonly encountered at the secondary level: (1) Summary of Performance (SOP), (2) extracurricular and nonacademic activities, (3) grading, (4) diploma and graduation, and (5) transfer of rights at age of majority.

Summary of Performance

The regulations (§300.305(e)(3)) require that schools provide a Summary of Performance (SOP) to a student with a disability who graduates with a regular diploma or ages out. As with transition planning, there is no required format that must be completed, so you are encouraged to find what your state or local district may require. Whatever format is used, the SOP must minimally contain a summary of the student's academic achievement, functional performance, and recommendations on how to support the student in meeting his or her postsecondary goals.

The SOP is a document that a student can voluntarily share with future employers, service providers, educational institutions, or other agencies that would support the student's attainment of postsecondary goals. Given the personal nature of information contained in the SOP, Shaw, Dukes, and Madaus (2012) emphasize the importance of having the student involved in its development. Helping develop the plan can serve as an educational activity that can help the student be an effective self-advocate. The National Collaborative on Workforce and Disability (NCWD) is a good source for self-advocacy materials and has a publication titled "The 411 on Disability Disclosure: A Workbook for Youth with Disabilities." This curriculum guide is available free of charge at **http://www.ncwd-youth.info/411-on-disability-disclosure**.

From the student perspective, it is important that the SOP contain information that will assist in achieving postsecondary goals. From the district perspective, it is also important that a legally compliant SOP be provided, because a student would have two years after graduating or aging out to challenge the quality of the SOP. If it was proven that a faulty SOP resulted in postsecondary failures, then districts may be liable (Norlin, 2010; Shaw, Dukes, & Madaus, 2012).

Extracurricular and Nonacademic Activities

We discussed LRE in Chapter 5 and noted that issues more commonly encountered at the secondary level would be discussed in this chapter. In this section, we are using the term extracurricular for activities that are not be specifically related to the curriculum or IEP goals and objectives for a student, whereas, cocurricular are those additional learning activities clearly related to the curriculum or IEP goals and objectives. Neither the law nor the regulations recognize cocurricular activities as we describe, but we mention it this way to emphasize that some extracurricular activities can incorporate learning goals and could be considered an extension of the curriculum. Whether an activity is best considered extracurricular or cocurricular would need to be determined on an individual basis. To help clarify our discussion consider the following examples.

For most students, playing on a school athletic team is an extracurricular activity. Membership on the team is competitive and not related to any specific learning targets. For example, there is no guarantee or expectation that all interested student can make the varsity football team; many get cut from the team and either don't play or are placed on a junior varsity team. However, for students with disabilities who cannot make the team, there are frequently assistant positions available. These assistant positions could provide excellent cocurricular opportunities. For example, a student with motor and communication goals might be able to work on those goals while acting as an assistant for the team by handing out equipment and communicating with players and coaches.

In contrast, participation in a club such as the Distributive Education Clubs of America (DECA) is clearly aligned with the marketing curriculum taught in vocational education and is an extension of the curriculum. All student who participate in the marketing courses are able to participate in DECA without passing a competitive cut as in sports. In either case, whether the activity is considered cocurricular or extracurricular, the district must comply with IDEA regulations. Pertinent sections of §300.107 and §300.117 follow.

§300.107 Nonacademic Services.

The State must ensure the following:

(a) Each public agency must take steps, including the provision of supplementary aids and services deemed appropriate and necessary by the child's IEP Team, to provide nonacademic and extracurricular services and activities in the manner necessary to afford children with disabilities an equal opportunity for participation in those services and activities.

(b) Nonacademic and extracurricular services and activities may include . . . athletics . . . special interest groups or clubs sponsored by the public agency . . .

§300.117 Nonacademic settings.

In providing or arranging for provision of nonacademic and extracurricular services and activities including meals, recess periods . . . must ensure that each child with a disability participates with nondisabled children in the extracurricular services and activities to the maximum extent appropriate to the needs of the child. . . . ensure that each child with a disability has the supplementary aids and services determined by the child's IEP Team to be appropriate and necessary for the child to participate in nonacademic settings.

For extracurricular activities, particularly those that are competitive in nature, districts must ensure equal opportunity (*Dear Colleague Letter*, 2016). This means that regardless of disability, students must have the opportunity to participate, but are not guaranteed participation in any sport or activity desired. If a student with a disability wants to participate in an extracurricular activity, then the district must consider whether modifications are warranted. For example, a modification for deaf student who cannot hear the starter pistol in a track meet may be use of a starter pistol that includes a light as a signal. The student would still need to meet the criteria to be on the track team, but the signal light is a reasonable accommodation.

As delineated in the *Dear Colleague Letter* (2016) providing equal opportunity for extracurricular activities does not mean:

- Compromising student safety;
- Changing the nature of selective teams—student with disabilities have to compete for a place on the team like everyone else;

- Giving a student with a disability an unfair advantage; or
- Changing essential elements that affect the fundamental nature of the game.

In essence, districts must ensure that students are provided equitable opportunities to participate in extracurricular activities, but as with other students participation is not guaranteed. It is crucial that students not be discriminated against based on disability and that reasonable accommodations be considered. In addition, IEP teams may want to consider what services and supports a child may need to participate in nonacademic activities (whether cocurricular or extracurricular) such as pep rallies, school dances, language clubs, DECA, etc.

Grading

District practices regarding assignment of course grades must not be discriminatory in nature. In *Letter to Runkel* (1996), the Office for Civil Rights (OCR) provided substantial guidance regarding grading practices and will be the source of information in the following discussion. First, students with disabilities may be awarded modified grades in courses; however, the decision should be made by the IEP team. Second, it would be appropriate for the IEP team to discuss collaborative grading efforts between general and special educators for a student who is completing a course in the general education classroom.

Third, transcripts can indicate that modifications or exceptions to the grading scale were made as long as students without disabilities are also treated accordingly. It is important that any coding on the transcript be relatively generic and not identify that it is used only with students with disabilities. Otherwise, the grading system may be a violation. For example, OCR recommended that a label such as "modified curriculum" might be acceptable, especially if that was also used with students who were in advanced level courses. Alternatively, the transcript could use terms such as "basic" or "level 1" rather than "special education" as those terms may also be useful for student without disabilities who are enrolled in remedial courses. Schools are cautioned about using terms such as "resource room" on the transcript, because that term is generally associated with disability and could violate issues of confidentiality. Since students frequently request high school transcripts are be released to potential employers or postsecondary schools/training facilities, students should be informed of what identifiers are included on the transcript.

The last grading issue we will discuss relates directly to student who may be attending a general education course, but working on skills other than academic content. For example, if a student with a low-incidence disability was attending a social studies course, not taking it for social studies credit, and working on IEP objectives related to communication skills, that student could receive a grade based on criteria outlined in the IEP.

Diploma and Graduation

The IDEA does not guarantee that every student who receives special education services will receive a regular high school diploma. While diploma alternatives are a local or state decision, the option of earning a regular diploma must be available to all students who meet standards.

In a 2001 Letter to the Florida Department of Education (102 LRP 37673), OCR stated that districts are not required to grant a regular diploma for students with disabilities who do not meet the standards, but stressed that districts must provide students with disabilities an equal opportunity to meet standards. These specific protections against discrimination (equal opportunity) are provided by Section 504 and Title II of the ADA. In that same letter, OCR made it clear that districts must notify students of specific requirements for earning a regular diploma and make appropriate testing accommodations.

In a 1989 Letter to Special School District of St. Louis County (MO), OCR noted that schools must notify parents if successful completion of the IEP will not result in a regular education diploma. In addition to keeping parents informed, this notification would allow students, parents, and schools to alter the course of study to enable student to complete the requirements for a regular diploma, if appropriate. Receipt of a special education diploma, GED, or certificate of mastery is not considered a substitute for a regular diploma (§300.102(a)(3)(iv)). Students with disabilities who have earned any of these nonregular education options could continue to receive special education and related services in a school setting, a transition setting, or other alternative as stipulated in the IEP. They could also complete requirements and earn a regular high school diploma.

IDEA eligibility terminates when a child graduates with a regular diploma or ages out. While this may vary by state, students typically age out of services at the end of the school year in which they turn 21. If a child ages out, then eligibility automatically ends, and the child is no longer eligible for special education services regardless of need. If however, the child has not aged out but has earned a regular education diploma, then the school has additional responsibilities. (Just a reminder that students who age out or earn a regular diploma, the child must receive a Summary of Progress.) For a student who graduates with a regular diploma, the graduation constitutes a change in placement, and the district must send Prior Written Notice. This document would ensure that parents and the student are fully aware of the termination of services upon graduation.

Finally, we want to note that student with disabilities should not be prohibited from participating in graduation ceremonies. That should already be an assumption for those student who will be graduating. For those student who will not be graduating, but will continue with services, IDEA does not prohibit their participation in the ceremony with their typically developing peers. They are able to walk with peers and participate in this important "coming of age" ceremony without that participation being considered an official graduation and termination of services. Some districts may not allow a student to participate in a ceremony until actually graduating, so you should check with your state laws.

Transfer of Rights at Age of Majority

In accordance with state law, once a student reaches age of majority, some or all of the rights afforded parents regarding special education may be transferred to the child. The language of the law is permissive, meaning that the rights transferred, if any, are determined by the state. However, if any rights will transfer to the student, IDEA requires that no later than one year before the child reaches age of majority, the IEP must include a statement that the child and parents have been notified of what rights will transfer (§300.320 (c)).

This transfer of right does not apply to a child who has been determined to be incompetent under state law. For a child who had been judged incompetent, the state must have a procedure for appointing the parent or other person as needed to represent the child's educational interests (§300.520 (b)).

So, if the age of majority is 18, then at least one year before the child reaches that age, the IEP team must discuss and document that transfer of rights has been discussed. Since IEPs are generally not conducted on birthdays, you probably aren't providing this information on the child's 17th birthday—exactly one year before he reaches age of majority. In practical terms, you will likely be discussing this earlier than one calendar year before the child reaches age of majority. It is imperative that you provide at least one year's notification as required by the law, because that early notice would ensure that neither parents nor students would be caught unprepared for the changes. It would also provide parents with time to request that the courts declare a child incompetent and award them a continuation of the rights, if necessary.

Chapter Summary

In this chapter, we provided information detailing the generally unacceptable postsecondary achievements of students with disabilities in order to support the contention that development of transition plans must be a thoughtful process designed to prepare youth for adult life. One requirement is the provision of transition services beginning with the IEP in effect when the child turns 16 years of age. The requirements for transition planning and the IEP team responsibility were briefly discussed. As we noted at the start of the chapter, transition is a complex topic and cannot be covered sufficiently in one short chapter in an IEP book. We recommend that those of you who will be working in the transition area complete coursework and/or training in this area. Absent that, we provided numerous web-based resources for you to conduct further investigation.

We also covered many issues that are more commonly encountered when developing IEPs for secondary age students. Overall, it is important to recognize that whether considering participation in extracurricular activities, graduation ceremonies, or other events, schools must ensure that students with disabilities are provided with equitable access. Access does not mean that just because a student has a disability, he or she should be on the track team; rather, it means that the student should not be penalized for the disability.

Chapter Activities

1. Review your state law and determine what rights, if any are transferred to a student upon reaching age of majority.

2. Review your state law and describe the procedure for determining if a child is incompetent. Is there an emergency provision for a determining competency for child who might have been in a serious accident shortly before the IEP meeting and without sufficient time for a court to rule on competence?

3. Obtain the grading policies of three or four school districts. How do they designate a modified curriculum on the transcript?

4. Develop a scenario for a secondary age student that includes Present Levels of Academic Performance and Present Levels of Functional Performance. Develop an IEP for that student and including transition.

5. Obtain a completed secondary level IEP and review it to ensure that all IEP components have been completed. In addition, use the Indicator 13 Checklist to determine whether the required transition components have been addressed. (Be sure that you have permission to use the IEP and that any identifying information has been removed. Identifying information may include specific life circumstances as well as a student's name or school.)

6. Visit a local school district to determine what type of transition programming is currently provided to students.

Chapter 8

Procedural Safeguards

Chapter Overview

In an earlier chapter, we noted that passage of special education law brought with it protections and safeguards for children with disabilities above and beyond those afforded to children without disabilities. As you may recall, prior to federal special education law, many states routinely denied students with disabilities an education, while at the same time mandating attendance of students without disabilities. If students with disabilities did receive services, they were generally provided with much less than was afforded children without disabilities, and received those services in separate settings, segregated from their peers. In addition, many of the activities that were provided lacked any educational merit and served as little more than a way to fill the time—oftentimes more similar to daycare than school. Passage of P.L. 94-142, Education for All Handicapped Children Act, in 1975 signified a new commitment on the part of the federal government to the education of children with disabilities and included the provision of procedural safeguards designed to equalize the playing field for children with disabilities and their families.

The procedures and safeguards identified in IDEA serve several purposes which include: 1) providing an option to keep parents informed and involved in making meaningful decisions regarding their child's education, 2) outlining some of the major protections that districts must afford children with disabilities, 3) ensuring methods for parents to challenge district actions, and 4) providing a mechanism for the resolution of disagreements between a district and parent regarding the delivery of special education services. It is important that you have a basic understanding of the safeguards to avoid inadvertently violating them and to enable you to explain the basic provisions to parents. For more in-depth guidance, you can always refer parents to the district administrators, including the special education director or to advocacy organizations, but teachers are frequently the first point of contact.

Procedural Safeguards

We have repeatedly stressed the importance of parents providing informed, written consent when granting permission for actions such as evaluation and placement in special education. That consent requirement is actually one of the safeguards, and it requires that parents be fully informed of the proposed actions and have an understanding of the procedural safeguards available to them. When preparing this chapter, we decided to write brief descriptions of the safeguards and refer you to the appropriate sources for more specific details, such as timelines, etc. We felt that for the most part, readers of this book would not need to know the exact timeline for more complex issues such as due process proceedings and most would simply not be interested in delving into the topic at that depth—at least not now. So, we will approach the task of reviewing the procedural safeguards by providing a very simple description of the content, and also provide you with some guiding questions to consider as chapter review activities.

When IDEA '04 was passed, the Department of Education was assigned the task of developing model forms for the IEP as well as a Procedural Safeguards Notice. The model IEP forms are not particularly helpful, but the Procedural Safeguards Notice was written for distribution to parents, and the language is relatively free of acronyms and the concepts are presented in an easy to understand manner. The Procedural Safeguards Notice model form and appropriate sections of the regulations (§ 300.500-300.537) are excellent sources for delving into the specifics of particular safeguards. The model notice form is available at **http://idea.ed.gov/static/modelForms**. We also encourage you to reference the notice developed by your state or school district as it should contain important information specific to your locale.

Our overall goal for you is to develop sufficient familiarity with the safeguards so that you will be able to provide an oral review of them in a few minutes at the beginning of an IEP meeting. While not required by the law, we recommend that a copy of the Procedural Safeguards Notice be sent with the Invitation to the IEP meeting. Even though you may have given a written copy of the safeguards to the parents prior to the IEP meeting, we recognize that not all parents have the time to read the document, some parents lack the reading skills and may be uncomfortable asking for a review, while others may feel overwhelmed and confused by the legal tone of the document. Therefore, we recommend beginning each IEP meeting with a brief review of the Procedural Safeguards. (You could even complete that review with the parents before other IEP team members join the meeting.) The important point is that parents be fully informed of the Procedural Safeguards.

Distribution of Safeguards

IDEA requires that schools provide parents of children who are eligible for special education or students referred for an evaluation with a notice that contains a full explanation of the procedural safeguards afforded. This requirement for a full explanation is one reason that the Procedural Safeguard Notice is so lengthy, but you will find that it is important information for parents to have. Occasionally, we have encountered individuals who were reluctant to provide the information to parents whom they felt might be difficult to work with, but that is exactly the wrong way to think. It is both a legal and ethical responsibility that districts provide parents with the information. The Procedural Safeguards Notice must be provided at the following times:

- Once every school year (which is why we suggest the annual IEP meeting) and again in the following situations:
  - Upon initial referral or request for an evaluation,
  - Upon receipt of the parent's first special education state complaint in a school year,
  - Upon receipt of the parent's first due process hearing complaint filed in a school year,
  - When the district decides to take a disciplinary action that constitutes a change in placement, and
  - Upon parental request.

The regulations specify that Notice of Procedural Safeguards addresses the following 13 items. We will provide a brief review of critical points for each item, but each of the 13 items listed below will not be addressed under a separate heading. In the section titled "Opportunity to present and resolve concerns," we will also discuss the interrelated topics of state level appeals, mediation, due process, and we will combine information regarding Interim Alternative Educational Placement (IAE) with placement during due process hearings.

(1) Prior Written Notice (PWN)

(2) Independent Education Evaluation (IEE)

(3) Consent

(4) Access to Records

(5) Opportunity to present and resolve concerns

(6) Availability of Mediation

(7) Child's placement during due process proceedings

(8) Interim Alternative Educational Placement (IAE)

(9) Unilateral placement of child in private schools by parents

(10) Due process

(11) State level appeals (if available in the state)

(12) Civil Actions

(13) Attorney fees

Prior Written Notice (PWN)

The purpose of Prior Written Notice (PWN) is to provide parents with information regarding certain actions that the district is proposing or refusing to with respect to the child. Specifically, PWN must be provided whenever a district proposes or refuses to initiate or change the identification, evaluation, placement, or provision of FAPE. The notice must be written in language understandable to the general public (avoid jargon) and provided in the native language of the parent or other mode of communication used by the parent unless that is clearly not feasible. If the native language or mode of communication is not a written language, then the district must ensure that the notice is translated orally or by other means in the parent's native language or mode of communication and that the parent understands the content of the notice. Some examples of when PWN may be required include:

- The district would like to conduct an initial evaluation or reevaluate a child to determine special education eligibility.

- The district would like to conduct an FBA to inform special education programming.

- The district plans to change the IEP or placement. (It is not necessary to provide PWN for a routine annual IEP meeting in which the Annual Goals and Short-Term Objectives are updated but the services and placement remain the same. However, if placement was changed as a result of the IEP, then PWN must be provided before the change of placement takes effect.)

- The student will be graduating with a regular diploma (but not aging out) and will no longer be eligible for special education services. This is a change in placement.

- The district is refusing a parent request for an initial evaluation or a request for change regarding identification, evaluation, placement, or FAPE.

- The parent has provided written notice revoking consent for provision of special education services. (If parents revoke consent, then they should be fully informed that the child will no longer be afforded the special education protections provided to children receiving special education support.)

- In some cases it may be required for postsecondary transition assessment, (See Post-secondary Transition chapter for further discusion).

Independent Educational Evaluations (IEE)

If parents disagree with an evaluation conducted by the district, they can request that an Independent Education Evaluation be conducted at public expense. Within 15 calendar days of the request for an IEE, the district must either agree to provide the IEE at public expense or file due process to try and demonstrate that their evaluation was appropriate.

If the district prevails in the due process hearing, it would not need to pay for an IEE. Sometimes parents have already had an independent evaluation completed at their own expense. In that case the district must consider the results. However, the district is not required to accept the findings.

Parent Consent and Revocation of Consent

Districts must obtain informed, written consent from parents at several times. The granting of consent means that the parent has been fully informed in his/her native language or mode of communication of all information relevant to the proposed action and provides permission for the action to take place. It also means that a parent understands that consent is optional and may be revoked in writing at any time. The times that consent must be provided include the following.

First, a parent must provide consent before the district conducts an *initial evaluation*. If during the assessment process, the parent revokes permission, then the district must stop the assessment process immediately. Should the parent deny consent, the district has the option of filing due process or using mediation procedures to try to obtain an authorization to conduct an evaluation, but is not required to do so.

Second, parents must also provide written consent before *initial placement* in special education. If a parent refuses to grant consent, then the district is not required to hold an IEP meeting and is not allowed to provide special education services. In addition, if a parent withholds consent for initial placement, the district is specifically prohibited from trying to compel parental consent through the use of mediation or due process.

A third time that consent is required is when new testing is part of the *reevaluation* to determine continuing eligibility. A district may pursue mediation procedures or due process to obtain parental agreement for assessment, but is not required to do so. As we noted previously, IDEA '04 allows districts to confirm continuing eligibility if the parent agrees, without conducting additional assessments.

Fourth, consent is required before conducting a Function Behavioral Assessment. It may also be required for some postsecondary assessment activities (see the corresponding chapters Disciplinary Issues (chapter 6) or Postsecondary Transition (chapter 7) for more in-depth discussion).

A fifth time that consent may be required is when a member of the IEP team is being excused and that member's area is being discussed. Absent consent for the excusal, the school must ensure that team member is at the IEP.

Finally, consent is required before the district releases personally identifiable information or educational records to outside agencies unless release of such records is allowed by Family Educational Rights to Privacy ACT (FERPA). For example, if a child were moving to another state and enrolled in a public school, then the district could share the information without obtaining consent. We provided the following link to the FERPA regulations earlier but provide it again for your convenience. **http://www2.ed.gov/policy/gen/guid/fpco/ferpa/index.html**

If a parent refuses to consent to special education services or revokes consent, then the child would be considered to be a child without a disability and would not be afforded any of the protections contained in the Procedural Safeguards. The district would be free to treat the child as it would any child without a disability, including the use of suspensions and other disciplinary actions. However, a parent who either refused or revoked consent for special education services could always refer the child for an initial evaluation at a later date.

If a child is receiving service and the parent revokes consent, the district must provide PWN indicating the date on which the special education services and associated procedural protections will end. The school district cannot compel a parent to keep a child in special education. Revocation of consent does not "undo" what has taken place and a district need not alter the child's records to eliminate any reference to special education services or evaluations.

Access to Records

Parents have a right to inspect and review IDEA related educational records maintained by the district. They can also request copies of that information. The district can charge for copying, provided that charging a fee does not have the effect of preventing the parent from getting the necessary information. One issue of concern is copyrighted test protocols from norm-referenced tests that many districts use as part of the eligibility process and ultimately keep as part of a child's educational records. Parents are allowed to view those materials, but are not allowed to make copies or write down questions. Doing so could be a violation of copyright law and a potential threat to the validity of the instrument by making the test questions known and readily accessible to individuals taking the test in the future.

If a parent believes that information contained in a child's records is inaccurate, misleading, or represents an invasion of privacy, the parent can request that the district make appropriate corrections. If the district refuses to change the records, then it must advise parents of the right to seek a hearing according to the district procedures under FERPA, as this is not an issue that would be resolved through an IDEA due process hearing. If the information in the child's records is not changed following a district level FERPA hearing, then the parents may submit a statement for inclusion in the child's records.

Opportunity to Present and Resolve Concerns

There are two ways to formalize complaints under IDEA, through a state complaint or a due process hearing. A state complaint may be filed by anyone who believes that a district, state, or other public agency violated a provision of IDEA. The state must develop procedures for processing state complaints, so you would need to reference your state guidelines for specific guidance in that area. States were also required to develop model forms to assist parties in filing a state complaint. If a state complaint and a due process complaint are filed for the same issue, then the state must delay action on any issues that are subject to a due process hearing pending the rendering of the decision.

While a state complaint can be filed by anyone regarding failure to comply with IDEA, a due process complaint can only be filed by a parent or school for issues regarding the proposal or refusal to initiate or change the identification, evaluation, placement, or provision of FAPE for a particular child. Beginning with IDEA '04, a two-year timeline was implemented which required that the complaint must be filed no more than two years before parents or school knew or should have known about the alleged violation. The two-year timeline does not apply to parents if: 1) the district misrepresented that the concern had been adequately addressed or 2) the district withheld information that it was required to provide under Part B.

The actual due process procedures are quite involved and we won't get into specifics here. For more detailed information, we recommend you consult the Procedural Safeguards Model form, the regulations, or contact your district counsel or special education director. Generally speaking, due process procedures are adversarial and both sides are represented by attorneys who argue the case before an impartial due process hearing officer. Unless prohibited by state law, parents may represent themselves throughout a due process, but the school district must inform parents of free or low cost legal support available in the area. In a due process hearing, the two sides can compel witnesses to attend, cross-examine them, and present evidence. It is unlikely that you will ever find yourself in the midst of a due process hearing, but if you do, the best thing you can do is be honest and support your statements with a record documenting that you followed the law. Be sure that you have meaningful, data-based IEPs that addressed all required components, provided services as agreed upon in the IEP, and involved parents in a meaningful way in the development of the IEP. Upon completion of the due process hearing, the hearing officer will issue a ruling that is final unless it is overturned upon appeal.

In addition to due process hearings, school districts must have in place a mechanism for solving disputes through mediation. Mediation generally does not involve attorneys but is carried out like a mini-due process hearing. In a mediation, both sides present their case to an impartial mediator who helps parents and the district arrive at a mutually agreed upon settlement that is enforceable in the courts. Unlike a due process, where parents may find themselves responsible for attorney fees, the entire cost of mediation is covered by the state. The discussion that takes place during a mediation are confidential and may not be used in any future due process or judicial proceedings. Finally, mediation is only an option and cannot be used to deter a parent from filing a due process complaint.

Civil Actions

The following is taken directly from the regulations. If parents have specific questions, we suggest that you have them contact district counsel or another attorney for clarification regarding their specific situation and issues. If the parent is considering a due process and the lawyer believes that the issue could go directly to the courts, then the lawyer should provide the parent with the proper guidance. "Nothing in Part B of IDEA restricts or limits the rights, procedures, and remedies available under the U.S. Constitution, the Americans with Disabilities Act of 1990, Title V of the Rehabilitation Act of 1973 (Section 504), or other Federal laws protecting the rights of children with disabilities, except that before the filing of a civil action under these laws seeking relief that is also available under Part B of IDEA, the due process procedures described above must be exhausted to the same extent as would be required if the party filed the action under Part B of IDEA. This means that you may have remedies available under other laws that overlap with those available under IDEA, but in general, to obtain relief under those other laws, you must first use the available administrative remedies under IDEA (i.e., the due process complaint; resolution process, including the resolution meeting; and impartial due process hearing procedures) before going directly into court" (§300.515(e)).

Child's Placement During Due Process

Unless agreed upon between the school district and the parent, once a due process complaint is filed, the child remains in his or her current placement until the complaint is resolved. Many due process complaints are resolved during the resolution process that occurs before the actual hearing. If there is a due process hearing, the hearing officer will issue a ruling on the issues, including placement if necessary. Consider the following example where, at the IEP meeting, the district proposed changing the child's placement from regular education setting to a special school. The district would have to provide the parents PWN describing the proposed change in placement and specifying the date the change would take effect. If the parents disagreed and filed a due process complaint before the change in placement was implemented, the child would remain in the regular education setting unless the parents and district agreed upon a different placement. This is commonly referred to as the "stay put" rule.

When there is a change of placement as a result of disciplinary actions, the procedures are a bit different. The IEP team determines the Interim Alternative Educational Placement (IAE) where the child will continue to receive special education services, but the disciplinary procedures regarding manifestation determination that were described in Chapter 6 must be followed. As noted in those guidelines, the child would be returned to the current placement if the behavior was determined to be a manifestation of the disability unless parents and district agreed upon a different placement or in the case of "special circumstances" (drugs, weapons, serious bodily injury). Remember that under "special circumstances," the school district may unilaterally change the child's placement for up to 45 days without regard for whether the behavior is determined to be a manifestation of the disability if the student: (1) carries a weapon to or possesses a weapon at school, on school campuses, or to a school function; (2) knowingly possesses or uses illegal drugs, or sells or solicits the sale of a controlled substance, while at school, on school premises, or at a school function; or (3) has inflicted serious bodily injury upon another person while at school, on school premises or at a school function. The parent may file due process, but the student could stay in the alternative placement for 45 days pending decision of the hearing officer. Under these conditions, the hearing should be conducted in an expedited manner. If the district believes that returning the child to the prior placement upon completion of the 45 school day removal is substantially likely to result in injury to the child or other children, then the district may seek the decision of a hearing officer to extend the time allowed for the child's removal.

Attorney Fees

The court, including a due process hearing officer, may award parents reasonable attorney fees if they prevail in an action. The regulations note that attorneys' fees should not exceed the prevailing rate. The court may reduce fees provided to parents under certain conditions including: billing for attorney fees that exceed the prevailing rates, charging for excessive time and legal services, and unreasonably delaying final resolution of the dispute. The district may be awarded fees if an attorney files complaints that were found to be frivolous, unreasonable, or without foundation.

Unilateral Placement of Child in Private Schools by Parents

Parents may request that the district reimburse them for the cost of enrolling their child in a private school without the consent of the school district under certain circumstances. If the district challenges parental placement of the child in the private school, then this issue is typically resolved through a due process hearing. The hearing officer may order the district to pay for the placement if it is determined that the district did not provide the child with FAPE in a timely manner before parents enrolled the child in a private school and the private placement is appropriate.

The reimbursement *may be reduced or denied* by the due process hearing officer if any of the following occurred:

(1) At the most recent IEP, parents failed to notify the district of their rejection of the proposed placement, explained their concerns regarding the provision of FAPE, and stated their intent to enroll the child in a private school at public expense, OR failure of parents to provide the district with written notice addressing these issues at least 10 business days prior to the child's removal from the public school.

(2) Prior to removal, the district provided PWN detailing its intent to evaluate the child and parents failed to make the child available for the evaluation.

(3) The hearing officer finds that the actions of the parent were unreasonable.

The reimbursement may not be reduced or denied for parental failure to provide notice if: 1) the school prevented the parents from providing notice, 2) parents had not been informed of their responsibility to provide notice, or 3) provision of notice would likely result in physical harm to the child. At the discretion of the hearing officer, the following may also be cause for not reducing or denying reimbursement: 1) the parents are not literate or cannot write in English, or 2) provision of notice would likely result in serious emotional harm to the child.

Chapter Summary

Parents of children with disabilities who receive special education services are afforded procedural safeguards. These safeguards were designed to ensure parental participation in educational decisions involving their child. As a teacher, you need not be familiar with every aspect of the Procedural Safeguards, but you should have a basic understanding to help you better serve students with disabilities and support their families.

Chapter Activities

1. Obtain a copy of the Procedural Safeguards Notice used by a local district or your state. Familiarize yourself with the guidelines so that you could review them in an efficient manner at the beginning of an IEP meeting.

2. When must you provide Procedural Safeguards Notice?

3. When must you provide Prior Written Notice? (hint: whenever a district is proposing or refusing ...)

    Identify two examples of when you would provide PWN.

4. When must parents provide written consent?

5. If a parent revokes consent for provision of special education services, would that be considered a change of placement? Would the district be required to provide PWN?

Chapter 9

Meeting the Needs of Students with an IEP in the Classroom

Chapter Overview

By now you should have an excellent idea of what goes into the Individualized Education Program (IEP) and how it is developed. A very fundamental question that we have not yet addressed is, quite simply and directly, "How do I, the general education teacher, include the student with an IEP in my classroom?" Or said a bit differently, "How am I to address this one student's individual needs and at the same time implement the curriculum for all of my typically developing students who have no IEP?" In spite of overwhelming support for the concept of inclusive programming for young children with disabilities there is little by way of published curricula to suggest how to accomplish the task in a way that benefits all of the children. We may have established that there is a strong empirical basis for the effectiveness of inclusive programming (e.g., Oh-Young & Filler, 2015), but there is still need for further study regarding the best strategies for an instructional approach that benefit all of the students in inclusive settings. Nevertheless, there are some very helpful strategies that have worked and you may find it helpful if we devote a few pages here at the end to discussing one of the more important characteristics of those strategies, careful team planning. We will refer to the early work of researchers at the Center of Disabilities at the University of Vermont (e.g., Fox & Williams, 1991) and to our work at the University of Nevada, Las Vegas (e.g., Filler & Xu, 2007) in developing a strategy for identification of adaptations and accommodations for an individual student but we acknowledge that there are numerous texts that have focused upon strategies for including students with significant disabilities in the general education setting.

To successfully address the needs of students with an IEP in the Least Restrictive Environment (i.e, the regular classroom) one must start with the realization that the education of this student, as for all students, is not the sole responsibility of any one person. So don't let yourself get trapped into a feeling that, because this student is in your class, that you alone are responsible for the timely attainment of goals and objectives specified in the IEP. In a very practical sense, you are only one member of a team that shares the responsibility for the program planning, design, and delivery. Other members of the team include a teacher who is appropriately credentialed in special education, parents and other family members, the principal or program administrator to whom you may report, related service personnel including speech and language specialists, occupational therapists, the school nurse and any other specialist who is providing a service that is listed in the IEP. Remember, special education is not a place, it's a set of services that follow the child whatever the setting.

Successful inclusion begins with a plan for how we are going to meet that student's needs and at the same time preserve the integrity of the curriculum for all of the other students who do not have IEPs. As Filler and Xu (2006) have stated:

> "In spite of what many parents and professionals may think, inclusion is not accomplished by simply placing a child with disabilities in a setting with his typically developing peers. It is realized only when we have succeeded in designing a set of activities that insure the full participation of all children, including (thus "inclusion") the child with disabilities. It is participation and not mere geographical proximity that is the necessary pre-condition for *achievement* and meaningful participation requires systematic planning." (p. 94)

While there is both a firm legal basis and widespread support for the concept of inclusive programming for students with disabilities, there is little by way of published curricula to suggest how to accomplish the task in a way that benefits all students. Traditional curriculum guides devote only a few pages to a discussion of the unique needs of children with disabilities. In spite of this lack of readily available published guides for curricular modification, there is a more general strategy that any teacher can use. Filler and Xu (2006) have described it as consisting of a six steps.

Step 1: Forming the Planning Team

According to Filler and Xu (2006), the formation of a team to plan for the inclusion of a student with disabilities is the first step in the inclusion process. It begins with a series of invitations issued to those who share in the daily education of the target student. It is this group of individuals who are responsible for the development of the plan. Included are those we have mentioned above (parents and/or primary caregivers, the special education teacher, related service personnel, the site principal, the regular class teacher in whose room the student with the IEP will be placed) and anyone else who plays a significant part in the daily activities of the student.

The first invitation to participate should be for the parents of the target student with the IEP. It should be issued by the general education teacher but only after prior discussion with, and agreement from, that teacher's supervisor or principal. The teacher should explain the purpose of the planning team being careful to distinguish the difference between the goal of this team from that of the IEP team which will have discussed earlier. While the IEP team goal was to develop the components of the entire education program, the role of the inclusion planning team is to determine how best to address needs documented in the IEP in the regular education setting.

Since the family is a critical component of planning efforts, discussion of a convenient time for the meeting is essential. We have found that most often this means a meeting either before or after school hours for it is unreasonable to expect parents to take time off from work or to rearrange a difficult schedule to attend a meeting during usual business hours. Arranging a time for the meeting can often be the most difficult part of the entire process and it may mean that not everyone you would like to attend will be able to do so. Remember, the parents or primary caregivers are critical members of the team and so every effort should be made to insure their full participation. This may mean that more than one meeting is necessary, but we have found that seldom more than two meetings, each lasting about an hour, are required to complete the initial phases of planning.

Step 2: Document the Curricular Activities of the General Education Setting

The planning meeting begins by a full discussion of exactly what the general education activities are for each day of the week in the classroom where our student with an IEP will be placed. When two meetings are required it is often the case that the first one is devoted entirely to a discussion of the activities that occur in the general education setting or classroom. It is critically important that everyone understands how they are conducted, what the curricular focus is for each, when they occur, and what materials are needed for each. A full understanding of these daily activities by each member of the team is critical for it is those activities planned for our general education students that will provide us with naturally occurring opportunities to address the needs of the student we are working to include. It is an essential requirement that we preserve the integrity of the general curriculum and not lessen its value for the general education student by making compromises for the sake of the student with the IEP.

For our discussion, we will assume that the class is a typical third grade class located in a typical public elementary school. Those members of the team who may not be familiar with the general layout and schedule for the class may wish to visit it and spend enough time to observe first hand the activities that occur throughout the day. Schedules usually vary with certain days indicated for "specials" like music or library so it will probably be necessary to distinguish those days from the usual or typical schedule days. The list of activities proceeds from the beginning of the day when the students arrive until they depart in the afternoon. For each activity it is important to record the length of time devoted to the activity. For example, it may take 25 minutes for students to arrive, put their things away and get seated before the day begins. Arrival and departure along with recess, bathroom breaks, and lunch are all activities that should be listed along with those academic activities that are part of the day such as math, reading, social studies, and so forth.

Step 3: IEP Goals and Objectives

Next, the team turns its attention to a careful specification of the goals and objectives in the IEP. Each should be written clearly enough to for all to understand including an exact specification of what is expected of the student along with the criterion and number of times and conditions under which the criterion performance is to be exhibited (see Chapter 4). If some or all are simply too vague to be clearly understood by each member of the team then it may be necessary to spend a bit of time to rewrite them. This does not mean that we are changing the IEP and, so, would have to convene another meeting to make modifications to the formal document but, merely, that we are translating IEP goals into instructional goals and objectives. For IEPs that do not include objectives for each goal it is a good idea to generate instructional objectives during this meeting or at least discuss the value of doing so. The generation of instructional objectives provides us with the starting point for the development of individual lesson plans that may be necessary in addition to the existing daily group activity plans that are used in the classroom. For a discussion of activity based programming and the use of both individual and group activity plans we suggest that you consult Pretti-Frontzac and Bricker's (2004) text entitled *An Activity Based Approach to Early Intervention*.

Step 4: Planning for Modifications

The determination of what modifications to the existing set of daily activities that are occurring in our example third grade classroom is the next task for the planning team. Each goal and/or objective in the IEP must be referenced to the existing daily in-class and out-of-class activities. The team must address a series of questions, one for each of the scheduled activities that have been listed during Step 2, "Does this activity provide an opportunity to address any of the targeted skills that are reflected in the goals and objectives in the IEP? And if so, which ones?" As answers are sought it is important to remember what the purpose of each daily activity is for the general education students in the class. By asking the question the way we have, we are simply determining whether or not an *opportunity* may exist to practice a skill in the IEP. If it seems possible that the activity in question may provide a natural context in which to address the target skill(s) of the student with an IEP, without completely destroying the meaningfulness of the activity for the general education students, then we must discuss the need for any changes in either content or method of deliver that might be needed for our student with a disability. For example, if the activity involves reading, a student with a visual disability might read from a text with very large print, or a student with a hearing impairment might use a communication device that allows his direct selection of symbols to be translated into intelligible speech when answering questions about the reading passage. One goal of all instruction should be to design activities that both engage the interest of students and at the same time provide opportunities for a wide range of participation. Modifying activities to meet needs of the student with an IEP often leads to the discovery of ways to more actively involve all students.

As Filler and Xu (2006) have noted, modifications to activities of the general education environment may be conceptualized as consisting of two distinct types, one involves individualizing the content of the activity to fit the specific needs of the student with an IEP. A change in content to reflect the needs of a student with a disability is referred to as an adaptation. For example, during math activity the general education students are working on two digit addition problems, but during the same activity our student with the IEP may be working on simple number recognition. Both are math skills but the level of difficulty is significantly different. The second kind of modification to the existing routine may involve an accommodation. Accommodations involve changes to the contextual environment in which the activity occurs. The example these authors use is that of a young child with a physical disability. Whereas his typically developing peers are seated in child size chairs he may be seated in a chair with supports at a cut-out table which supports upright posture. Other accommodations that may be included in the IEP could go so far as calling for an additional instructional aide to work with the general education teacher during part or even all of the day. Some have suggested that an accommodation by way of reduction in class size is also a reasonable considerations when students with intensive needs are included in the general education classroom (Sailor, Halvorsen, Anderson, Doering, Filler, & Goetz, 1989).

Step 5: Related Services

The next phase of planning involves a discussion of how the target student is to receive any related services that might be included in his or her IEP. Students with an IEP often will need such related services as speech therapy, occupational therapy along with periods of one-on-one instruction by a certified special educator. While, it is important to remember that all of what is needed by our student, including related services, must be provided in any setting in which he or she is placed, that does not mean that it is always necessary or even desirable to provide them in the classroom. Services like speech or occupational therapy may more reasonably occur on a pull-out basis. Numerous times during the day typical general education students who do not have an IEP may leave the room for some service or activity and, so, may a student with an IEP also leave the classroom to receive a required service. Some examples of pull-out activities for general education students would include participation in gifted and talented programs, counseling for students whose parents may be going through divorce and/or participation in a reading improvement program. It may well be possible (and desirable) to provide some of the services in the classroom including other students in an activity that provides an opportunity for all to benefit. But everyone on the team should have clear understanding of how frequent and how long for any specified related service is to occur and the setting in which it is to be provided. Whenever it is the judgment of the team that a related service is more appropriately provided outside of the classroom, the team must decide when the student will be receiving that service and what general education in class activity that he will need to miss to do so.

Step 6: Parent/Family Prioritization

Throughout, we have stressed the importance of parent and family involvement in both the development and implementation of the IEP. As one plans for how to include a student with an IEP into the general education setting and to do so in a way that not only references the general education curriculum but supports it and extends it, one must consider the priorities of the parents and families. Parents must be given the opportunity to state what they feel is most important for the child to learn. We know much from research over the past several decades about what aspects of the curriculum parents most value. For example, parents and teachers alike tend to rate social skills as very important for young children with disabilities (Baumgart, Filler, and Askvig, 1991). We may each have our own opinion of what among the various curricular components is most important, but more that anyone else parents and family values must be taken into consideration, if we expect that what we teach in the classroom will generalize to the outside world in which we hope to see those skills practiced on a daily basis.

It is important to recognize that families may have priorities that are best addressed outside of typical educational settings. A good example is toileting. Many young children need to learn to toilet independently and certainly instruction to do so at school is important, but teaching a child to toilet who has not learned to do so by third grade, with all of the necessary component skills, requires the active participation of the family. Naturally occurring opportunities to work on toileting skills will occur at times when the child is not at school. Another example that recently emerged from a planning meeting attended by one of the authors involved the child's behavior while attending church with his family. Mom and Dad wanted him to learn to occupy himself without shouting out during the main service so that he could sit with them and not have to hear the service from the "cry room" accompanied by one parent. It would be out of the question to consider providing school sponsored community-based instruction on a Sunday during church services, but a suggestion as to how the family might implement procedures used at school to accomplish a similar goal at church were welcomed with enthusiasm.

There are several different ways to illicit the feelings of family members, which lessen the understandable reluctance many may feel when in the company of so many "experts". One that we have found effective is the MAPS (Vandercook et al., 1989). The MAPS (McGill Action Planning System) involves a meeting with the parents, family members, friends of the student, and others that might be invited. This meeting usually occurs separate from either the IEP or the inclusion planning team meeting. During the MAPS meeting significant individuals in the life of the student, and if at all possible the student as well, are asked to introduce themselves by describing their relationship to the student, tell what their dreams and fears are about the education of the student, and describe what they each feel are the important educational needs of the student. In this nonjudgmental context family members often feel that they are more able to express themselves with less feeling of pressure that may come from a room full of professionals trying to guide the discussion according to a set legalistic requirements as may be the case in an formal IEP meeting.

The Activity Matrix

Filler and Xu (2006) described a format for summarizing the planning activities discussed above which they adapted from the earlier suggestions of Fox and Williams (1991). We will use their activity matrix format to summarize the steps discussed above but you may prefer a different way to portray the results of the meeting (or meetings). Looking at Figure 9-1 you will see that this summary is for Timothy, a child with an IEP who will be in a typical regular education third grade class in the Fall. While the example we use is for an elementary age student, the same process is equally applicable to middle school or even high school. Of course adjustments would need to be made to accommodate class schedules. Rotations from class to class throughout day would replace transitions from activity to activity within the classroom.

In our example, two meetings occurred to develop the plan during the summer preceding the fall start of school. Since the family was generally familiar with the school and the classroom that Timothy would attend visits to observe were not deemed to be necessary. However, there was much discussion concerning the nature of each activity including how the activities for Tuesday and Thursday (when visits to the school library and music activities were scheduled) differed from those for Monday, Wednesday, and Friday. But, to illustrate, how a completed summary matrix might look we will focus on the schedule for Monday, Wednesday, and Friday. A second matrix would be used for Tuesday and Thursday to reflect the different schedule for those days. This plan was developed for Timothy, an 8-year-old student with moderate cognitive delay and a physical disability that required the use of support (cane and walker).

As a close look at Figure 9-1 will reveal, all of the steps in the planning process that we have discussed are represented. The layout of the form is by columns and rows. Immediately below the student and class identifiers each of the activities that occur each Monday, Wednesday, and Friday in his third grade class are listed, one for each column in the section labeled "Typical Daily Activities." Below each is an indication of how much time in minutes is usually and normally devoted to the activity. On the left lower portion of the form there are a number of rows in a section titled "Skill Areas from Current IEP" and below that are listed, one for each row, a short-hand notation for each goal that needs to be targeted for instruction. These are taken directly from Timothy's IEP.

Also taken directly from the IEP is the list of the related services he will need to receive and/or any pull-out instruction with a special education teacher that may be needed. Below each service, there is an indication of how much time is to be devoted to each. These are listed in the section labeled "Related Services" and appear along with the typical daily activities in

Student: Timothy Age: 8 years Class: Ms. Jones- 3rd Grade Days: Mon./Wed./Fri.

Alternative Activities Listed by Number	1	1								2										Special Education/Related Services							Home/Family
																				1	2						
TYPICAL DAILY ACTIVITIES (Mon./Wed./Fri.)	Flag Salute	Welcome/Warm-up	Language Arts	Snack/Recess	Math	Lunch	Silent Reading\ Cursive	Social Studies\ Science	Spanish\ PE	Clean Up\ Departure										Speech Therapy	Special Ed. Resource						Quietly occupies self during church service
Length of Time for Activity	15 mins.	25 mins.	40 mins.	30 mins.	60 mins.	50 mins.	40 mins.	40 mins.	30 mins	15 mins										30 mins.	45 mins.						
Adaptation: Modified content			X		X		X		X																		
Accommodation: Modified arrangement/staffing				X		X			X																		
SKILL AREAS FROM CURRENT IEP (√ indicates skill is a family priority)																											
Reading: 70 wds/min			X		X		X	X																			
Math: Single digit addition			X		X																						
Expressive Voc.: Uses words	X	X	X	X	X	X	X	X	X	X																	√
Motor: Walk w/o support				X		X																					√
Social Skill: Plays and/or works cooperatively			X	√		√			X	X																	√
Social: Raises hand to be recognized	X	X	X		X		X	X																			√

NOTES: Family places high priority upon opportunities to practice sharing and cooperative interactions with peers and wants Timothy to "behave" in church as indicate by a √ instead of X.

FIGURE 9-1. Example 3rd Grade Activity Matrix

columns at the top right of the form. If these services are to occur weekly they will have to be scheduled to occur in place of one or more of the typical class activities. But if the IEP team feels that biweekly or less often than weekly is sufficient to meet his needs the NOTES section at the bottom of the form provides space to describe when and the conditions under which they are to occur.

Once each of the daily activities for the class are included on the form, along with the amount of time scheduled for each, current targets for Timothy from the goals in his IEP and the related services or other "special activities" like intensive specialized instruction for a special education teacher are included, the heart of the planning begins. Planning now focuses upon an activity-by-activity determination of whether or not each provides an opportunity to address any of the goals in Timothy's IEP. As inspection of Figure 9-1 reveals, there is a box where goals and activities intersect. An "X" is entered for each activity out to the right of each goal that may be addressed during that activity. The need for either an adaptation or accommodation is noted by an X placed above where it was felt that one or the other or both are necessary, before the general education activity could actually constitute a realistic opportunity to address the goal from his IEP.

Looking at Figure 9-1, we see that the first activity of the day, "Flag Salute," was deemed to be an activity wherein two of Timothy's goals could be addressed, using word (expressive vocabulary) and raising his hand to be recognized (social skills). The team did not feel that any adaptations to the content of the activity or any accommodations for Timothy in the way the activity was normally and usually conducted were necessary. However, if one looks at one of the same goals later during "Language Arts" an adaption, or modification of the content, is necessary before that activity can serve as an opportunity to address his need to work on expressive vocabulary. Similarly, we see that an accommodation, perhaps an extra staff person, is needed in order to work on the expressive vocabulary goal during snack/recess. So the need for either adaptations or accommodations is related directly to the nature of each activity. As we said before, a primary concern is to preserve the meaningfulness of each activity for the students who do not have an IEP but to adapt and accommodate, only when necessary and within reasonable bounds, to allow those activities to be just as meaningful for students like Timothy.

As the note at the bottom of the form indicates, any activity or goal that the parent or primary caregiver thinks is critically important is indicated by the substitution of a "√" in place of an "X." For example, we see that there is a √ at the intersection of the goal for social skills (plays or works cooperatively) and the activity "snack/recess." It means that the parent or primary caregiver felt strongly about the need for Timothy to learn to play and work cooperatively with his friends. Similarly, we see a "√" entered for the same goal during lunch when he would be with his friends. When we plan for Timothy to leave the group for his speech therapy or for one-on-one work with the special education teacher, we do not want it to be during recess or when everyone else is at lunch since these activities provide opportunities to work on high-priority goals.

After we have discussed the alignment of typical daily general education activities with Timothy's goals for his IEP, the need for any adaptations or accommodations and family priorities attention turns to a discussion of when best to plan for his out of class related service needs. As indicated under the section entitled "related services" two are called for in his IEP. On a weekly basis, Timothy is to receive 30 minutes of speech therapy to work on his expressive pronunciation and an additional 40 minutes of one-on-one resource special education where he will receive extra help learning strategies for solving math problems. We indicate when a related service will occur by placing the identifying number of that service above the activity. We can leave for later the determination of the day of the week when these will occur but we should not forgo a discussion of what daily activities he will miss in order to receive these services. Too often such a decision is left, by default, to logistical considerations relative to the schedule demands of related service professionals. While that is certainly understandable, if at all possible students should miss only those activities that are least relevant to their IEP goals and objectives. Accordingly, we see that Timothy is scheduled to receive his speech therapy first thing in the morning, missing flag salute and welcome/warm-up. While these activities are important, by looking under each we see that they provide an opportunity to address only two of Timothy's six goals and those same two goals are addressed during numerous other activities. In a similar fashion we see that the team felt the most appropriate time for Timothy to visit the resource teacher was at the end of the day during the 30 minutes scheduled for Spanish/PE and for 15 minutes of the scheduled 30 minutes for "Clean Up and Departure." On the days he is at resource there will be no need for the adaptation or the accommodation that is needed to address his two IEP goals (expressive vocabulary and social skills) while in "Spanish/PE."

Conclusion

Inclusive planning is essential to successful inclusive programming. That planning should be conducted by a team of those individuals most directly responsible for the daily instruction of students. Teachers, parents, and site administrators related service personnel are all essential members of the planning team. But perhaps even more than planning is the shared sense of responsibility that can come from a team approach to the planning process. We are all responsible for the education of our students and that responsibility extends to those with the most intensive needs who may come to school with very complex IEPs. To meet the challenges that may arise it matters less that we use the matrix strategy we have discussed here than it does that we proceed with a common commitment to success and an approach to solving the challenges of programming for students with IEPs in the regular classroom that reflects the best thoughts of parents and professionals alike. When that occurs we believe all students will benefit.

Chapter Activities

1. Now that you have acquired a certain amount of expertise with IEPs, it is time to put your skills to work. In small groups, develop a scenario for a specific student (you can use the Present Level examples provided in Chapter 4 as a starting point if necessary). Once you have a description of the student, conduct a mock IEP meeting and write an IEP using he blank forms and the IEP Checklist provided in the Appendices. Then meet as a group and role-play an Inclusion Planning Team meeting and complete an Activity Matrix, using the blank form contained in the Appendix.

2. Repeat exercise 1 for a student with more intensive needs. This could be a student with a significant intellectual disability, or one with significant physical and intellectual disabilities who also uses either a wheel chair or walker for moving around the classroom, school, and community.

3. Search the internet for sites that may have suggestions for adaptations and/or modifications that would be useful when developing activity matrices for students with IEPs who may be placed in your classroom.

Chapter 10

Wrap Up: Transfer Students, Private Schools, Home Schools, and Computerized/Draft IEPs

Chapter Overview

If you have mastered the material presented in this text, then you have the skills and knowledge needed to support the IEP team develop educationally relevant and legally compliant IEPs for the vast majority of students and situations. You also have an idea of what it will take to implement appropriate instruction in the LRE. Of course, the longer you stay in the profession, the more likely it is that you will encounter a unique circumstance when developing an IEP. In such a situation, remember that the IEP is a team process, meaning that no single individual is responsible for its development or implementation. Should you need additional information before completing an IEP, you can always reconvene the IEP in a day or two and finish up after you have obtained the necessary information. It is just important that the provision of special education services not be unnecessarily delayed.

Before ending the text, we wanted to inform you of a few other important items that didn't fit neatly in the previous chapters. So, we will briefly address the following items:

(1)   Students with an IEP transferring to your school,

(2)   Students in private schools,

(3)   Students who are home schooled, and

(4)   Computerized IEP forms/Draft IEP.

Students with an IEP Transferring to Your School

Generally speaking, if a student has an IEP and transfers to your school, then you must implement the IEP. If the student is from the same state, then there should not be any concern with eligibility; however, if the student moved from a different state, then the school should implement the IEP while conducting any necessary assessment or evaluation to determine whether the child remains eligible in the new state. Just because a child comes to your school with an IEP doesn't mean that the current IEP is appropriate. It is entirely feasible that your team could review the IEP and make significant changes, including placement. (On a side note, remember that any suspensions or removals conducted at the previous school must be considered should disciplinary removals be conducted at the new school.)

Following are some common questions and answers regarding transfer students that you may find useful. This information was taken directly from the IEP Questions and Answers document on the U. S. Department of Education website, Building the Legacy: IDEA 2004 **http://idea.ed.gov/**

Question A-1: What if a student whose IEP has not been subject to a timely annual review, but who continues to receive special education and related services under that IEP, transfers to a new public agency in the same State? Is the new public agency required to provide a free appropriate public education (FAPE) from the time the student arrives?

Answer: If a child with a disability who received special education and related services pursuant to an IEP in a previous public agency (even if that public agency failed to meet the annual review requirements in 34 CFR §300.324(b)(1)(i)) transfers to a new public agency in the same State and enrolls in a new school within the same school year, the new public agency (in consultation with the parents) must, pursuant to 34 CFR §300.323(e), provide FAPE to the child (including services comparable to those described in the child's IEP from the previous public agency), until the new public agency either (1) adopts the child's IEP from the previous public agency; or (2) develops, adopts, and implements a new IEP that meets the applicable requirements in 34 CFR §§300.320 through 300.324.

Question A-2: What options are available when an out-of-state transfer student cannot provide a copy of his/her IEP, and the parent identifies the "comparable" services that the student should receive?

Answer: The regulations in 34 CFR §300.323(g) require that, to facilitate the transition for a child described in 34 CFR §300.323(e) and (f)—

(1) the new public agency in which the child enrolls must take reasonable steps to promptly obtain the child's records, including the IEP and supporting documents and any other records relating to the provision of special education or related services to the child, from the previous public agency in which the child was enrolled, pursuant to 34 CFR §99.31(a)(2); and

(2) the previous public agency in which the child was enrolled must take reasonable steps to promptly respond to the request from the new public agency.

After taking reasonable steps to obtain the child's records from the public agency in which the child was previously enrolled, including the IEP and supporting documents and any other records relating to the provision of special education or related services to the child, if the new public agency is not able to obtain the IEP from the previous public agency or from the parent, the new public agency is not required to provide special education and related services to the child pursuant to 34 CFR §300.323(f).

Even if the parent is unable to provide the child's IEP from the previous public agency, if the new public agency decides that an evaluation is necessary because it has reason to suspect that the child has a disability, nothing in the IDEA or its implementing regulations would prevent the new public agency from providing special education services to the child while the evaluation is pending, subject to an agreement between the parent and the new public agency. However, if the child receives special education services while the evaluation is pending, the new public agency still must ensure that the child's evaluation, which would be considered an initial evaluation, is conducted within 60 days of receiving parental consent for the evaluation or within the State-established timeframe within which the evaluation must be conducted, in accordance with 34 CFR §300.301(c)(1). Further, under 34 CFR §300.306(c)(1)-(2), if the new public agency conducts an eligibility determination and concludes that the child has a disability under 34 CFR §300.8 and needs special education and related services, the new public agency still must develop and implement an IEP for the child in accordance with applicable requirements in 34 CFR §§300.320 through 300.324 even though the child is already receiving special education services from the new public agency.

If there is a dispute between the parent and the new public agency regarding whether an evaluation is necessary or the special education and related services that are needed to provide FAPE to the child, the dispute could be resolved through the mediation procedures in 34 CFR §300.506 or, as appropriate, the due process procedures in 34 CFR §§300.507 through 300.516. If a due process complaint requesting a due process hearing is filed, the public agency would treat the child as a general education student while the due process complaint is pending. 71 FR 46540, 46682 (Aug. 14, 2006).

Question A-3: Is it permissible for a public agency to require that a student with a disability who transfers from another State with a current IEP that is provided to the new public agency remain at home without receiving special education and related services until a new IEP is developed by the new public agency?

Answer: No. Under 34 CFR §300.323(f), if a child with a disability (who had an IEP that was in effect in a previous public agency in another State) transfers to a public agency in a new State, and enrolls in a new school within the same school year, the new public agency (in consultation with the parents) must provide the child with FAPE (including services comparable to those described in the child's IEP from the previous public agency), until the new public agency (1) conducts an evaluation pursuant to 34 CFR §§300.304 through 300.306 (if determined to be necessary by the new public agency); and (2) develops and implements a new IEP, if appropriate, that meets the applicable requirements in 34 CFR §§300.320 through 300.324.

Thus, the new public agency must provide FAPE to the child with a disability when the child enrolls in the new school in the public agency in the new State, and may not deny special education and related services to the child pending the development of a new IEP.

Question A-4: What is the timeline for a new public agency to adopt an IEP from a previous public agency or to develop and implement a new IEP?

Answer: Neither Part B of the IDEA nor the regulations implementing Part B of the IDEA establish timelines for the new public agency to adopt the child's IEP from the previous public agency or to develop and implement a new IEP. However, consistent with 34 CFR §300.323(e) and (f), the new public agency must take these steps within a reasonable period of time to avoid any undue interruption in the provision of required special education and related services.

Question A-5: What happens if a child with a disability who has an IEP in effect transfers to a new public agency or LEA in a different State and the parent refuses to give consent for a new evaluation?

Answer: Under 34 CFR §300.323(f), if a child with a disability (who has an IEP in effect) transfers to a public agency in a new State, and enrolls in a new school within the same school year, the new public agency (in consultation with the parents) must provide the child with FAPE (including services comparable to those described in the child's IEP from the previous public agency), until the new public agency (1) conducts an evaluation pursuant to §§300.304 through 300.306 (if determined to be necessary by the new public agency); and (2) develops and implements a new IEP, if appropriate, that meets the applicable requirements in §§300.320 through 300.324. Nothing in 34 CFR §300.323(f) would preclude the new public agency in the new State from adopting the IEP developed for the child by the previous public agency in another State. If the new public agency determines that it is necessary to conduct a new evaluation, that evaluation would be considered an initial evaluation because the purpose of that evaluation is to determine whether the child qualifies as a child with a disability and to determine the educational needs of the child. 71 FR 46540, 46682 (Aug 14, 2006). The public agency must obtain parental consent for such an evaluation in accordance with 34 CFR §300.300(a). However, 34 CFR §300.300(a)(3)(i) provides that if a parent does not provide consent for an initial evaluation, or fails to respond to a request to provide consent, the new public agency may, but is not required to, pursue the initial evaluation by utilizing the Act's consent override procedures, if permissible under State law. The Act's consent override procedures are the procedural safeguards in subpart E of 34 CFR Part 300 and include the mediation procedures under 34 CFR §300.506 or the due process procedures under 34 CFR §§300.507 through 300.516.

Because the child's evaluation in this situation is considered an initial evaluation, and not a reevaluation, the stay-put provision in 34 CFR §300.518(a) does not apply. The new public agency would treat the student as a general education student and would not be required to provide the child with comparable services if a due process complaint is initiated to resolve the dispute over whether the evaluation should be conducted. 71 FR 46682. Also, 34 CFR §300.300(a)(3)(ii) is clear that the public agency does not violate its obligation under 34 CFR §§300.111 and 300.301 through 300.311 (to identify, locate, and evaluate a child suspected of having a disability and needing special education and related services) if it declines to pursue the evaluation. Similarly, if the parent does not provide consent for the new evaluation and the new public agency does not seek to override the parental refusal to consent to the new evaluation, the new public agency would treat the student as a general education student.

Students Enrolled in Private Schools and Home-Schooled Children

The regulations regarding provision of services to children in private schools are detailed, but we will provide a simple summary of the major provisions and refer you to §300.130-300.148 for more specific regulatory guidance. We further encourage interested individuals to consult state and local guidelines as there may be important differences in service provision requirements according to state law. For example, federal law allows provision of special education services at religious schools in certain circumstances but only if permitted under state law. However, if services are provided at a religious school, it is crucial that the provision of such services not violate the establishment clause of the First Amendment of the U.S. Constitution. Your state laws should provide sufficient guidance to ensure that any programming you design is allowable and does not violate important constitutional protections.

There are three ways in which students can be placed in private school settings. The first two possibilities involve provision of FAPE and would likely be resolved with upper level district representation on the IEP team. These two situations can be quite involved, and we will simply describe the options so you know they are available for children but will spend little time describing the numerous possibilities, as discussion of all likelihoods is beyond the scope of this text and probably beyond what you would be expected to know.

One option for placement in a private school is due to a recommendation by the school district that such a placement is necessary for the child to receive FAPE. The recommended placement could include a specialized school or even a residential treatment facility. The second option would be placement in a private school by parents who requested that the placement be at public expense because the district's plan did not provide FAPE, an option we discussed briefly in Chapter 7.

It is more likely that you will encounter situations in which children are placed in private schools when FAPE is not an issue, but the parents prefer the private school placement. The issues and district responsibilities are a bit different for these children than for those placed in private schools due to issues with FAPE. In those cases, children would generally receive an IEP and the district would be required to ensure that all necessary services are provided to ensure FAPE. For children placed in private school when FAPE is not an issue, the district need not develop an IEP, but must develop a service plan that identifies the special education and related services that will be provided to the child by the district. A representative of the private school must attend the meeting when the service plan is developed or be allowed to participate via other options such as individual or conference phone calls (§300.137(c)(2)). It is also important to note that students who receive service plans have no right to receive some or all of the special education and related services that the child would receive if enrolled in a public school (§300.137(a)). In many cases, a child may receive special education services at a site other than the private school. If so, the district may be required to provide transportation services (§300.139).

States have different regulations and options for children who are home-schooled, so you must consult your local regulations for guidance. Some states have arrangements where home-schooled students also attend an alternative public school cooperative for some time during the week and are therefore classified similar to students placed in private schools by their parents when FAPE is not an issue. Those students would be eligible for special education either through a service plan or an IEP, depending upon state law. The overarching guideline regarding eligibility of home-schooled students is that special education services would be available only if the state recognized home schools or home day care as private schools. If not, then the states have no responsibility to provide special education services (71 Fed. Reg. 46594, 2006).

Computerized IEP Forms and Draft IEPs

Computerized IEP forms are becoming more common and may streamline the IEP meeting if used appropriately. For example, the IEP could be projected so all in the meeting could view the form as the goals and objectives were written. This use of technology could actually help team members keep focused on the topic because the information on the form could be readily accessed by all. Contrast that with the paper and pencil method of writing an IEP with the team either huddling around a form or passing it around the table, and you can imagine the numerous benefits of using a computer projected IEP form. Many of the computerized forms can also assist the IEP team by ensuring that all the appropriate sections of the IEP are completed.

However, one must exercise caution when using some of the computerized forms. It is incumbent upon the district to ensure that any computerized form does not conflict with the law and regulations. In Chapter 4, we spent a considerable amount of time discussing the development of Annual Goals and Short-Term Objectives. As you should recall, the first part of an objective was a statement of the antecedents or the conditions under which the behavior would be exhibited. Some of the computerized IEP programs actually begin objectives by requiring that a placement decision be made. For example, the program may force you to select a statement from several programmed options, which may include statements such as "in the special education classroom", which will be placed at the beginning of an objective before the antecedent statement. This could be problematic, because it implies that the placement decision has been made before the objective was even written, much less before the team had considered supplementary aids and supports that would allow the child to meet the objective in the regular education environment. As you know, the placement decision can only be made at the end of the IEP, not when writing goals and objectives. Should you find yourself using a program that forces you to make this type of choice, then select the item that does not indicate a placement decision; a safe option could be something such as "on school grounds" depending upon the Goal or Objective.

Some computerized programs also provide samples of Annual Goals and Short-Term Objectives. These may serve as a valuable resource, but an IEP is an *Individualized* Education Program and the preprogrammed objectives that accompany computerized IEP programs may not be appropriate for your student. While it is possible that some of the prewritten objectives may work for a particular student, you must not be limited to selecting objectives from a predetermined list. If appropriate, you could select and/or modify an objective from a list, but it must be selected on an individual basis to meet the needs of the child, and you must be allowed to write your own objectives independent of any computerized objective bank.

The last item we want to address is the use of draft IEPs. Prior to IDEA '04, the presentation of a written, draft IEP at the beginning of a meeting was specifically prohibited. However, that changed with IDEA '04 which allows the use of a draft IEP at a meeting provided the parents are informed that it is a draft, are allowed to participate in developing the final version, and the draft does not inhibit parental participation. Even though it is allowed, the Department of Education (DOEd) strongly discourages the use of a draft IEP (71 Fed. Reg, 46678, 2006), and we concur with that recommendation. There is just too much risk of alienating parents or minimizing parental input associated with the practice. If a draft is used, the DOEd recommends that parents be provided a copy of the draft prior to the IEP meeting so they have sufficient time to review the document and consider any changes or identify their questions.

An acceptable alternative to use of a draft IEP is drafting the Annual Goals and Short-Term Objectives before the meeting. Then they could be reviewed at the meeting and changes could be made before writing them on the actual IEP form. You could even send draft goals and objectives to the parents to review before the meeting. An important consideration is whether parents will be less likely to participate if a form is completed, even if presented as a draft. It is critical that you conduct IEP meetings where parents will be allowed to participate in a meaningful manner.

Concluding Thoughts

Throughout the text, we have continually emphasized key concepts and requirements, such as informed parental consent, LRE, FAPE, and measurability. We did so not to be redundant but to remind you how the different interrelated components of the IEP impact each other and to help you develop the habit of considering all components as you develop the IEP. We hope that we have relayed to you the importance of family involvement in both the IEP development and implementation. We want to stress the importance of data-based decision making in IEP development and implementation that embraces the intent of the LRE provisions of the law. In our opinion, there are few things worse than being unnecessarily segregated, because that segregation bears with it the risk of marginalization and exclusion rather than membership and empowerment. However, an inclusive placement does not guarantee either membership or empowerment; it is imperative that you ensure that all children with whom you work develop a social network and contribute meaningfully to the instructional environment. To do so, you may find that you will need to continually learn new interventions and refine your current skills as you encounter children with differing needs, both children with and without disabilities. We encourage you to continue with professional development opportunities, join professional organizations, and attend conferences. As educators, we have a professional and ethical responsibility to the children and families with whom we work, part of which includes our staying informed about changes in the field and implementing interventions in a reliable manner. Many of the hyperlinks we have provided in the various chapters will provide you with valuable assessment and intervention suggestions that are directly applicable to the classroom setting.

Appendix A: Mock IEP

Student Name: John Vanberg   **Date of Birth:** 9-16-2005   **Age:** 7   **Student ID:** 154632

Home Address: 1521 1ˢᵗ Ave South   Independence   WA   98989

           (Street)   (City)   (State)   (Zip)

Phone: 555-9090   **Alternate Phone:** 555-1475   **Primary Language:** English

Parent(s)/Guardian(s): Marc and Sylvia Vanberg

Purpose of Meeting: __X__ Initial IEP   ____ Revision   ____ Annual IEP

Signature of IEP Team Members in Attendance

(Note: Signature documents attendance, not agreement with the IEP.)

_____   _____
(Parent/Guardian)   (Parent/Guardian)

_____   _____
Student (as needed)   (General Education Teacher)

_____   _____
(Special Education Teacher)   (Administrator of Designee)

_____   _____
(Other, specify _____)   (Other, specify _____)

_____   _____
(Other, specify _____)   (Other, specify _____)

Present Levels of Academic Achievement (Include a description of student strengths, results of initial or most recent evaluation.)

MATH CALCULATION

John adds and subtracts single-digit numbers with 100% accuracy at a rate of 35 per minute with 0 errors when given worksheets with only addition or subtraction problems. His speed and accuracy decline when given a worksheet with 30 single-digit addition and subtraction problems mixed. Then, he solves 15 per minute with 2 or fewer errors. He adds and subtracts multi-digit numbers without carrying at 100% accuracy but does not add or subtract multi-digit numbers with regrouping. On the Woodcock-Johnson III, John received a standard score of 85 (16ᵗʰ percentile) on the math calculation subtest and a standard score of 70 (2ⁿᵈ percentile) on the math fluency subtest.

Present Levels of Functional Performance, for example, communication, behavior, self-help skills, etc. (Include a description of student strengths, results of initial or most recent evaluation.)

John behaves well in class and is well liked by peers and staff. He communicates clearly.

Description of how the child's disability affects the child's involvement in and progress in the general education curriculum (i.e., the same curriculum as for nondisabled children); or for preschool children, how the disability affects the child's participation in appropriate activities

John actively participates in all aspects of the general education math curriculum, but at a level lower than that expected of a student his age and grade. His lack of fluency negatively impacts his acquisition of math skills. He spends a considerable amount of time deciphering basic math facts, which interferes with his performance with work and application problems in math. He does understand the questions posed in the application problems when verbally explained to him.

Parental concerns related to enhancing the education of their child

Parents are happy with his social performance at school. He has made friends and likes school, except he expresses a dislike for math. Parents would like him to improve his math skills and hope that as he becomes better at math, he will begin to like it more.

Consideration of Special Factors

(1) Does the child's behavior impede learning of self or others?   ____ Yes _X_ No

       If yes, consider the use of positive behavioral interventions and supports and other strategies to address that behavior.

(2) Does the child have limited English proficiency?   ____ Yes _X_ No

       If yes, consider language needs as they relate to the IEP.

(3) Is the child blind or visually impaired?   ____ Yes _X_ No

       If yes, provide instruction in Braille and the use of Braille unless the IEP team determines, after an evaluation, that instruction in Braille or the use of Braille is not appropriate,

(4) Does the child have special communication needs?   ____ Yes _X_ No

       In the case of a child who is deaf or hard of hearing, consider opportunities for direct communication with peers and professionals in the child's language and mode of communication.

(5) Does the child require assistive technology devices and services?   ____ Yes _X_ No

Measureable Annual Goals and Short-Term Objectives

Area of Need: _Math Calculation_____

Measurable Annual Goal When presented with 50 single-digit, mixed addition and subtraction problems using numerals (0–9), John will write the correct answer to 48 problems within 60 seconds.

Short-Term Objective 1 Given a worksheet with 30 single-digit **addition** problems (0–9) and a direction to complete it, John will write the correct answer to 29 problems within 60 seconds on three consecutive opportunities.

Short-Term Objective 2 Given a worksheet with 30 single digit **subtraction** problems (0–9) and a direction to complete it, John will write the correct answer to 29 problems within 60 seconds on three consecutive opportunities.

Describe how progress will be measured: John's progress will be measured on timed fluency measures.

Progress Report

Identify when periodic progress reports regarding the student's progression on annual goals and/or objectives will be made: Progress reports for IEP goals and objectives will be provided at the regular quarterly report card distribution time.

State and District Mandated Assessments

Student will be taking standard assessment: If the student will be participating in the assessment but needs modifications or adaptations for any of the sections, identify what modifications or adaptations will be allowed and for what assessment.

John will be allowed up to twice the allotted time for completion of math application sections of the assessment that are not timed fluency measures. He will be allowed to complete the assessment in an alternative setting, such as the office or resource room or other quiet setting.

Student will **NOT** be taking standard assessment: If the IEP team determined that the standard assessment would not be appropriate, answer the following:

1. Describe why the student cannot participate in the standard assessment.
    _____
    _____

2. Describe why the particular alternative assessment selected is appropriate for the student.
    _____
    _____

Special Education, Related Services, and Accommodations/Adaptations

Describe the special education and related services, based on peer-reviewed research to the extent available, that will be provided to enable the student to: 1) make adequate progress toward meeting annual goals and/or objectives, 2) to be involved and make progress in the general education curriculum, including extracurricular and nonacademic activities, and 3) to be educated with other students with and without disabilities. Include any modifications or supports provided to school personnel.

Special Education	Begin Date	Frequency	Location	Duration	Person Responsible
Small group instruction	9-10-2012	Daily	Regular Ed Classroom	20 minutes	Special and Regular Ed. Teachers

Related Service	Begin Date	Frequency	Location	Duration	Person Responsible

Accommodations/Adaptations: None needed

Supports provided to school personnel: None needed

Least Restrictive Environment

Provide an explanation of the extent, if any, that the child will not be participating with children without disabilities in the regular class and extracurricular or nonacademic activities. _____

_____

_____

Percentage of time in general education setting ___100%_____

Extended School Year

Is the child eligible for Extended School Year Services? ____ Yes ____ No

Decision will be made by __May 1, 2013_____

Positive Behavioral Supports

Does the child have a Positive Behavior Support plan? ____ Yes _X_ No (If yes, attach to the IEP)

Appendix B: Blank IEP Forms

Student Name:_____ Date of Birth:_____ Age:_____ Student ID:_____

Home Address: _____ _____ _____ _____
             (Street)   (City)   (State)   (Zip)

Phone: _____ Alternate Phone: _____ Primary Language: _____

Parent(s)/Guardian(s): _____

Purpose of Meeting: ____ Initial IEP ____ Revision ____ Annual IEP

Signature of IEP Team Members in Attendance

(Note: Signature documents attendance, not agreement with the IEP)

_____   _____
(Parent/Guardian)   (Parent/Guardian)

_____   _____
Student (as needed)   (General Education Teacher)

_____   _____
(Special Education Teacher)   (Administrator of Designee)

_____   _____
(Other, specify _____)   (Other, specify _____)

_____   _____
(Other, specify _____)   (Other, specify _____)

Present Levels of Academic Achievement (Include a description of student strengths, results of initial or most recent evaluation.)

Present Levels of Functional Performance, for example, communication, behavior, self-help skills, etc. (Include a description of student strengths, results of initial or most recent evaluation.)

Description of how the child's disability affects the child's involvement in and progress in the general education curriculum (i.e., the same curriculum as for nondisabled children); or for preschool children, how the disability affects the child's participation in appropriate activities

Parental concerns related to enhancing the education of their child

Consideration of Special Factors

1. Does the child's behavior impede learning of self or others?   ____ Yes ____ No

    If yes, consider the use of positive behavioral interventions and
    supports and other strategies to address that behavior.

2. Does the child have limited English proficiency?   ____ Yes ____ No

    If yes, consider language needs as they relate to the IEP.

3. Is the child blind or visually impaired?   ____ Yes ____ No

    If yes, provide instruction in Braille and the use of Braille unless the IEP team
    determines, after an evaluation, that instruction in Braille or the use of Braille
    is not appropriate.

4. Does the child have special communication needs?   ____ Yes ____ No

    In the case of a child who is deaf or hard of hearing, consider opportunities
    for direct communication with peers and professionals in the child's language
    and mode of communication.

5. Does the child require assistive technology devices and services?   ____ Yes ____ No

Measureable Annual Goals and Short-Term Objectives

Area of Need: _____

Measurable Annual Goal

_____

_____

Short-Term Objective 1

_____

_____

Short-Term Objective 2

_____

_____

Short-Term Objective 3

_____

_____

Describe how progress will be measured:

_____

_____

Area of Need: _____

Measurable Annual Goal

_____

_____

Short-Term Objective 1

_____

_____

Short-Term Objective 2

_____

_____

Short-Term Objective 3

_____

_____

Describe how progress will be measured:

_____

_____

Progress Report

Identify when periodic progress reports regarding the student's progression on annual goals and/or objectives will be made: _____

State and District Mandated Assessments

<u>Student will be taking standard assessment</u>: If the student will be participating in the assessment but needs modifications or adaptations for any of the sections, identify what modifications or adaptations will be allowed and for what assessment.

_____

_____

_____

<u>Student will **NOT** be taking standard assessment</u>: If the IEP team determined that the standard assessment would not be appropriate, answer the following:

1. Describe why the student cannot participate in the standard assessment.

   _____

   _____

2. Describe why the particular alternative assessment selected is appropriate for the student.

   _____

   _____

Special Education and Related Services

Describe the special education and related services, based on peer-reviewed research to the extent available, that will be provided to enable the student to: 1) make adequate progress toward meeting annual goals and/or objectives, 2) to be involved and make progress in the general education curriculum, including extracurricular and nonacademic activities, and 3) to be educated with other students with and without disabilities. Include any modifications or supports provided to school personnel.

Special Education	Begin Date	Frequency	Location	Duration	Person Responsible

Related Service	Begin Date	Frequency	Location	Duration	Person Responsible

Accommodations/Adaptations:

Supports provided to school personnel:

Least Restrictive Environment

Provide an explanation of the extent, if any, that the child will not be participating with children without disabilities in the regular education setting including extracurricular and nonacademic activities.

_____

_____

_____

Percentage of time in general education setting _____

Extended School Year

Is the child eligible for Extended School Year Services? ____ Yes ____ No

Decision will be made by _____

Positive Behavioral Supports

Does the child have a Positive Behavior Support plan? ____ Yes____ No (If yes, attach to the IEP)

Invitation to Individualized Education Program Meeting

Parent/Guardian:_____ Date: _____

Student:_____ Student#: _____

The purpose of this letter is to invite you to an IEP meeting scheduled on _____ at

(Date)

_____. The IEP meeting should be held at a mutually agreed upon time. Should

(Time and Location)

you need to change the meeting time, please contact _____ at _____ to

(Name)   (Phone)

reschedule.

If you are unable to meet at the school, please contact us so we can try to arrange an alternative way for you to participate.

At this meeting, we will be discussing:

_____ Annual IEP Review   _____ IEP Revision

_____ Manifestation Determination   _____ Placement Issues

_____ Extended School Year   _____ Other: _____

The district is required to notify you of the individuals who will attend the IEP meeting. Following is a listing of those individuals. If your child is transitioning from Early Intervention Services for young children age birth through two years to special education and you would like your Service Coordinator to attend, we will invite that person. Please contact _____ at _____ with the name of your Service Coordinator and contact information.

Individuals who the district will bring to the IEP:

_____   _____

_____   _____

_____   _____

_____   _____

It is important that you attend the meeting, and we welcome your participation. Once again, please contact us if you need to reschedule.

Parent IEP Preparation Sample Letter

Date _____

Dear _____,

On _____, we will be meeting to develop an Individualized Education Program (IEP) for _____. In that meeting, we will review your child's progress as well as discuss areas of difficulty and develop learning goals. Your input is very important in this process, and we value your participation in this important activity. Sometimes when at a meeting, it can be easy to forget to ask questions or share because the meeting moves too quickly. With that in mind, we would like you to consider the following items and encourage you to ask questions and participate in the meeting. (You don't have to complete this form, and at the IEP meeting, we only ask that you share information you are comfortable sharing.)

1. What questions, if any, do you have about special education and the IEP?

2. What are some of your child's strengths and interests?

3. What concerns do you have regarding your child's learning? Don't feel that you have to limit this to academic skills only. If you have other concerns, such as behavior or communication, please list them.

4. Describe how you would view the ideal school day for your child.

5. Other questions or concerns…

Prior Written Notice

This Prior Written Notice is being provided to formally notify you of any actions that the district proposes or refuses to conduct regarding the identification, evaluation, placement, or provision of a Free Appropriate Public Education for your child.

Parent/ Guardian: _____ Date: _____

Student: _____ Student #: _____

This notice is written to inform you that we are:

☐ Proposing ☐ Initiate

o ***To*** or

☐ Refusing ☐ Change

☐ Identification ☐ Evaluation ☐ Placement ☐ FAPE

1. Description of the action proposed or refused:

_____

_____

2. Explanation of Reason for proposed or refused action:

_____

_____

3. Description of each evaluation procedure, assessment, record, or report used as a basis for the proposed or refused action:

_____

_____

4. Other options considered and rejected. Reason(s) for rejection of options:

_____

_____

5. Other factors relevant to the proposal or refusal:

_____

_____

6. Your child has procedural protections under the Individuals with Disabilities Education Act. If this prior written notice was provided as part of: 1) an initial evaluation or referral, 2) a reevaluation, or 3) a disciplinary action resulting in a change of placement, a copy of the procedural safeguards is enclosed.

7. We will begin this action on _____

If you did not receive a copy of the procedural safeguards or would like assistance understanding the content, please contact _____

Written Parent Consent

Parent/ Guardian: _____   Date: _____

Student: _____   Student #: _____

We are requesting your consent to conduct one of the following actions:

_____ Initial Evaluation

_____ Initial Provision of Special Education and Related Services

_____ Re-evaluation

If this permission is for an **Initial evaluation or Re-evaluation**, we will collect information in areas related to the suspected disability that will assist in eligibility determination and educational planning.

The concerns prompting this evaluation are:

_____

_____

The evaluation will consist of the following types of test and assessments:

_____

_____

If this consent is sought for the **Initial Provision of Special Education and Related Services**, then this permission is granting your consent for implementation of the initial Individualized Education Program.

Description of any records that will be released and to whom:

_____

_____

By granting consent, you are acknowledging that you have been fully informed of all information relevant to the activity for which consent is sought. You also understand that your consent is voluntary and may be revoked at any time; however, if you revoke consent, it is not retroactive. That means it does not negate any actions taken prior to your revocation.

_____ I grant consent

_____ I DO NOT grant consent

_____   _____
Signature   Date

Appendix C: IEP Checklist

Pre-Meeting

- If the child already has an IEP, obtain information regarding the child's progress toward goals and objectives.

- Collect information for development of Present Levels

    - Obtain information from general education teachers

    - Obtain any information from Curriculum-Based Assessment or Observations, etc.

    - Obtain information from any standardized testing or reevaluation

    - Write Present Levels (Be sure to include strengths)

- Obtain schedule information from school personnel needed at IEP – don't forget general education teachers and related service providers, if needed. Remember all general education teachers do not need to attend. In the following cases, required IEP team members can be excused from the IEP meeting.

    (1) Parent and LEA agree that particular member is not necessary because the member's curricular area or related services are not modified or discussed. Written parent consent is required.

    (2) Member can be excused when discussion or modification relate to member's area if: parents & LEA agree and excused member submits in writing to the parent and IEP team before the IEP meeting. Written parent consent is required.

- Contact parents/guardians or adult student and verify IEP meeting date and time.

    - Send out following forms: Invitation to IEP (Keep track of these dates in a log).

    - As a general rule, after the third no-show by the parents to a scheduled IEP meeting, the school should develop the IEP and mail a copy to parents/caregivers or adult student. (This is only an option if writen consent for services has already been obtained.)

    - It is critical that parents/guardians/adult students are fully informed participants, so obtain an interpreter if needed.

    - If using an interpreter, remember to talk to the parents and not the interpreter. Don't worry about hurting the interpreter's feelings, well trained interpreters don't expect that you speak to them, except for a greeting.

- You can develop suggested goals and objectives before the meeting, but do not write them on the IEP until they are agreed upon in the meeting. (While having a draft IEP is allowable, we agree with the DOEd and recommend against this practice, because it may inadvertently discourage with parental participation.) You may discuss your suggested IEP goals and objectives with parents prior to the meeting or send them home for review prior to the meeting.

Meeting

(Depending on the actual IEP form, some of these items may be conducted in a slightly different order)

- Introductions and purpose of meeting

- Review *Procedural Safeguards.* Parents must be provided with a copy of Procedural Safeguards once per year. You may want to provide them the copy with the Invitation and review the contents at the beginning of the IEP meeting.

- Ensure that demographic information is correct.

- Review child progress toward attainment of goals and objectives from the current IEP, if the child already has an IEP.

- Review *Present Levels* and obtain parent information. Be sure that you include student strengths and interests in the IEP document.

- Review how the child's disability impacts progress in the general education curriculum.

- Address special considerations: behavior, language, vision, communication needs, assistive technology.

- Develop *Measurable Annual Goals and Objectives,* based on Present Levels of Academic and Functional Performance. IDEA 04 only requires that short-term objectives be written for students who will be participating in an alternative assessment; however, best practice would be to write short-term objectives for each annual goal. Student progress on the objectives will serve as the measurement for the annual goal.

- For each goal and/or objective, determine what special education service will be provided. In addition, identify other *related services, adaptations, or modifications* are needed for the child to benefit from special education. You should also give thoughtful consideration to the provision of supplementary aids and services that will allow the child to meet the goals and objectives in the regular education setting.

- State how student *progress toward goals and objectives* will be measured and reported to parents.

- Determine how student will participate in state and district mandated *assessments*. Identify any allowable accommodations or modifications.

- Complete Summary of Service Matrix.

- Discuss *Extended School Year* services. You may make a decision regarding a child's eligibility for ESY at this time or delay the decision.

- If the student must be removed from the regular education environment in order to receive FAPE, justify that removal.

- Have participants sign form. (This signing does not indicate agreement, it just documents who was at the meeting.)

- Don't forget to write a behavior plan and attach it to the IEP if needed. If aversive procedures are part of the behavior plan, they must be clearly described in the IEP.

- Give a copy of the IEP to parents, file a copy and keep a copy for your use. Ensure that all school personnel who this information to ensure compliance with the IEP get copies or detailed summaries of the appropriate sections.

- If needed, this would be a good time to have parents sign *permission for exchange of confidential information*, (e.g., Permission for you to share information with a psychiatrist).

Additional Issues for Secondary level IEP Teams

- Address postsecondary transition in the IEP that will be in effect when the student turns 16.

- If current program will not lead to a regular diploma, inform parents and student.

- At least one year prior to the student reaching age of majority, inform the student and parents which, if any, rights will transfer to the student.

Appendix D: Indicator 13 Checklist

NSTTAC Indicator 13 Checklist Form A
(Meets Minimum SPP/APR Requirements)

Percent of youth with IEPs aged 16 and above with an IEP that includes appropriate measurable postsecondary goals that are annually updated and based upon an age appropriate transition assessment, transition services, including courses of study, that will reasonably enable the student to meet those postsecondary goals, and annual IEP goals related to the student's transition services needs. There also must be evidence that the student was invited to the IEP Team meeting where transition services are to be discussed and evidence that, if appropriate, a representative of any participating agency was invited to the IEP Team meeting with the prior consent of the parent or student who has reached the age of majority. (20 U.S.C. 1416(a)(3)(B))

1. Are there appropriate measurable postsecondary goals in the areas of training, education, employment, and, where appropriate, independent living skills?	Y N
Can the goals be counted? Will the goals occur *after* the student graduates from school? Based on the information available about this student, do the postsecondary goals seem appropriate for this student? • If *yes* to all three guiding questions, then circle Y OR if a postsecondary goal is *not* stated, circle N	
2. Are the postsecondary goals updated annually?	Y N
Were the postsecondary goals addressed/ updated in conjunction with the development of the current IEP? • If *yes*, then circle Y OR if the postsecondary goals were *not* updated with the current IEP, circle N	
3. Is there evidence that the measurable postsecondary goals were based on age appropriate transition assessment(s)?	Y N
Is the use of transition assessment(s) for the postsecondary goals mentioned in the IEP or evident in the student's file? • If *yes*, then circle Y OR if *no*, then circle N	
4. Are there transition services in the IEP that will reasonably enable the student to meet his or her postsecondary goals?	Y N
Do the transition services listed in the student's IEP that the student needs to reach the postsecondary goals include, as needed, *instruction, related service (s), community experience, development of employment and other post-school adult living objectives, and if appropriate, acquisition of daily living skills and provision of a functional vocational evaluation* • If *yes*, then circle Y OR if *no*, then circle N	
5. Do the transition services include courses of study that will reasonably enable the student to meet his or her postsecondary goals?	Y N
Do the transition services include courses of study that align with the student's postsecondary goals? • If *yes* , then circle Y OR if *no*, then circle N	
6. Is (are) there annual IEP goal(s) related to the student's transition services needs?	Y N
Is (are) an annual goal(s) included in the IEP that is/are related to the student's transition services needs? • If *yes*, then circle Y OR if *no*, then circle N	
7. Is there evidence that the student was invited to the IEP Team meeting where transition services were discussed?	Y N
For the current year, is there documented evidence in the IEP or cumulative folder that the student was invited to attend the IEP Team meeting , (e.g. a letter inviting the student to the meeting)? • If *yes*, then circle Y OR if *no*, then circle N	
8. If appropriate, is there evidence that a representative of any participating agency was invited to the IEP Team meeting with the prior consent of the parent or student who has reached the age of majority?	Y N NA
For the current year, is there evidence in the IEP that representatives of any of the following agencies/services were invited to participate in the IEP development including but not limited to: *postsecondary education, vocational education, integrated employment (including supported employment), continuing and adult education, adult services, independent living or community participation* for the postsecondary goals? Was prior consent obtained from the parent (or student who has reached the age of majority)? • If *yes* to both, then circle Y • If *no* invitation is evident and a participating agency is likely to be responsible for providing or paying for transition services and there was consent to invite them to the IEP meeting, then circle N • If it is too early to determine if the student will need outside agency involvement, or no agency is likely to provide or pay for transition services, circle NA • If parent or individual student consent (when appropriate) was *not* provided, circle NA	
Does the IEP meet the requirements of Indicator 13? (Circle one) **Yes** (all Ys or NAs for each item (1 –8) on the Checklist or **No** (one or more Ns circled)	

Instructions for Completing NSTTAC Indicator 13 Checklist

1. **Are there appropriate measurable postsecondary goals in the areas of training, education, employment, and, where appropriate, independent living skills?**

    - Find the postsecondary goals for this student
    - If there are appropriate measurable postsecondary goals that address *Training* after high school, *Education* after high school, and *Employment* after high school, and (where appropriate) independent living *Skills* after high school **and** if the identified postsecondary goals for *Training, Education, and Employment*, and (where appropriate) *Independent Living Skills* appear to be appropriate for the student, based on the other information regarding Present Levels of Academic and Functional Performance and / or the student's strengths, preferences, and interests, circle Y
    - If a student's postsecondary goals in the areas of *Training* and *Education* address both training for a career and other education after high school (e.g., enrollment in an adult education program focused on both job and independent living skills; enrollment in a college program in preparation for a career in architecture), circle Y
    - *"it may not always be necessary for the student to have separate postsecondary goals for training and education in these instances. Based on the individual needs of the student and the student's plans after leaving high school, it may be reasonable for an IEP Team to interpret the areas of training and education as overlapping in developing postsecondary goals for a student. In these instances, an IEP Team could develop a combined postsecondary goal in the areas related to training and education. Employment is a distinct activity from the areas related to training and education, and each student's IEP must include a separate postsecondary goal in the area of employment. For further information see Questions and Answers on Secondary Transition, Revised September 2011, OSEP, Retrieved http://idea.ed.gov/explore/view/p/%2Croot%2Cdynamic%2CQaCorner%2C10%2C).*
    - If there are postsecondary goals that address *Training* after high school, *Education* after high school, and *Employment* after high school, and (where appropriate) *Independent Living Skills* after high school, but these goals are not measurable, circle N
    - If there is misalignment between the student's postsecondary goals, based on the information available (e.g., present levels of performance, student strengths, student interests, student preferences), circle N
    - If there is not a postsecondary goal that addresses *Training* after high school, circle N
    - If there is not a postsecondary goal that addresses *Education* after high school, circle N
    - If there is not a postsecondary goal that addresses *Employment* after high school, circle N

2. **Are the postsecondary goal(s) updated annually?**

    - If the postsecondary goals for *Training, Education, Employment*, and where appropriate *Independent Living Skills* are documented in the student's current IEP, circle Y
    - If the postsecondary goals for *Training, Education, Employment*, and where appropriate *Independent Living Skills* are not documented in the student's current IEP, circle N
    - If this is the student's first IEP that addresses secondary transition services because the student just turned 16, it is considered an update for purposes of this checklist, so circle Y

3. **Is there evidence that the measurable postsecondary goals were based on age appropriate transition assessment(s)?**

    - Find where information relates to assessment(s) and the transition component on the IEP (either in the IEP or the student's file)
    - For each postsecondary goal, if there is evidence that at least one age appropriate transition assessment was used to provide information on the student's needs, strengths, preferences, and interests regarding the postsecondary goals circle Y

- For each postsecondary goal, if there is **no** evidence that age appropriate transition assessment(s) provided information on the student's needs, taking into account the student's strengths, preferences, and interests [regarding the postsecondary goals,] circle N
- If a postsecondary goal area was addressed in item #1, but was not measurable and if there is age appropriate transition assessment information, from one or more sources, regarding the student's needs, taking into account the student's strengths, preferences, and interests [regarding this postsecondary goal], circle Y
- If a postsecondary goal area was addressed in item #1, but was not measurable and if there is **not** age appropriate transition assessment information provided on the student's needs, taking into account the student's strengths, preferences, and interests [regarding this postsecondary goal], circle N

4. **Are there transition services in the IEP that will reasonably enable the student to meet his or her postsecondary goals?**
   - Find where transition services/activities are listed on the IEP
   - For each postsecondary goal, is there a transition service such as instruction, related service, community experience, development of employment and other post-school adult living objectives, and if appropriate, acquisition of daily living skill(s), and provision of a functional vocational evaluation) listed that will enable the student to meet the postsecondary goal, circle Y
   - For each postsecondary goal, if there is **no** transition service that relates to a specific postsecondary goal, (a) type of instruction, (b) related service, (c) community experience, (d) development of employment and other post-school adult living objective, (e) if appropriate, acquisition of a daily living skill, or (f) if appropriate, provision of a functional vocational evaluation listed in the IEP that will enable the student to meet the postsecondary goal, circle N
   - If a postsecondary goal area was addressed in item #1, but was not measurable and there is a transition service that will enable the student to meet that postsecondary goal, circle Y
   - If a postsecondary goal area was addressed in item #1, but was not measurable and there is **no** transition service listed that will enable the student to meet that postsecondary goal, circle N

5. **Do the transition services include courses of study that will reasonably enable the student to meet his or her postsecondary goals?**

   - Locate the course of study (instructional program of study) or list of courses of study in the student's IEP
   - Are the courses of study a multi-year description of coursework from the student's current to anticipated exit year that is designed to help achieve the student's desired post-school goals? If yes, go to next instruction bullet. If no, circle N
   - Do the courses of study align with the student's identified postsecondary goals? If yes, circle Y. If no, circle N

6. **Is (are) there annual IEP goal(s) that is (are) related to the student's transition services needs?**

   - Find the annual goals, or, for students working toward alternative achievement standards, or States in which short-term objectives are included in the IEP, short-term objectives on the IEP
   - For each of the postsecondary goal areas circled Y in question #1, if there is an annual goal or short-term objective included in the IEP related to the student's transition services needs, circle Y
   - For each of the postsecondary goals mentioned in question #1, if there is **no** annual goal or short-term objective included in the IEP related to the student's transition services needs, circle N
   - If a postsecondary goal area was addressed in #1, but was not measurable, and an annual goal is included in the IEP related to the student's transition services needs, circle Y
   - If a postsecondary goal area was addressed in #1, but was not measurable, and there is **no** annual goal included in the IEP related to the student's transition services needs, circle N

7. **Is there evidence that the student was invited to the IEP Team meeting where transition services were discussed?**

    - Locate the evidence that the student was invited, (e.g., a copy of the student's invitation to the IEP conference) Was the student invitation signed (by the LEA) and dated prior to the date of the IEP conference. If yes, circle Y. If no, circle N

8. **If appropriate, is there evidence that a representative of any participating agency [that is likely to be responsible for providing or paying for transition services] was invited to the IEP Team meeting with the prior consent of the parent or student who has reached the age of majority?**
    - Find where persons responsible and/or agencies are listed on the IEP
    - Are there transition services listed on the IEP that are likely to be provided or paid for by an outside agency? If yes, continue with next instruction bullet. If no, circle NA.
    - Was parent consent or student consent (once student has reached the age of majority) to invite an outside agency(ies) obtained? If yes, continue with next instruction bullet. If no, circle NA
    - If a postsecondary goal area was addressed in item #1, but was not measurable and there is evidence that agency(ies) for which parent/student had given their consent to invite, were invited to the IEP meeting to discuss transition, circle Y
    - If a postsecondary goal area was addressed in item #1, but was not measurable and there is **no** evidence that agency(ies) for which parent/student had given their consent to invite, were invited to the IEP meeting to discuss transition, circle N
    - If it is too early to determine if this student will need outside agency involvement, circle NA

Does the IEP meet the requirements of Indicator 13?

- If all Ys or NAs for each item (1 – 8) on the Checklist, then circle **Yes**
- If one or more Ns are circled, then circle **No**

Appendix E: Activity Matrix

Student: _____ Age: _____ Class: _____ Days: _____

Alternative Activities Listed by Number														Special Activities								Home/ Family
														1	2	3	4	5	6	7	8	
TYPICAL DAILY ACTIVITIES																						
Length of Time for Activity																						
Adaptation: Modified content																						
Accommodation: Modified arrangement/staffing																						
TARGET CHILD SKILL AREAS FROM CURRENT IEP (✓ indicates skill is a family priority)																						

Appendix F: List of Hyperlinks

Chapter 1 Introduction

1. Federal site for information related to special education regulations
   http://idea.ed.gov/
2. Office for Civil Rights Section 504 page
   http://www2.ed.gov/about/offices/list/ocr/504faq.html
3. Library of Congress information on 14th Amendment
   http://www.loc.gov/rr/program/bib/ourdocs/14thamendment.html
4. The ARC, advocacy for individuals with intellectual disabilities
   http://www.thearc.org/
5. Section 504 manual
   http://www.psesd.org/index.php?option=com_content&task=view&id=586&Itemid=342
6. Disability is Natural
   http://www.disabilityisnatural.com/

Chapter 2 Eligibility and Referral Procedures

1. Department of Education Site providing easy access to IDEA (both Part C and Part B)
   http://idea.ed.gov/
2. Readily accessible information for RtI
   http://www.interventioncentral.org/
   http://www.rtinetwork.org/
3. Keith Stanovich discusses the Matthew effect
   http://www.youtube.com/watch?v=IF6VKmMVWEc

Chapter 3 The Individualized Education Program (IEP)

1. U. S. Department of Education, Office of Special Education Programs—information on assessment
   http://www.osepideasthatwork.org/
2. First Circuit Court Decision in Timothy W. v. Rochester (1989)
   http://law.justia.com/cases/federal/appellate-courts/F2/875/954/179023/

3. U. S. Supreme Court Decision in Irving v. Tatro (1984)

   http://supreme.justia.com/cases/federal/us/468/883/case.html

4. Link to article by Giangreco, Edelman, Luiselli, & MacFarland (1997), *Helping or Hovering*.

   http://www.uvm.edu/~cdci/archives/mgiangre/helpinghovering.pdf

5. Department of Education, IEP Questions and Answers

   http://www2.ed.gov/policy/speced/guid/idea/iep-qa-2010.pdf

Chapter 4 Writing Meaningful Present Levels, Annual Goals, and Short-Term Objectives

1. Dynamic Indicator of Basic Early Literacy Skills—site at University of Oregon that provides information related to CBM and early literacy for young children

   https://dibels.uoregon.edu/

2. Intervention Central—provides readily accessible information on RtI

   http://www.interventioncentral.org/

3. RtI Network—informative site covering information related to RtI

   http://www.rtinetwork.org/

4. Individual Growth and Developmental Indicators for Infants and Toddlers

   http://www.igdi.ku.edu/

Chapter 5 Least Restrictive Environment

1. Ninth Circuit Court Decision in Clyde K. v. Puyallup

   http://openjurist.org/35/f3d/1396/clyde-v-puyallup-school-district-no-clyde-k

2. Fifth Circuit Court Decision in Daniel R. R. v. State Board of Education

   http://openjurist.org/874/f2d/1036/daniel-rr-v-state-board-of-education

3. Fourth Circuit Court Decision in Hartmann v. Loudoun County Board of Education

   http://openjurist.org/118/f3d/996/hartmann-hartmann-v-loudoun-county-board-of-education-b

4. Sixth Circuit Court Decision in Roncker v. Walter

   http://openjurist.org/700/f2d/1058/roncker-roncker-v-b-walter-n

5. Ninth Circuit Court Decision in Sacramento v. Holland

   http://openjurist.org/14/f3d/1398/sacramento-city-unified-school-district-board-of-education-v-rachel-h-holland

Chapter 6 Disciplinary Issues, Harassment, and Bullying

1. Center for Effective Collaboration and Practice
   http://cecp.air.org/center.asp

2. Controlled Substances Act, Section 202 (c)) (21 U.S.C. 812 (c))
   http://www.gpo.gov/fdsys/pkg/USCODE-2010-title21/pdf/USCODE-2010-title21-chap13-subchapl-partB-sec812.pdf

3. Family Educational Rights and Privacy Act (FERPA)
   http://www2.ed.gov/policy/gen/guid/fpco/ferpa/index.html

4. Goss v. Lopez decision
   http://laws.findlaw.com/us/419/565.html

5. Honig v. Doe decision
   http://laws.findlaw.com/us/484/305.html

6. Office of Special Education Programs Center on Positive Behavior Interventions and Supports
   http://www.pbis.org/

7. National Association of School Psychologists zero tolerance and suspension
   http://www.nasponline.org/publications/cq/mocq375zerotolerance.aspx

8. Questions and Answers document prepared by OSERS—Disciplinary Procedures
   http://idea.ed.gov/explore/view/p/%2Croot%2Cdynamic%2CQaCorner%2C7%2C

9. TASH: The cost of waiting to end restraint and seclusion
   http://tash.org/tash-shows-%E2%80%98the-cost-of-waiting%E2%80%99-to-end-restraint-seclusion/

10. U. S. Department of Education: Restraint and Seclusion Resource Document
    http://www2.ed.gov/policy/seclusion/restraints-and-seclusion-resources.pdf

11. United States DOE Colleague letter
    http://www2.ed.gov/about/offices/list/ocr/letters/colleague-bullying-201410.pdf

12. Positive Behavior and Interventions & Supports
    www.pbis.org

13. StopBullying.gov
    www.stopbullying.gov

14. National Suicide Prevention Lifeline
    suicidepreventionlifeline.org

15. Safe Supportive Learning
    safesupportivelearning.ed.gov

Chapter 7 Postsecondary Transitions and Other Common Issues on Secondary Age IEPs

1. Economic Picture of the Disability Community Project
   http://www.dol.gov/odep/pdf/20141022-KeyPoints.pdf

2. SPP/APR Related Requirements
   http://www2.ed.gov/policy/speced/guid/idea/bapr/2008/5relstedrequirements081308.pdf

3. ODEP Integrated Employment
   http://www.dol.gov/odep/topics/IntegratedEmployment.htm

4. National Technical Assistance Center on Transition
   http://transitionta.org

5. Seattle U Center for Change in Transitions Services
   https://www.seattleu.edu/ccts/about/

6. George Washington University Directory of Transitions Websites
   http://heath.gwu.edu/directory-of-transition-websites

7. Illinois State Board of Education Secondary Transition
   http://www.isbe.net/spec-ed/pdfs/parent_guide/ch8-secondary_transition.pdf

8. Virginia Transition Assessment
   http://www.doe.virginia.gov/special_ed/transition_svcs/transition_assessment.pdf

9. Massachusetts DOE Technical Assistance Advisory 2014
   http://www.doe.mass.edu/sped/advisories/2014-4ta.html

10. National Collaborative on Workforce and Disability 411 on Disability Disclosure
    http://www.ncwd-youth.info/411-on-disability-disclosure

11. NTACT sample transition plans
    Alex, 17, autism
    http://transitionta.org/sites/default/files/dataanalysis/I13_Alex.pdf
    Allison, 18, learning disability
    http://transitionta.org/sites/default/files/dataanalysis/I13_Allison.pdf
    Jamarreo, 19, behavior, hearing
    http://transitionta.org/sites/default/files/dataanalysis/I13_Jamarreo.pdf
    Jodi, 17, mild intellectual disability
    http://transitionta.org/sites/default/files/dataanalysis/I13_Jodi.pdf
    Kevin, 18, significant intellectual disability
    http://transitionta.org/sites/default/files/dataanalysis/I13_Kevin.pdf
    Paulo, 18, mild intellectual disability and autism
    http://transitionta.org/sites/default/files/dataanalysis/I13_Paulo.pdf

Chapter 8 Procedural Safeguards

1. Model Forms developed by the Department of Education

   http://idea.ed.gov/static/modelForms

2. Family Educational Rights and Privacy Act

   http://www2.ed.gov/policy/gen/guid/fpco/ferpa/index.html

Chapter 9 Meeting the Needs of Students with an IEP in the Regular Classroom

1. Including Samuel: A powerful video that explores the reasons for and impacts of inclusion. The site also has links to valuable reference materials.

   http://includingsamuel.com/home.aspx

2. Inclusion Network: A site that provides information supporting inclusive practices.

   http://www.inclusion.com/inclusionnetwork.html

References

Alberto, P. A., & Troutman, A. C. (2013). *Applied behavior analysis for teachers* (8th ed.). Upper Saddle River, NJ: Pearson.

Arter, J. A., & Jenkins, J. R. (1979). Differential diagnosis-prescriptive teaching: A critical appraisal. *Review of Educational Research, 49,* 517–555.

Assistance to States for the Education of Children With Disabilities and Preschool Grants for Children With Disabilities; Final Rule, 71 Fed. Reg. (Monday, August 14, 2006).

Bateman, B. D., & Herr, C. M. (2006). *Writing measurable IEP goals and objectives.* Verona, WI: Attainment Company.

Bateman, B. D., & Linden, M. A. (2012). *Better IEPs: How to develop legally correct and educationally useful programs* (5th ed.). Verona, WI: Attainment Company.

Baumgart, D., Filler, J., & Askvig, B. (1991). Perceived importance of social skills: A survey of teachers, parents and other professionals. *Journal of Special Education, 25,* 236–252.

Bell, M. H. (1914). What the Montessori method means to me. *Freedom for the Child, 1,* 7–10.

Bennett, R. E. (1982). The use of grade and age equivalent scores in educational assessment. *Diagnostique, 7,* 139–146.

Biklen, D. (1982). The least restrictive environment: Its application to education. *Child and Youth Services, 5,* 121–144.

Blankenship, C. S. (1985). Using curriculum-based assessment data to make instructional decisions. *Exceptional Children, 52,* 233–228.

Blatt, B., & Kaplan, F. (1966). *Christmas in purgatory: A photographic essay on mental retardation.* Boston, MA: Allyn & Bacon.

Bowe, F. G. (2000). *Birth to five early childhood special education* (2nd ed.). Albany, NY: Delmar.

Bricker, D., Capt, B., Johnson, J., Pretti-Frontczak, K., Straka, E., Wassell, M. S., & Slentz, K. (2002). *Assessment, Evaluation, and Programming System for Infants and Children (AEPS)* (2nd ed.). Baltimore, MD: Brookes.

Bricker, D., & Waddell, M. (2002). Curriculum for Three to Six Years. Assessment Evaluation, and Programming System for Infants and Children (AEPS), (Second ed. Vol. 4) Baltimore, MD: Paul H. Brookes Publishing Co.

Browder, D. M. (2012). Finding the balance: A response to Hunt and McDonnell. [Response]. *Research & Practice for Persons with Severe Disabilities, 37,* 157–159.

Brown v. Board of Education, 347 U.S. 483, 74 S.Ct. 686, 98 L.Ed.873 (1954).

Brown, F., Lehr, D., & Snell, M. E. (2011). Conducting and using student assessment. In M. E. Snell & F. Brown (Eds.), *Instruction of student with severe disabilities* (7th ed., pp. 73–121). Upper Saddle River, NJ: Pearson.

Buck, G. H., Polloway, E. A., Smith-Thomas, A., & Cook, K. W. (2003). Prereferral intervention processes: A survey of state practices. *Exceptional Children, 69,* 349–360.

Carter, S. (2001). Common Developmental Problems. Retrieved from http://www.pediatrics.emory.edu/divisions/neonatology/dpc/defn.html#cp

Chambers, D. (1972). Alternatives to civil commitment of the mentally ill: Practical guides and constitutional imperatives. *Michigan Law Review, 70,* 1108.

Clyde K. v. Puyallup School District, No. 3, 33 F.3d 1396 (9th Cir. 1994).

Cook, R. E., Klein, M. D., & Tessier, A. (2008). *Adapting early childhood curricula for children with special needs* (7th ed.). Upper Saddle River, NJ: Pearson.

Daniel R. R. v. State Bd. Of Educ., 874 F.2d 1036 (5th Cir. 1989).

Danile, P.T. K. (1997). Educating students with disabilities in the least restrictive environment: A slippery slope for educators. *Journal of Educational Administration, 35,* 397–410.

Danneker, J. E., & Bottge, B. A. (2009). Benefit and barriers to elementary student-led Individualized Education Programs. *Remedial and Special Education, 30,* 225–233. doi: 10.1177/0741932508315650

Deal v. Hamilton County Board of Education, 392 F3d 840 (6th Cir, 2004).

Dear Colleague Letter. (2000). 111 LRP 45106.

Dear Colleague Letter. (2010). 55 IDELR 174.

Dear Colleague Letter. (2013). 61 IDELR 263.

Dear Colleague Letter. (2014). 64 IDELR 115.

Dear Colleague Letter. (2016). 62 IDELR 185.

DePaoli, J. L., Fox, J. H., Ingram, E. S., Maushard, M., Bridgeland, J. M., & Balfanz, R. (2015). Building a Grad Nation: Progress and Challenge in Ending the High School Dropout Epidemic. Annual Update, Everyone Graduates Center at the School of Education at Johns Hopkins University.

Downing, J. E. (2008). *Including students with severe and multiple disabilities in typical classrooms: Practical strategies for teachers* (3rd ed.). Baltimore, MD: Paul H. Brookes Publishing Co.

Drobnicki v. Poway Unified School District, 358 F. App'x 788 (9th Cir, 2009).

Education for All Handicapped Children Act of 1975 (P.L. 94-142), 20 U.S.C. §1400 *et seq.*

Espino v. Bestiero, 520 F.Supp. 905 (S.D.Tx.1981).

Family Educational Rights and Privacy Act of 1974 (FERPA) (P.L. 93-380), 20 U.S.C.1232g, FERPA:34 C.F.R. 99.1 *et seq.*

Filler, J. (1996). A comment on inclusion: Research and social policy. *Society for Research in Child Development Social Policy Report, 10*(2-3), 31-33.

Filler, J. W., Jr., Robinson, C. C., Smith, R. A., Vincent-Smith, L., Bricker, D. D., & Bricker, W. A. (1975). Mental retardation. In N. Hobbs (Ed.) *Issues in the classification of children* (Vol. 1., pp. 194-238). San Francisco, CA: Jossey-Bass.

Filler, J., & Xu, Y. (Winter 2006/2007). Including children with disabilities in early childhood education programs: Individualizing developmentally appropriate practices. *Childhood Education, 83*(2), 92-98.

Fox, T. J., & Williams, W. (1991). *Implementing best practices for all students in their local school.* Burlington, VT: Center for Developmental Disabilities, The University of Vermont.

Frost, L., & Bondy, A. (2002). *The Picture Exchange Communication System training manual* (2nd ed.). Newark, DE: Pyramid Educational Consultants, Inc.

Fuchs, D., & Fuchs, L. S. (1994). Inclusive schools movement and the radicalization of special education reform. *Exceptional Children, 60*, 294-309.

Fuchs, D., Fuchs, L., & Vaughn, S. (Eds.) (2007). *Response to intervention: A framework for reading educators.* Newark, DE: International Reading Association.

Gargiulo, R. M., & Metcalf, D. (2013). *Teaching in today's inclusive classrooms: A universal design for learning approach* (2nd ed.). Belmont, CA: Cengage.

Giangreco, M. F. (2011). Educating students with severe disabilities: Foundational concept and issues. In M. E. Snell & F. Brown (Eds.), *Instruction of student with severe disabilities* (7th ed. pp. 1-30). Upper Saddle River, NJ: Pearson.

Giangreco, M. F., & Doyle, M. B. (Eds.). (2007). *Quick guides to inclusion: Ideas for educating students with disabilities* (2nd ed.). Baltimore, MD: Paul H. Brookes Publishing Co.

Giangreco, M. F., Edelman, S., Luiselli, T. E., & MacFarland, S. Z. (1997). Helping or hovering? Effects of instructional assistant proximity on students with disabilities. *Exceptional Children, 64*(1), 7-18. PDF version posted with permission of the Council for Exceptional Children at http://www.uvm.edu/~cdci/archives/mgiangre/paraprofessional.html

Ginsburg, H., & Baroody, A. (2003). *Test of early mathematics ability* (3rd ed.). Austin, TX: Pro-Ed.

Good, R. H., III, & Jefferson, G. (1998). Contemporary perspectives on curriculum-based measurement. In M. R. Shinn (Ed.), *Advanced applications of curriculum-based measurement* (pp. 61-88). New York, NY: Guilford Press.

Goss v. Lopez, 419 U.S. 565, 95 S. Ct. 729 (1975).

Gould, S. J. (1996). *The mismeasure of man (revised and expanded).* New York, NY: W.W. Norton & Company.

Habib, D. (2009). *Including samuel.* Concord, NH: Institute on Disability at the University of New Hampshire.

Hamre-Nietupski, S., & Nietupski, J. (2008). Integral involvement of severely handicapped students within regular public schools. *Journal of the Association for the Severely Handicapped, 6*(2), 30-39.

Hargrove, L. J., Church, K. L., Yssel, N., & Koch, K. (2002). Curriculum-based assessment: Reading and state academic standards. *Preventing School Failure, 46*, 148-151.

Hartmann v. Loudoun County Board of Education, 118 F.3d (4th Cir. 1997), cert. denied, *118 S. Ct. 688 (1998).*

Hendrick Hudson Dist. Bd. of Ed. v. Rowley, 458 U.S.176 (1982).

Heward, W. L. (2006). *Exceptional children: An introduction to special education* (8th ed.). Upper Saddle River, NJ: Pearson.

Heward, W. L. (2013). *Exceptional children: An introduction to special education* (10th ed.). Upper Saddle River, NJ: Pearson.

Honig v. Doe, 484 U.S. 305, 108 S. Ct. 592 (1988).

Horner, R. H., Albin, R. W., Todd, A. W., Newton, J. S., & Sprague, J. R. (2011). Designing and Implementing Individualized Positive Behavior Support. In M. E. Snell & F. Brown (Eds.), *Instruction of student with severe disabilities* (7th ed., pp. 257–303). Upper Saddle River, NJ: Pearson.

Hosp, J., Hosp, M., & Howell, K. W. (2007). *The ABCs of CBM: A practical guide to curriculum-based measurement.* New York, NY: Guilford Press.

Hosp, J., Hosp, M., Howell, K., & Allison, R. (2014). *Curriculum-based evaluation: Using assessment data to plan instruction.* New York, NY: Guilford Press.

Howell, K. (1976). *Inside special education.* Columbus, OH: Merril Publishing.

Howell, K. W., & Davidson, M. R. (1997). Programming: Aligning teacher thought processes with the curriculum. In J. W. Lloyd, E. J. Kameenui, & D. Chard (Eds.), *Issues in educating students with disabilities* (pp. 101–128). Mawah, NJ: Lawrence Earlbaum Associates.

Hunt, P., McDonnell, J., & Crockett, M. A. (2012). Reconciling an ecological curricular framework focusing on quality of life outcomes with the development and instruction of standards-based academic goals. [Position]. *Research & Practice or Persons with Severe Disabilities, 37,* 139–152.

Hyatt, K. J. (2007). Braingym: Building stronger brains or wishful thinking? *Remedial and Special Education, 28,* 117–124.

Hyatt, K. J., & Filler, J. (2011). LRE re-examined: misinterpretations and unintended consequences. *International Journal of Inclusive Education, 15,* 1031–1045.

Hyatt, K. J., & Howell, K. W. (2004). Curriculum-based measurement of students with emotional and behavioral disorders: Assessment for data-based decision making. In R. B. Rutherford, M. M. Quinn, & S. R. Mather (Eds.), *Handbook of research in emotional and behavioral disorders* (pp. 181–198). New York, NY: Guilford Press.

Hyatt, K. J., Stephenson, J., & Carter, M. (2009). A review of three controversial educational practices: Perceptual motor programs, sensory integration, and tinted lenses. *Education and Treatment of Children, 32,* 313–342.

Individuals with Disabilities Education Act Amendments of 1997, 20 U.S.C. § 1401 *et seq.*

Individuals with Disabilities Education Improvement Act of 2004, 20 U.S.C. 1400 *et seq.* (2004).

Individuals with Disabilities Education Improvement Act Final Regulations (2006), 34 C.F.R. Parts 301 and 303.

Irving Indep. School Dist. v. Tatro, 703 F.2d 823 (5th Cir. 1983), aff'd in part, rev'd in part, 486 U.S. 883, 104 S. Ct. 3371 (1984).

Itard, J. M. (1932). *The wild boy of averyron* (G. a. M. Humphrey, Trans.). NewYork, NY: Century.

Jimerson, S. R., Burns, M. K., & VanDerHeyden, A. M. (Eds.). (2007). *Handbook of Response to Intervention: The science and practice of assessment and intervention.* New York, NY: Springer.

Johnson, C. E. (2004). *Transition Flowchart,* Retrieved from Center for Change in Transition Servcies website: http://www.seattleu.edu/ccts

K.J. v. Fairfax County Sch. Bd., 361 F App'x 435 (4th Cir. 2010).

Kauffman, J. M. (1995). Why must we celebrate a diversity of restrictive environments? *Learning Disabilities and Practice, 10,* 225–232.

Kauffman, J. M. (2010). Curtains for special education: An open letter to educators. Retrieved from spedpro.org/wp-content/documents/Curtains_PDK.pdf

Kauffman, J. M., & Hallahan, D. P. (2005). *The illusion of full inclusion: A comprehensive critique of a current special education bandwagon.* Austin, TX: Pro-Ed.

Kavale, K. A., & Forness, S. R. (1987). Substance over style: Assessing the efficacy of modality testing and teaching. *Exceptional Children, 54,* 228–239.

Kavale, K. A., & Forness, S. R. (1997). Defining learning disabilities: Consonance and Dissonance. In J. W. Lloyd, E. J. Kameenui, & D. Chard (Eds.), *Issues in educating students with disabilities* (pp. 3–26). Mahwah, NJ: Lawrence Earlbaum Associates.

Kubick, R. J. (2008). Best practices in making manifestation determinations. In A. Thomas & J. Grimes (Eds.) *Best practices in school psychology V* (Vol. 3., pp. 827–838). Bethesda, MD: The National Association of School Psychologists.

Lachman v. Illinois State Board of Education, 852 F.2d (7th Cir. 1988).

Lake, S. E., & Norlin, J. W. (2006). *The current legal status of inclusion: Updated and expanded!* Horsham, PA: LRP Publications.

Letter to Christiansen. (2007). 48 IDELR 161.

Letter to Florida Department of Education. (2001) 102 LRP 37673.

Letter to Gray. (2008). 50 IDELR 198.

Letter to Grether. (1994). 21 IDELR 60.

Letter to Myer. (1989). 213 IDELR 255.

Letter to Runkel. (1996). 25 IDELR 387.

Letter to Special School District of St. Louis county (MO). (1989). 16 IDELR 307.

Letter to Wessels. (1992). 19 IDELR 584.

Lynch, S., & Adams, P. (2008). Developing standards-based individualized education program objectives for students with significant needs. *TEACHING Exceptional Children, 40(3)*, 36–39.

McClean, M., Wolery, M., & Bailey, D., (2004). *Assessing infants and preschoolers with special needs* (3rd ed.). Columbus, OH: Merrill.

Mills v. District of Columbia Board of Education, 348 F. Supp 866 (D.D.C. 1972); contempt proceedings, EHLR 551:643 (D.D.C. 1980).

Montessori, M. (1917). *The advanced Montessori method: Scientific pedagogy as applied to the education of children from seven to eleven years.* London: Heinmann.

National Association of State Directors of Special Education. (2005). Response to Intervention: Policy Considerations and Implementation. Alexandria, VA.

Neubert, D. A., & Leconte, P. J. (2013). Age appropriate transition assessment: The position of the Division on Career Development and Transition. *Career Development and Transition for Exceptional Individuals, 36(2)*, 72–83.

Norlin, J. W. (2010). Postsecondary Transition Services: An IDEA Compliance Guide for IEP Teams. Horsham, PA: LRP Publications.

Oberti v. Board of Educ. of Clementon School Dist., 789 F.Supp. 1322, 1336 (D.N.J. 1992) (Oberti I).

Oh-Yung, C., & Filler, J. (2015). A meta-analysis of the effects of placement on academic and social outcome measures of student with disabilities. *Research in Developmental Disabilities, 47,* 80–92.

O'Neill, R. E., Horner, R. H., Albin, R. W., Sprague, J. R., Storey, K., & Newton, J. S. (1997). *Functional assessment and program development for problem behavior: A practical handbook* (2nd ed.). Pacific Grove, CA: Brooks/Cole.

Osborne, A. G., & Russo, C. J. (2009). *Discipline in special education.* Thousand Oaks, CA: Corwin.

Osgood, R. L. (2008). *The history of special education: A struggle for equality in american public schools.* Westport, CN: Praeger.

Overton, T. (2011). *Assessing learners with special needs: An applied approach* (7th ed.). Upper Saddle River, NJ: Pearson.

Pennsylvania Ass'n for Retarded Children (PARC) v. Commonwealth of Pennsylvania, 334 F. Supp. 1257 (E.D. Pa. 1971); 343 F. Supp. 279 (E.D. Pa. 1972).

Petrou, A., Angelides, P., & Leigh, J. (2009). Beyond the difference: From the margins to inclusion. *International Journal of Inclusive Education, 13,* 439–448.

Pierangelo, R., & Giuliani, G. (2007). *The educator's step-by-step guide to understanding, developing, and writing effective IEPs.* Thousand Oaks, CA: Corwin Press.

Pretti-Frontczak, K., & Bricker, D. D. (2004). *An activity based approach to early intervention* (3rd ed.). Baltimore, MD: Paul H. Brookes Publishing Co.

Rehabilitation Act of 1973, as amended in 1974 (P. L. 93-651), 29 U.S.C. sec 794, Sec. 504, 34 C.F.R. 104-104.61.

Reid, D., Hresko, W. I., & Hammill, D. (2001). *Test of early reading ability* (3rd ed.). Austin, TX: Pro-Ed.

Reschly, D. J., & Hosp, J. L. (2004). State SLD policies and practices. *Learning Disability Quarterly, 27,* 197–213.

Rich, J. (2010). *A parent and educator guide to free and appropriate public education (Under Section 504 of the Rehabilitation Act of 1973).* Renton, WA: Puget Sound Educational Service District.

Rivera, G. (1972). *Willowbrook: A report on how it is and why it doesn't have to be that way.* New York, NY: Vintage Books.

Roncker v. Walter, 700 F.2d 1058 (6th Cir. 1983), cert, denied, 464 U.S. 864 (1983).

Rosa's Law, 20 U.S.C 1400. (2010).

Sacramento City School District v. Rachel H., 14 F.3d 1398 (9th Cir. 1994), cert. denied sub nom., Sacramento City Unified School Dist. v. Holland, 114 S. Ct. 2679 (1994).

Sailor, W., Anderson, J. L., Halvorsen, A. T., Doering, K., Filler, J., & Goetz, L. (1989). *The comprehensive local school: Regular education for all students with disabilities.* Baltimore, MD: Paul H. Brookes.

Sanford, C., Newman, L., Wagner, M., Cameto, R., Knokey, A. M., & Shaver, D. (2011). The Post High School Outcomes of Young Adults with Disabilities up 6 Years After High School. Key Findings From the National Longitudinal Transition Study-2 (NLST2)(NCSER 2011-3004). Melno Park, Ca: SRI International.

Salvia, J., Ysseldyke, J. E., & Bolt, S. (2013). *Assessment in special and inclusive education* (12th ed.). Belmont, CA: Wadsworth Cengage.

San Francisco Unified School District, 2009, 53 IDELR 31.

Schrank, F. A., Mather, N., & McGrew, K. S. (2014). *Woodcock-Johnson IV Tests of Achievement.* Rolling Meadows, IL: Riverside.

Seguin, E. (1856). Origin of the treatment and training of idiots. *American Journal of Education, 2,* 145–152.

Shaw, S. F., Dukes, L. L., & Madaus, J. W. (2012). Beyond compliance: Using the summary of performance to enhance transition planning. *Teaching Exceptional Children, 44,* 6–12.

Shinn, M. R. (Ed.) (1989). *Curriculum-based measurement: Assessing special children.* New York, NY: Guilford Press.

Shinn , M. R. (Ed.) (1998). *Advanced applications of curriculum-based measurement.* New York, NY: Guilford Press.

Shinn, M. R. (2008). Best practice in using curriculum-based measurement in a problem-solving model. In A. Thomas & J. Grimes (Eds.), *Best practices in school psychology* (Vol. 2., pp. 243–262). Bethesda, MD: NASP Publications.

Slentz, K. L., & Hyatt, K. J. (2008). Best practice in applying curriculum-based assessment in early childhood. In A. Thomas & J. Grimes (Eds.), *Best practices in school psychology* (Vol. 2., pp. 519–534). Bethesda, MD: NASP Publications.

Snow, K. (2012). People first language. Retrieved from http://www.disabilityisnatural.com/images/PDF/pfl09.pdf

Sparrow, S. S., Cicchetti, D. V., & Balla, D. A. (2005). *Vineland adaptive behavior scales* (2nd ed.). Upper Saddle River, NJ: Pearson.

Spielberg v. Henrico County Pub. Sch., 441 IDELR 178 (4th Cir. 1988).

Spooner, F., & Brower, D. (2006). Why teach the general curriculum? In F. Spooner & D. Browder (Eds.), *Teaching language arts, math, & science to students with significant cognitive disabilities* (pp. 1-13). Baltimore, MD: Brookes.

Stanovich, K. E. (1986). Matthew effects in reading: Some consequences of individual differences in the acquisition of literacy. *Reading Research Quarterly, 21,* 360–407.

Steege, M. W., & Watson, T. S. (2008). Best practices functional behavior assessment. In A. Thomas & J. Grimes (Eds.), *Best practices in school psychology V* (Vol. 2., pp. 337–348). Bethesda, MD: The National Association of School Psychologists.

Steubing, K. K., Fletcher, J. M., LeDoux, J. M., Lyon, G. R., Shaywitz, S. E., & Shaywitz, B. A. (2002). Validity of IQ-discrepancy classifications of reading disabilities: A meta-analysis. *American Educational Research Journal, 39,* 469–518.

T.Y. v. New York City Dep't of Educ., 584 F3d 412 (2d Cir. 2009), cert, denied, 130 S. Ct. 3277 (2010).

Taylor, S. J. (1988). Caught in the continuum: A critical analysis of the principle of the least restrictive environment. *Journal of the Association for Persons with Severe Handicaps, 13,* 45–53.

Taylor, S. J. (2001). The continuum and current controversies in the USA. *Journal of Intellectual and Developmental Disability, 26,* 15–33.

Thoma, C. A., & Wehman, P. (Eds.). (2010). *Getting the most out of IEPs: An educator's guide to the student-directed approach.* Baltimore, MD: Paul H. Brookes Publishing.

Thousand, J. S., Villa, R. A., & Nevin, A. I. (Eds.). (2002). *Creativity and collaborative learning: The practical guide to empowering students, teachers, and their families* (2nd ed.). Baltimore, MD: Paul H. Brookes Publishing Co.

Turnbull, R. H., Stowe, M. J., & Huerta, N. E. (2007). *Free appropriate public education: The law and children with disabilities* (7th ed.). Denver, CO: Love Publishing Company.

Turnbull, R. H., & Turnbull, A. P. (1998). *Free appropriate public education: The law and children with disabilities* (5th ed.). Denver, CO: Love Publishing Company.

U.S. Department of Education Office of Special Education and Rehabilitative Services. (2002).

A New Era: Revitalizing Special Education for Children and their Families. Washington, DC.

U.S. Department of Education, Office of Special Education and Rehabilitative Services, Office of Special Education Programs, 30th Annual Report to Congress on the Implementation of the Individuals with Disabilities Education Act, 2008, Washington, D.C., 2011.

Vandercook, T., York, J., & Forest, M. (1989). The McGill Action Planning System (MAPS): A Strategy for Building the Vision. [Reports - Descriptive]. *Journal of the Association for Persons with Severe Handicaps (JASH), 14*, 205–215.

Villa, R. A., & Thousand, J. S. (2003). Making inclusive education work. *Educational Leadership, 61*, 19–23.

Watson, T. S., & Steege, M. W. (2003). *Conducting school-based functional behavioral assessment: A practitioner's guide.* New York, NY: Guilford Press.

Wechsler, D. (2004). *Wechsler intelligence scale for children* (4th ed.). San Antonio, TX: Psychological Corporation.

Wehman, P. (2013). Transition from school to work: Where are we and where do we need to go? *Career Development and Transition for Exceptional Individuals, 36(1)*, 58–66.

Wilkinson, G. S., & Robertson, G. J. (2007). *Wide range achievement test 4.* Lutz, FL: Psychological Assessment Resources.

Williams-Diehm, K. L., & Benz, M. R. (2008). Where are they now? Lessons from a single district follow-up study. *Journal for Vocational Special Needs Educaiton, 30(2)*, 4–15.

Winzer, M. A. (2009). *From integration to inclusion: A history of special education in the 20th century.* Washington, DC: Gallaudet University Press.

Yell, M. L. (2006). *The law and special education* (2nd ed.). Upper Saddle River, NJ: Pearson.

Ysseldyke, J. M., & Christenson, C. (2002). *Functional assessment of academic behavior.* Longmont, CO: SoprisWest.

Zirkel, P. A. (2006). Manifestation determinations under the Individuals with Disabilities Education Act: What the new causality criteria means. *Journal of Special Education Leadership, 19*, 3–12.

Zirkel, P. A. (2011). What does the law say? *Teaching Exceptional Children, 43*, 56–67.

Index

CPSIA information can be obtained
at www.ICGtesting.com
Printed in the USA
LVHW020432030719
623004LV00001B/2/P